10 0014974 7
AF845135
UNIVERSITY OF BRISTOL
LIBRARY

Staff and Research Students	Other Borrowers
Date Borrowed	Date due back
15. APR. 1970	19. OCT. 1971
14. DEC. 1970	18. MAR. 1974
	21. NOV. 1977
	9. DEC. 1978

CAPITAL ALLOCATION THEORY

BUSINESS SERIES

Stanley F. Teele* and David W. Ewing, Editors

Dean S. Ammer, *Manufacturing Management and Control*

Gerald A. Fleischer, *Capital Allocation Theory: The Study of Investment Decisions*

Samuel Fox, *Management and the Law*

Thomas M. Garrett, *Business Ethics*

Thomas M. Garrett, Raymond C. Baumhart, Theodore V. Purcell, and Perry Roets, *Cases in Business Ethics*

David J. Luck and Arthur E. Prell, *Market Strategy*

Richards C. Osborn, *Financing Small Business*

William H. Reynolds, *Products and Markets*

Israel Unterman, *Personal Money Management*

Chester R. Wasson, *The Economics of Managerial Decision*

Chester R. Wasson, *Research Analysis for Marketing Decision*

Albert K. Wickesberg, *Management Organization*

Walter E. Willets, *Fundamentals of Purchasing*

* Deceased, May 29, 1967.

GERALD A. FLEISCHER
University of Southern California

CAPITAL ALLOCATION THEORY:

The Study of Investment Decisions

University of Bristol
WITHDRAWN

APPLETON-CENTURY-CROFTS
EDUCATIONAL DIVISION
MEREDITH CORPORATION New York

Copyright © 1969 by
MEREDITH CORPORATION
All rights reserved

This book, or parts thereof, must
not be used or reproduced in any
manner without written permission.
For information address the publisher,
Appleton-Century-Crofts, Educational Division,
Meredith Corporation, 440 Park Avenue
South, New York, N. Y. 10016.

6-10-8-1

Library of Congress Card Number: 69-19430

249781

PRINTED IN THE UNITED STATES OF AMERICA

390-31800-0

To

EUGENE L. GRANT

Scholar

Mentor

Inspiration

ACKNOWLEDGMENTS

The manuscript typing and editorial assistance of Miss Maureen Groarke and Miss Judy Toyama are gratefully acknowledged. We are also indebted to our many colleagues, both past and present, without whose encouragement, inspiration, and critical judgment this text would not have been written.

FOREWORD

Gerald A. Fleischer is a careful and experienced student of capital allocation theory. After receiving his Ph.D. in 1962 in Engineering–Economic Planning from Stanford University, he remained on the teaching faculty briefly prior to joining an AID-sponsored University of Michigan team in Brazil. In 1964 he became an associate professor in the Department of Industrial and Systems Engineering at the University of Southern California, Los Angeles, and since then has taught graduate and undergraduate sections in engineering economic analysis and operations research. Much of the research he has done has led to publications in a wide variety of professional journals and monographs. In addition to his work in Brazil, Dr. Fleischer recently served in Venezuela as a specialist in engineering economics for the United Nations. He has also been active as a consultant for various agencies of the U.S. government as well as private industry. Prior to taking his doctorate, he worked for several organizations on the West Coast.

This volume is one of a series of original texts by eminent authorities on business administration. Like its companion books, it is designed for use in business school courses or in-company training programs. It may also be used in schools of engineering or public administration, indeed, wherever students are interested in problems dealing with the allocation of capital to and among competing investment proposals. *Capital Allocation Theory* can be used either as a basic text or as a supplementary text. The author has sought to distill a large mass of material into the comparatively brief length of this book. It represents a compact analysis of highlights and key topics of capital allocation theory. Hence businessmen, too, should find it useful for enlarging their understanding of management problems.

David W. Ewing

PREFACE

The study of optimal investment decisions, as an area of special concern, is of relatively recent interest to both academicians and industrial managers. "Engineering economy," the analysis of the economic effects of engineering decisions, has its genesis in Arthur M. Wellington's classic text, *The Economic Theory of Railway Location*, published in 1887. As the engineers subsequently expanded and refined the techniques of engineering economy, certain economists and "financial managers" were in the process of developing a parallel theory, especially directed to capital budgeting decisions at senior management levels. This text represents a consolidation of current and relevant views of engineering economists and financial managers to present a unified theory of capital allocation appropriate to all levels within the business enterprise.

Parenthetically, it is of interest to note that the theory presented here is equally appropriate to individual (non-business) investment decisions as to those of government or non-profit organizations. These techniques are suitable wherever decisions must be made to select from among alternate investment opportunities.

The text begins with a qualitative discussion of certain principles from which a unified theory may be developed. The necessary mathematics of compound interest are then derived, and the principal techniques of economic evaluation — annual cost, present worth, and rate of return — are discussed. After devoting some attention to certain problems and applications of special interest, two "real-world" complications are explored: tax consequences of investment decisions and the effects of uncertainty associated with estimates about the future. The text concludes with an extensive discussion of management policy with respect to capital structure and administrative procedures to be employed in order to implement the foregoing theory.

G.A.F.

CONTENTS

3 / EQUIVALENT METHODS FOR SELECTING FROM AMONG ALTERNATIVES

4 / SOME INCORRECT AND / OR APPROXIMATE METHODS COMMONLY USED TO SELECT FROM AMONG ALTERNATIVES

5 / MULTIPLE ALTERNATIVES

6 / EFFECTS OF DEPRECIATION ON TAXABLE INCOME

7 / TAXES AND PROFITABILITY

8 / SPECIAL PROBLEMS OF REPLACEMENT AND RETIREMENT

9 / THE UNCERTAIN FUTURE

10 / COST OF CAPITAL

11 / CAPITAL BUDGETING PROCEDURES

1

AN INTRODUCTION TO CAPITAL BUDGETING

THE CAPITAL BUDGETING PROBLEM

Numerous investment opportunities are normally available to individual investors, business firms, and agencies of government. With respect to private industry in particular, continued investment (and reinvestment) is a fact of economic life if the firm is to survive as a viable entity in a competitive economic environment. Supplies and materials must be purchased; new equipment must be acquired and obsolescent equipment replaced; physical plant must be maintained and, in many cases, expanded; new products must be researched, developed, and marketed; etc. Moreover, investment by one company in another (in the form of stock ownership), purchase of government securities, and cash dividends distributed to the owners of the firm[1] represent just a few of the many other investment possibilities which may be considered as alternatives of capital demand.

Suppose that we lived in a world of unlimited capital resources. Given such an idealized environment, there would be no need for a text such as this one. *All* proposals requiring the expenditure of funds would be acceptable provided only that a very simple criterion were met; total cash revenue must exceed total cash expenses. Indeed, even this simple test is unnecessary in

[1] Distribution of the earnings of the firm in the form of cash dividends is frequently cited as an example of "disinvestment." The semantic distinction between "investment" and "disinvestment" is of little interest to us at this time; the difference will always be clear in context.

our make-believe world since the assumption of unlimited resources precludes the incentive to increase existing wealth. The man who has plenty to eat — and is assured that he will always have plenty to eat — does not devote his energies to the acquisition of more food.

In our real, finite world, it is clear that resources *are* limited. In all but the most pathological of cases, the available *capital supply* is not sufficient to meet all available demand. Although it is true that available capital may be increased by additional borrowing or, in some cases, by taking in additional partners, management is generally unable to take advantage of all available investment opportunities because of capital limitations. This, then, is the cardinal problem of capital budgeting: *Which of the many available investment alternatives should be selected* (*and which should be rejected*) *in order that the long-term wealth of current owners of the enterprise will be maximized?*[2] The following discussion is addressed to the development and application of a systematic and valid basis for answering this question.

Conceptually, the solution to the capital budgeting problem may be viewed as a determination of the point at which the *marginal cost* of capital supply is equal to the expected *marginal revenue*, or "payoff," of capital demand. Stated another way, alternatives should be accepted until the point at which the last (marginal) alternative accepted is expected to yield a return less than the cost of the capital necessary to finance it. At this point, no additional capital funds should be obtained and no additional investment proposals should be accepted. Figure 1-1 has been constructed by way of illustration.

Point A represents the total cost of all those investments (and reinvestments) necessary to maintain the existence of the firm, A1 denotes expected return from this level of investment, and A2 denotes the cost of the capital funds necessary to support these investments. Point B represents the total investment dollar required for level A plus the next project under consideration, and B1 and B2 denote the expected return and incremental (marginal) cost, respectively, from the next project. Since the marginal return is greater than the marginal cost, the project should be accepted. In like manner, the proposal leading to C appears attractive but those leading to D and E should be rejected.

The conceptual solution to the capital budgeting problem is deceptive in its simplicity since it fails to answer (or focus upon) such essential issues as definition of an appropriate measure for capital cost and profitability, determination of project "return" and cost of capital, and treatment of the un-

[2] Numerous authors have discussed the explicit objectives towards which capital management must be directed. It is the consensus of current thinking that the relevant goal is the maximization of the present worth of the current owners of the enterprise. As will be illustrated in later chapters, "present worth" refers to the discounted present value of long-run net earnings.

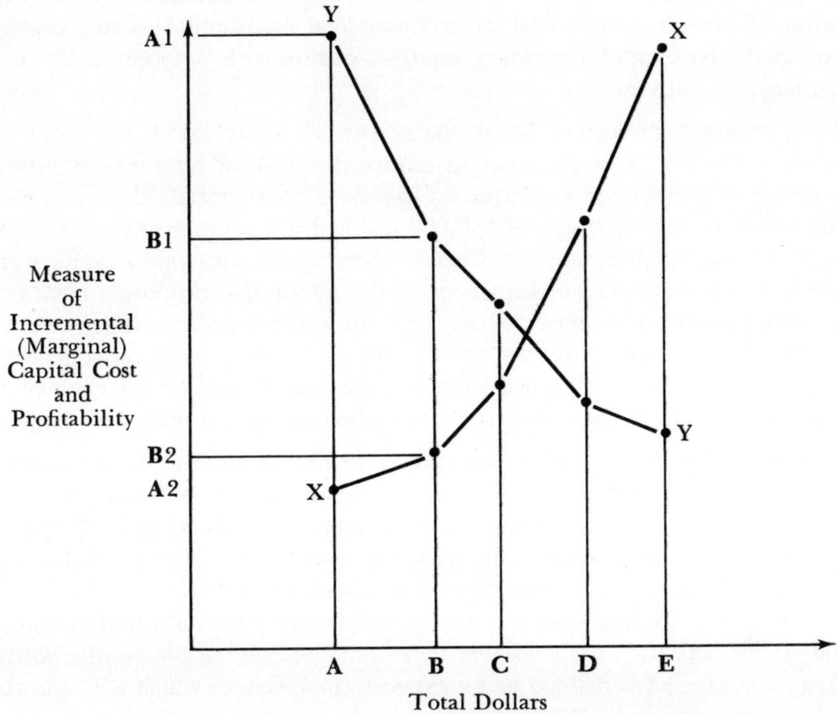

Fig. 1-1. Conceptual determination of the optimal capital budget.

certainty inherent in all predictions about future outcomes. These, as well as certain other relevant issues, are discussed in the following chapters.

FUNDAMENTAL PRINCIPLES OF CAPITAL ALLOCATION

Before developing the mathematical structure necessary to the evaluation of capital proposals, it is well to postulate certain qualitative principles which give rise to the rationale of capital budgeting. Moreover, certain of these principles lead directly to the quantitative techniques developed in the chapters following.

1. ALL DECISIONS ARE AMONG ALTERNATIVES. To illustrate, prospective investment in new equipment costing $100,000 is simply not a feasible alternative if the money is not, and cannot, be obtained and if no other financing opportunities are available. Similarly, management need not consider the possibility of distributing corporate profits as cash dividends if this action has been

temporarily prohibited by lenders. Since courses of action not feasible because of certain contractual or technological considerations are properly excluded, the capital budgeting analysis begins with determination of all *feasible* alternatives.

2. A COMMON DENOMINATOR IS NECESSARY SO AS TO MAKE CONSEQUENCES COMMENSURABLE. Is a proposal to reduce direct labor by 3,000 man-hours superior to another which is expected to reduce raw materials requirements by 500 tons? Is an investment of $10,000 justified if it promises to shorten production time by three weeks? Clearly, these questions cannot be answered unless the prospective consequences of the alternative proposals have been described in common units. All decisions are made in a single dimension, and money units — dollars, francs, pesos, yen, etc. — seem to be most generally suitable. Thus, after all consequences have been described for each of the feasible alternatives, they should be transcribed into the common denominator.

3. ONLY DIFFERENCES AMONG ALTERNATIVES ARE RELEVANT. Those prospective consequences which are common to all contending alternatives need not be considered in the analysis since their inclusion can only result in all alternatives being affected equally. This is akin to adding (or subtracting) the same number to both sides of an equation. The equality is undisturbed.

As a direct consequence of this principle, an important axiom may be stated: *All sunk costs are irrelevant to the economic choice among alternatives.* Here, a sunk cost is defined as an expense (or revenue) which has occurred *prior* to the decision. When considering the question of whether or not to replace certain manufacturing equipment, for example, the original cost of the equipment is "sunk" and hence of no direct interest.[3] The cost three weeks ago of a major overhaul of the equipment is also irrelevant. All events taking place prior to the decision are common to whichever alternative may be selected, and hence sunk costs are not differences among alternatives.

4. CRITERIA FOR INVESTMENT DECISIONS SHOULD RECOGNIZE THE TIME VALUE OF MONEY AND RELATED PROBLEMS OF CAPITAL RATIONING. Which of the following are more economically attractive? ALTERNATIVE A requires an expenditure of $100 today and promises a return of $200 five years hence. ALTERNATIVE B also requires an initial expenditure of $100, but in this case a payoff of $500 is expected ten years hence. There is no simple, direct answer to this problem since the expected returns occur at different points in time. We will not choose B over A simply because $500 is greater than $200. Without reading further in this text, it should be evident that the appropriate solution somehow must consider the opportunities available to the investor in the interval between year five and year ten. Indeed, since resources are limited in our finite world, money can be invested elsewhere, and hence it has

[3] As we discuss in a later section, the original cost of equipment may be of interest in certain instances insofar as this information is needed to determine subsequent depreciation expenses for tax purposes.

a "value" which increases over time. This phenomenon must be formally considered in any criterion used to select from among alternative investment opportunities.

5. SEPARABLE DECISIONS SHOULD BE MADE SEPARATELY. This principle requires that all capital allocation problems be carefully evaluated to determine the number and type of decisions required. For example, the analyst may be called upon to make recommendations concerning the technological alternative (e.g., the equipment to be acquired) as well as the financial alternative (the source of funds to finance the acquisition). If care is not taken to treat separable decisions separately, it is possible that optimal solutions will be obscured in the analysis.

6. SOME WEIGHT SHOULD BE GIVEN TO THE RELATIVE DEGREES OF UNCERTAINTY ASSOCIATED WITH VARIOUS FORECASTS. All capital budgeting decisions are based upon a series of estimates concerning the future. Since these estimates are at best only predictions of future events it is possible — indeed, it is probable — that the actual outcomes will differ in a greater or lesser degree from the original estimates. The future is uncertain, and any analysis which fails to consider this uncertainty implies a false omniscience. On the other hand, it cannot be inferred that specific solutions are invalid or useless because of the uncertainty associated with input data. Formal consideration of the type and degree of uncertainty serves to insure that the quality of the solution is evident to those responsible for capital allocation decisions.

7. DECISIONS SHOULD GIVE WEIGHT TO CONSEQUENCES NOT REDUCED TO MONEY TERMS. Selection from among candidates for limited capital resources requires that the prospective differences among alternatives be clearly specified. Wherever possible, of course, these differences should be reduced to a single common denominator (generally a monetary unit) to provide a basis for selection, but not all alternatives are capable of this reduction. One proposal may be expected to result in an increase in employee "comfort and convenience"; another may result in a production delay; still another may be expected to result in an increased share of the market for the firm. Although the analyst does not always have the available time or resources to reduce these consequences to equivalent money terms, decisions may be directly affected by their amount and direction. The "irreducible" as well as monetary consequences of proposed alternatives should be clearly specified in order that managers of capital be given all reasonable data upon which to base their decisions.

8. THE EFFICACY OF CAPITAL BUDGETING PROCEDURES IS A FUNCTION OF THEIR IMPLEMENTATION AT VARIOUS LEVELS WITHIN THE ORGANIZATION. Responsibility for capital budgeting decisions does not rest solely with the corporate board of directors or the most senior levels of management. Decisions affecting significant capital receipts and expenditures are made at many levels

within the organization, especially among those staff activities such as engineering design, marketing, and new product research and development. Moreover, the technical description of alternatives for the consideration of top-level management review generally requires preselection from among a larger number of sub-alternatives by lower level personnel. Thus it is necessary that capital budgeting procedures be clearly described and understood at all levels within the organization having responsibility, in whole or in part, for these decisions.

9. POST-DECISION AUDITS IMPROVE THE QUALITY OF DECISIONS. As indicated above, all capital budgeting analyses require estimates of expected consequences of the various alternatives, and thus the quality of decisions is directly affected by the ability of analysts to forecast with reasonable precision. The only way in which predictive ability can be judged, of course, is by auditing the results of the decision at some later date. In this way it is possible to determine the extent of predictive bias on the part of the analyst — some may be consistently optimistic, others pessimistic, and still others may evidence random bias — as well as to evaluate the strengths and weaknesses of over-all budgeting procedures. The capital budgeting function should be viewed as extending to post-decision audits in order to provide relevant feedback for improving future decisions.

Parenthetically, it should be noted that a post-decision audit is inherently incomplete. This is to say that, if only one of several alternative courses of action was selected, we can never know *with exactitude* what would have happened if one of the other alternatives had been chosen. "What might have been if . . ." is at best conjecture, and all post-decision audits should be made with this reservation in proper perspective.

SUMMARY

Capital budgeting is the process of selecting from among alternative investment (or disinvestment) proposals to maximize the long-term interests of current owners of the enterprise.[4] Although this process is usually thought of in terms of a firm's acquisition of physical assets (capital demand), the sources and amount of investment funds (capital supply) are also relevant.

Prior to the development of quantitative techniques and criteria for evaluating alternatives, a number of principles may be expressed which form the rational basis for capital budgeting procedures:

1. All decisions are among alternatives.

[4] When considering capital budgeting within the context of an agency of government, the "owners of the enterprise" may be viewed as the taxpayers or citizens of the governmental unit in question.

2. Monetary units are used as a common denominator to make consequences commensurable.

3. Only differences among alternatives are relevant. (Sunk costs are irrelevant to decisions about the future.)

4. Criteria for investment decisions should recognize the time value of money and related problems of capital rationing.

5. Separable decisions should be made separately.

6. Some weight should be given to the relative degrees of uncertainty associated with various forecasts.

7. Decisions should give weight to consequences not reduced to money terms.

8. The efficacy of capital budgeting procedures is a function of their implementation at various levels within the organization.

9. Post-decision audits improve the quality of decisions.

2

CONCEPTS AND MATHEMATICS OF COMPOUND INTEREST

EQUIVALENCE AS A FUNDAMENTAL CONCEPT

Essential to all valid approaches to capital budgeting problems is the fundamental concept of equivalence, that is, a sum of money may be *equivalent* to a different sum at a different point in time under certain specific conditions. This easily demonstrated principle leads to development of a methodology necessary to our discussion in future sections of this text.

To illustrate the concept of equivalence, consider a loan of $1,000 which is to be repaid at the end of five years along with all accrued interest. Further, assume that the interest rate associated with the loan is 10% and interest is to be compounded annually. From the calculations shown in Table 2-1, it is clear that the lender must repay $1,610.51 at the end of the five-year loan period. Thus we may say that $1,000 today is *equivalent* to $1,610.51 five years from today if interest is computed at the rate of 10% per year.

In addition, consider Table 2-2. Here the lender agrees to repay his borrowed $1,000 with equal end-of-year payments (uniform series) over a five-year period. Assuming an interest rate of 10% per annum, $1,000 today is *equivalent* to a uniform series of payments of $263.80 at the end of each and every year for five years. Moreover, this "uniform series" plan is equivalent to the "single payment" plan illustrated in Table 2-1.

Table 2-1

A Plan to Repay $1,000 Loan at the End of 5 Years with Interest Assumed at 10% Per Annum

Year	Owed at Start of Year	Annual Interest on Debt	Owed Prior to End-of-Year Payment	End-of-Year Payment
1	$1,000.00	$100.00	$1,100.00	
2	1,100.00	110.00	1,210.00	
3	1,210.00	121.00	1,331.00	
4	1,331.00	133.10	1,464.10	
5	1,464.10	146.41	1,610.51	$1,610.51

Table 2-2

A Plan to Repay $1,000 Loan with 5 Equal End-of-Year Payments with Interest Assumed at 10% Per Annum

Year	Owed at Start of Year	Annual Interest on Debt	Owed Prior to End-of-Year Payment	End-of-Year Payment
1	$1,000.00	$100.00	$1,100.00	$263.80
2	836.20	83.62	919.82	263.80
3	656.02	65.60	721.62	263.80
4	457.82	45.78	503.60	263.80
5	239.80	23.98	263.78[a]	263.80[a]

[a]Inequality ($0.02) caused by rounding error.

INTEREST

It is an undeniable fact that we live in a world of limited resources. Except for a few very special cases, companies (as well as individuals, family units, and governments) find it necessary to ration limited wealth. When a portion of one's assets is invested, it is reasonable to expect that a "rent" will be charged the "borrower" to reimburse the lender for the lost opportunity to invest elsewhere. *Interest*, the "rent" charged for the use of borrowed money, would be of little import to the lender whose own capital is unlimited.

Another feature of interest is the risk associated with various lending situations. (It should be noted, of course, that investments come in many forms: outright loans to borrowers, purchase of capital equipment, installation of an inventory control system, an advertising campaign, etc.) Since returns from investments may not occur as originally planned, it is reasonable to expect that investors will adjust for uncertainty by adding an interest element to their loan. Even the most casual observer will note the obvious interdependence of risk and rate of interest. Just as investors demand a return to compensate for the loss of alternative uses for their limited capital, so do they expect some measure of return in anticipation of losses resulting from uncertain investments.

SOME ADDITIONAL TERMINOLOGY

Before proceeding further, it will be helpful at this point to define and explain some key words and phrases commonly used in connection with compound interest calculations.

A *cash flow* is simply a receipt or payment of an amount of money. It is an actual income or expenditure, not merely a financial obligation or accrual. Diagrams and tabular presentations are frequently used to portray the amount and timing of cash flows in a clear and concise manner. Tables 2-1 and 2-2 are examples of *cash flow tables*; the corresponding *cash flow diagrams* are shown as Figure 2-1.

Interest was defined earlier as money charged for the use of borrowed money. It is stated in monetary units and should not be confused with the interest rate which is a pure number. The *interest rate*, generally written as a percentage rather than a decimal, is the ratio of the interest charged during an *interest period* to the amount of money owed at the beginning of the interest period. The length of the period must be stated or understood. (Through common usage, "interest rate" is frequently abbreviated to "interest." For example, one may speak of "6% interest" in connection with a home mortgage, omitting "per year." Although strictly improper, this should not be bothersome because the meaning is usually clear in context.)

Simple interest is merely the interest produced in the first interest period multiplied by the total number of periods. Referring to the earlier example (Table 2-1), the simple interest is $\$1,000 \times 10\% \times 5 = \$500$. *Compound interest*, on the other hand, is computed periodically on the total amount owed at the start of each period. Compound interest is illustrated in Table 2-1; in that example the total interest paid at the end of five years was \$610.51. Compound interest is always greater than simple interest because the former computes "interest on interest." Simple interest is rarely used in our economy.

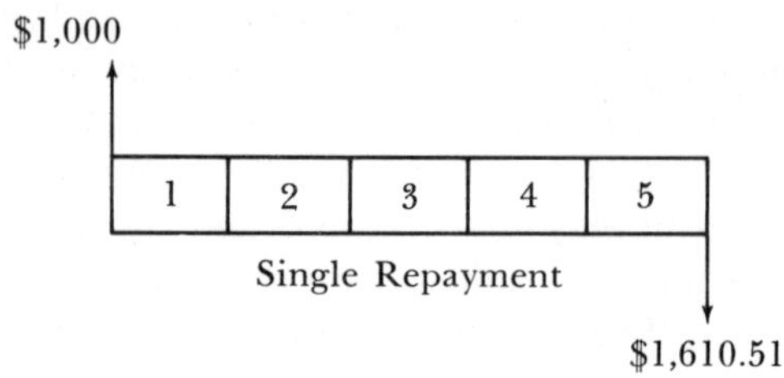

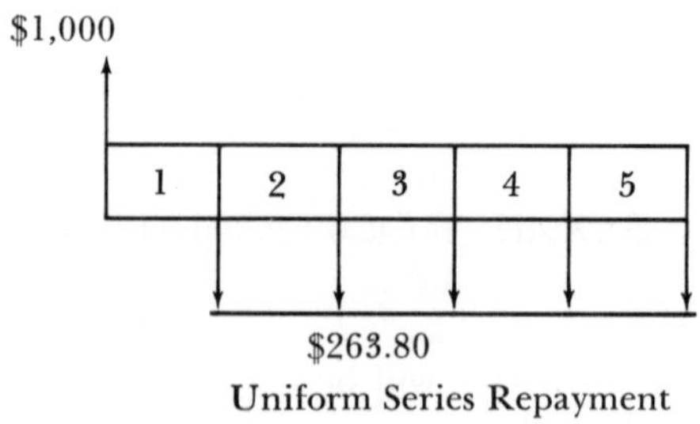

Fig. 2-1. Cash flow diagrams of two equivalent plans to repay a $1,000 loan over a five-year period with interest at 10% per annum. (Note that, from the point of view of the borrower, the arrow pointing upward indicates a positive cash flow whereas the downward direction indicates a negative cash flow. This is merely a suggested convention which, if followed consistently, may prove useful.)

NOTATION[1]

The following symbols will be used in the discussion of the mathematics of compound interest:

i effective interest rate per interest period.

r nominal interest rate per year.

N number of interest periods (days, months, years, etc.).

M number of compounding periods per year.

P present value of a sum of money.

F a future sum of money at the end of N periods which is equivalent to P with interest rate i.

A a uniform series (or "annuity") of cash flows taking place at the end of each and every period for N periods, the entire series equivalent to P with interest rate i.

[1] These and other symbols used throughout the text are summarized in the Glossary on pp. 203–204.

$\bar{F}$ a cash flow taking place continuously during the Nth period, the sum equivalent to P with interest rate i.

$\bar{A}$ cash flows taking place continuously during each and every period from the first through the Nth period, the entire series equivalent to P with interest rate i.

G uniform (gradient) period-by-period increase or decrease in cash flow.

L expected net residual salvage value upon disposal of an asset.

EQUIVALENT VALUES OF A SINGLE CASH FLOW

Table 2-3 illustrates the effect of period-by-period compounding. It shows that a present value P is equivalent to a future sum F (at the end of the Nth period) if P is multiplied by the factor $(1 + i)^N$.

This inductive proof, then, leads to the useful equation:

$$F = P(1 + i)^N \tag{2.1}$$

Further, dividing both sides of the equation by $(1 + i)^N$, it follows that:

$$P = F(1 + i)^{-N} \tag{2.2}$$

Mnemonic forms are frequently adopted to preclude writing out the

Table 2-3

Period	Sum of Money Owed at Start of Period	Interest Accumulated During the Period	Sum of Money Owed at End of Period
1	P	iP	$P + iP = P(1+i)$
2	$P(1+i)$	$iP(1+i)$	$P(1+i) + iP(1+i) = P(1+i)^2$
3	$P(1+i)^2$	$iP(1+i)^2$	$P(1+i)^2 + iP(1+i)^2 = P(1+i)^3$
.	.	.	.
.	.	.	.
.	.	.	.
N	$P(1+i)^{N-1}$	$iP(1+i)^{N-1}$	$= P(1+i)^N$

factors each time they are used. In this text, the mnemonic forms for the two single payment factors are:

$$(CA - i\% - N) = (1 + i)^N$$
$$(PW - i\% - N) = (1 + i)^{-N}$$

In the first instance, $(CA - i\% - N)$ should be read "*single payment compound amount factor* with interest rate i and N interest periods." $(PW - i\% - N)$ is the "*single payment present worth factor* with interest rate i and N interest periods."

Compound interest tables are commonly used to avoid the necessity of calculating new values for the factors each time different values of i and N are assumed. The first two columns of the Appendix contain values for the single payment compound amount factor and the single payment present worth factor, respectively.

To illustrate the use of the factors and the tables, consider a borrower who receives \$1,000 on March 15, 1969, and who agrees to repay this debt at the end of five years. Assuming an interest rate of 10% per year with interest compounded annually, the amount to be repaid on March 15, 1974, is:

$$\begin{aligned} F &= P(CA - 10\% - 5) \\ &= \$1{,}000(1.611) \\ &= \$1{,}611 \end{aligned}$$

Note that this is precisely the same result as determined by the "brute force" method illustrated in Table 2-1.

As another example, suppose that we desire to determine how much must be deposited in the bank on March 15, 1969 in order to have exactly \$1,611 in the account on March 15, 1974, assuming interest is compounded annually at an effective rate of 10% per year.

$$\begin{aligned} P &= F(PW - 10\% - 5) \\ &= \$1{,}611(0.6209) \\ &= \$1{,}000 \end{aligned}$$

This answer is not surprising, of course. The example has been chosen to reinforce the earlier discussion.

EQUIVALENT VALUES OF A UNIFORM SERIES OF CASH FLOWS

Figure 2-2 illustrates a series of cash flows occurring at the end of each and every period for N periods. The value of the cash flow at the end of each of the N periods is A. Since this pattern frequently occurs in industry, and

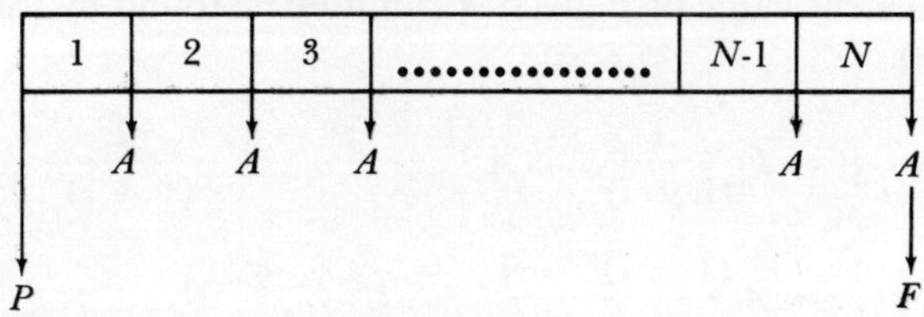

Fig. 2-2. Cash flow diagram: Uniform Series.

since certain irregular series may be reasonably approximated by a uniform series, it is often necessary to find equivalent present values or future sums and, conversely, to convert from present values or future sums to equivalent uniform series.

To convert a uniform series to an equivalent value F, we may take each value of A, one by one, and find its equivalent value by use of equation (2.1). Then the individual values of F_j can be summed thus:

$$F_1 = A_1(1+i)^{N-1}$$
$$F_2 = A_2(1+i)^{N-2}$$
$$\vdots$$
$$F_{N-1} = A_{N-1}(1+i)^1 = A(1+i)$$
$$F_N = A_N(1+i)^0 = A$$

Summing:

$$F = \sum_{j=1}^{N} F_j = A \sum_{j=0}^{N-1} (1+i)^j$$

Multiplying by $(1+i)$:

$$F(1+i) = A \sum_{j=1}^{N} (1+i)^j$$

Thus:

$$F(1+i) - F = A(1+i)^N - A(1+i)^0$$
$$iF = A[(1+i)^N - 1]$$
$$F = A\frac{(1+i)^N - 1}{i} \tag{2.3}$$

and:

$$A = F\frac{i}{(1+i)^N - 1} \tag{2.4}$$

The equivalent value of P given A can now be found by using equations (2.2) and (2.3).

$$P = F\frac{1}{(1+i)^N} = A\frac{(1+i)^N - 1}{i} \cdot \frac{1}{(1+i)^N}$$

$$= A\frac{(1+i)^N - 1}{i(1+i)^N} \tag{2.5}$$

and

$$A = P\frac{i(1+i)^N}{(1+i)^N - 1} \tag{2.6}$$

The names by which these factors are generally known, and their mnemonic forms, are as follows:

Equation	Mnemonic Form	Factor Name
$\frac{(1+i)^N - 1}{i}$	$(SCA - i\% - N)$	Uniform Series Compound Amount Factor
$\frac{i}{(1+i)^N - 1}$	$(SF - i\% - N)$	Sinking Fund Factor
$\frac{(1+i)^N - 1}{i(1+i)^N}$	$(SPW - i\% - N)$	Uniform Series Present Worth Factor
$\frac{i(1+i)^N}{(1+i)^N - 1}$	$(CR - i\% - N)$	Capital Recovery Factor

Each of the factors is tabulated in the Appendix for various values of i and N.

EQUIVALENT VALUES OF A GRADIENT SERIES[2]

Another frequently observed cash flow series is one which results from a uniform, period-by-period increase (or decrease) in cash flow. Figure 2-3 illustrates this gradient pattern. Note that the increase (or decrease) first occurs at the end of the *second* interest period, not the first. The reason for this peculiarity becomes apparent when the reader attempts to solve problems combining both uniform and gradient series.

[2] The uniform gradient discussed in this section describes an *arithmetic* series, i.e., the cash flow increase (or decrease) from period to period is constant. A *geometric* series, on the other hand, describes cash flows which increase (or decrease) at a constant *rate* from period to period. In the latter case, factors for determining the equivalent present values are presented in: Fleischer, G. A., and Basil Mikhalkin, "Discounting the Geometric Series," *The Engineering Economist*, Vol. 12, No. 4, July–August 1967, pp. 217–28.

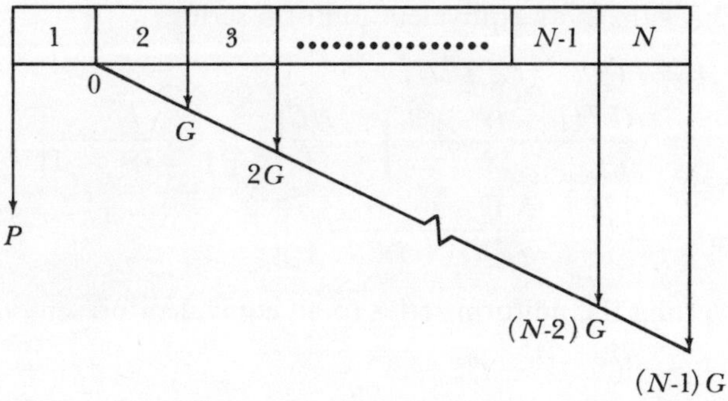

Fig. 2-3. Cash flow diagram: Gradient Series.

The gradient series may be converted to an equivalent present value by use of a factor which is derived by first dividing the gradient series into N uniform series. Each of the uniform series is then converted to an equivalent sum F_j, the F_j's totaled, and then converted to an equivalent present value.

Thus:

$$F_1 = 0$$

$$F_2 = G(SCA - i\% - [N-1]) = G\frac{(1+i)^{N-1} - 1}{i}$$

$$F_3 = G(SCA - i\% - [N-2]) = G\frac{(1+i)^{N-2} - 1}{i}$$

.

.

.

$$F_{N-1} = G(SCA - i\% - 2) = G\frac{(1+i)^2 - 1}{i}$$

$$F_N = G(SCA - i\% - 1) = G\frac{(1+i)^1 - 1}{i}$$

Summing:

$$F = \sum_{j=1}^{N} F_j = \frac{G}{i}[(1+i)^{N-1} + (1+i)^{N-2} + \ldots + (1+i)^1 + (N-1)(-1)]$$

$$= \frac{G}{i}\left[\sum_{j=0}^{N-1}(1+i)^j\right] - \frac{NG}{i}$$

Recognizing that the value in [brackets] is the $(SCA - i\% - N)$,

$$F = \frac{G}{i}\left[\frac{(1+i)^N - 1}{i}\right] - \frac{NG}{i}$$

Converting this sum to an equivalent uniform series,

$$\begin{aligned} A &= F(SF - i\% - N) \\ &= \left\{\frac{G}{i}\left[\frac{(1+i)^N - 1}{i}\right] - \frac{NG}{i}\right\} \cdot \left\{\frac{i}{(1+i)^N - 1}\right\} \\ &= G\left\{\frac{1}{i} - \frac{N}{i}\left[\frac{i}{(1+i)^N - 1}\right]\right\} \end{aligned} \tag{2.7}$$

Finally, converting the uniform series to an equivalent present value,

$$\begin{aligned} P &= A(SPW - i\% - N) \\ &= G\left\{\frac{1}{i} - \frac{N}{i}\left[\frac{i}{(1+i)^N - 1}\right]\right\} \cdot \left\{\frac{(1+i)^N - 1}{i(1+i)^N}\right\} \end{aligned} \tag{2.8}$$

The mnemonic forms for equations (2.7) and (2.8) are $(GUS - i\% - N)$ and $(GPW - i\% - N)$, respectively. Although these equations appear to be mathematically cumbersome, it is clear that:

$$\begin{aligned} A &= G\left\{\frac{1}{i}\,[1 - N(SF - i\% - N)]\right\} \\ &= G(GUS - i\% - N) \end{aligned}$$

and

$$\begin{aligned} P &= G(GUS - i\% - N)(PW - i\% - N) \\ &= G(GPW - i\% - N) \end{aligned}$$

The *gradient uniform series factor* and the *gradient present worth factor* are both tabulated in the Appendix for various values of N and i.

EFFECTIVE VS. NOMINAL INTEREST RATES

Suppose we are offered the opportunity to borrow money at an interest rate of 1% per month. Will we be paying the equivalent of 12% per year? Yes and no. More precisely, we are paying an *effective* rate of 1% per month and a *nominal* rate of 12% per year. When the interest period is less than one year, the nominal (annual) rate r is determined by multiplying the effective rate per interest period i by the number M of interest periods per year. Note here that $i = r/M$.

It is clearly of interest to be able to convert from nominal interest rates to effective interest rates per annum. A simple equation for this conversion may be easily derived by considering the following figure.

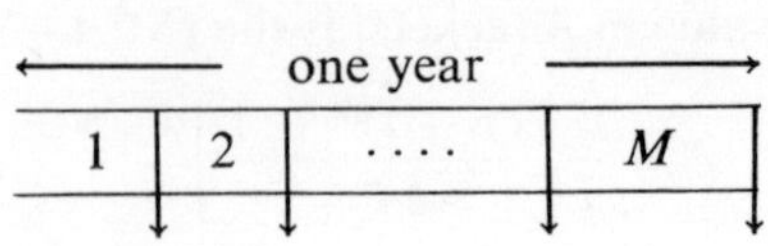

Each compounding takes place at rate r/M, and there are M such compoundings during the year. If i' represents the effective interest rate per annum, then:

$$(1 + i')^1 = \left(1 + \frac{r}{M}\right)^M$$

Thus:

$$i' = \left(1 + \frac{r}{M}\right)^M - 1 \tag{2.9}$$

It will be noted from the equation that the difference between the effective and nominal rates increases as r and/or M increase.

Returning to our original example, now, what is the effective interest rate per annum if interest is compounded at 1% monthly?

$$\begin{aligned} i' &= \left(1 + \frac{12\%}{12}\right)^{12} - 1 = (1 + 0.01)^{12} - 1 \\ &= 1.127 - 1 \\ &= 12.7\% \end{aligned}$$

THE CONTINUOUS COMPOUNDING CONVENTION

Except for the discussion of nominal interest, in previous sections it was assumed that interest is compounded just once during each interest period, at the end of the period. In the real world, of course, compounding may or may not occur in accordance with this assumption. Interest may be compounded twice during the period, four times, twelve times, or perhaps 365 times. In fact, it may be closer to the truth to assume *continuous* rather than end-of-period compounding in any particular case. Since a different set of compound interest factors is necessary under this assumption, two of the most important factors are derived here.

Determination of the effective interest rate (and resulting factors) is analogous to the situation discussed in the preceding section. However, in this instance there are an infinite number of compoundings during the period.

From equation 2.9: $i = \left(1 + \frac{r}{M}\right)^M - 1$

$$= \left[\left(1 + \frac{1}{M/r}\right)^{M/r}\right]^r - 1$$

Letting $k = M/r$, $\quad i = \left[\left(1 + \frac{1}{k}\right)^k\right]^r - 1$

Algebraic note: e represents the base of the natural (Naperian) system of logarithms. Its definition and approximate value is

$$e = \lim_{k \to \infty} \left(1 + \frac{1}{k}\right)^k \simeq 2.72$$

Since continuous compounding implies that k tends to infinity as M tends to infinity,

$$i = e^r - 1 \tag{2.10}$$

To find P or F under conditions of continuous compounding[3]:

$$F = P(1 + i)^N = P[1 + (e^r - 1)]^N$$
$$= Pe^{rN} \tag{2.11}$$

and

$$P = Fe^{-rN} \tag{2.12}$$

CONTINUOUS COMPOUNDING AND CONTINUOUS CASH FLOW

Just as real world situations may call for the use of the continuous compounding convention, so is it possible that the assumption of *continuous cash flow* may be a most reasonable approximation. For example, firms may, in certain situations, receive and dispense cash daily, a pattern which is more nearly approximated by an assumption of continuous cash flow than by the end-of-period (end-of-year) convention. In order to be consistent in our comparison of capital budget proposals — consistent in the use of effective interest rates for comparable time periods — it is necessary at this point to develop compound interest factors based on effective interest rates, which may be used when continuous cash flow and continuous compounding appear to be the most reasonable assumptions.

First, consider a single year. Let $1/M$ be the size of each uniform receipt (or disbursement) during the year.

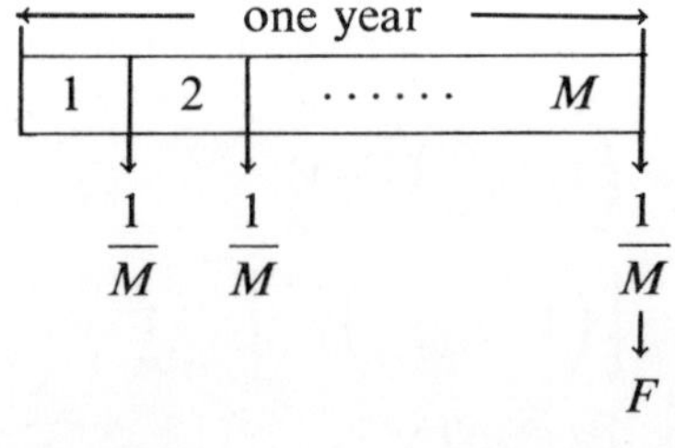

[3] Equations (2.11) and (2.12) are stated in terms of the *nominal* interest rate. To convert to (or from) an *effective* rate, use equation (2.10).

From equation 2.3: $F = A\dfrac{(1+i)^N - 1}{i}$.

But here $A = \dfrac{1}{M}$, $i = r/M$, and $N = M$.

Thus:

$$F = \frac{\frac{1}{M}\left(1+\frac{r}{M}\right)^M - 1}{r/M}$$

$$= \frac{\left[\left(1+\frac{1}{M/r}\right)^{M/r}\right]^r - 1}{r}$$

$$= \frac{\left[\left(1+\frac{1}{k}\right)^{k}\right]^r - 1}{r}, \text{ where } k = M/r.$$

$$\lim_{M\to\infty} F = \lim_{k\to\infty} F = \frac{e^r - 1}{r}$$

But $e^r - 1 = i$, and from this we see that $r = log_e(1+i)$.

Thus:

$$F = \frac{i}{log_e(1+i)} = \frac{i}{ln(1+i)}$$

Assuming continuous compounding, the above equation may be used to convert one dollar flowing continuously during the period to an equivalent end-of-period value.[4] Since the previous factors have been based on the end-of-period convention, it is now a simple matter to derive factors based on the assumptions of continuous compounding and continuous cash flow.

In Figure 2-4a, an amount $\bar{F}$ is shown flowing continuously throughout the Nth period. The "*continuous*" *single payment present worth factor* is used to find its equivalent present value.

$$P = \bar{F}\left\{\left[\frac{i}{ln(1+i)}\right]\cdot\left[(1+i)^{-N}\right]\right\} \tag{2.13}$$

$$= \bar{F}(\overline{CPW} - i\% - N)$$

[4] Using the appropriate identities, it may be shown that:

$$\frac{i}{ln\,(1+i)} = \frac{e^r - 1}{r}$$

Some authors refer to this expression as the "funds-flow conversion factor."

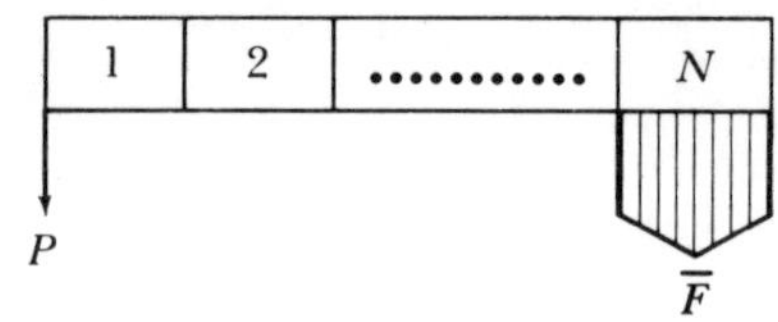

Fig. 2-4a. Cash Flow Diagram for an amount flowing uniformly and continuously during the Nth period.

An amount flowing continuously throughout each and every interest period from the 1st through the Nth period is illustrated in Figure 2-4b. $\bar{A}$ indicates

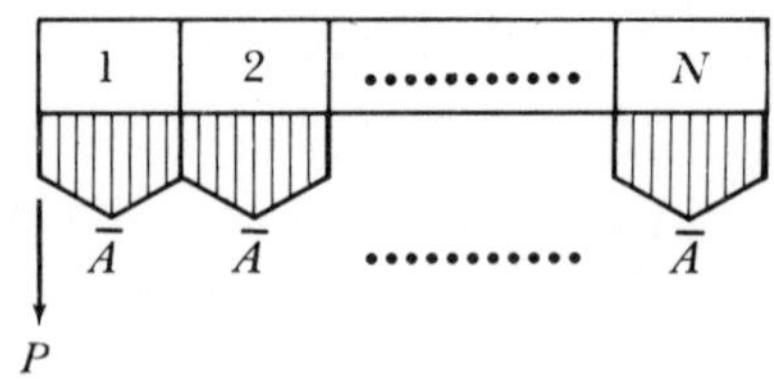

Fig. 2-4b. Cash Flow Diagram for an amount flowing uniformly and continuously throughout each and every period from time 0 through the Nth period.

the amount each period. To find the equivalent present value, we use the "*continuous*" *uniform series present worth factor.*

$$P = \bar{A}\left\{\left[\frac{i}{ln(1+i)}\right] \cdot \left[\frac{(1+i)^N - 1}{i(1+i)^N}\right]\right\} \tag{2.14}$$

$$= \bar{A}\,(\overline{CSPW} - i\% - N)$$

Values for the $\overline{CPW}$ and $\overline{CSPW}$ have been tabulated for various values of i and N and are shown in the Appendix.[5]

SUMMARY

Money amounts cannot be fairly compared unless they are stated as occurring at the same point in time. But since expenditures and receipts resulting from alternative capital investments almost always yield dissimilar cash flow patterns, it is necessary to determine equivalent values through the use of appropriate compound interest calculations. Some of the factors most commonly employed have been derived and are summarized in Table 2-4.

The distinction between nominal and effective interest rates should be clearly understood since the relative difference between these two rates can be

[5] The letter "*C*" in the mnemonic forms of equations (2.13) and (2.14) represents continuous compounding. The bar above the letters "*CPW*" denotes continuous cash flow.

Table 2-4

Summary of Important Equations

A. To Find Equivalent Values of a Single Cash Flow

(2.1) $F = P(1+i)^N = P(CA-i\%-N)$

$P = F\dfrac{1}{(1+i)^N} = F(PW-i\%-N)$

B. To Find Equivalent Values of a Uniform Series of Cash Flows

(2.3) $F = A\dfrac{(1+i)^N-1}{i} = A(SCA-i\%-N)$

(2.4) $A = F\dfrac{i}{(1+i)^N-1} = F(SF-i\%-N)$

(2.5) $P = A\dfrac{(1+i)^N-1}{i(1+i)^N} = A(SPW-i\%-N)$

(2.6) $A = P\dfrac{i(1+i)^N}{(1+i)^N-1} = P(CR-i\%-N)$ *NOTE:* $(CR) = (SF) + i$

C. To Find Equivalent Values of a Gradient Series

(2.7) $A = G\left\{\dfrac{1}{i}-\dfrac{N}{i}\left[\dfrac{i}{(1+i)^N-1}\right]\right\} = G(GUS-i\%-N)$

(2.8) $P = G\left\{\dfrac{1}{i}-\dfrac{N}{i}\left[\dfrac{i}{(1+i)^N-1}\right]\right\}\cdot\left\{\dfrac{(1+i)^N-1}{i(1+i)^N}\right\}$

$= G(GPW-i\%-N)$

D. Nominal and Effective Interest Rates

(2.9) $i' = (1+r/M)^M - 1$

E. Equivalent Values of a Single Cash Flow under Continuous Compounding

(2.10) $i = e^r - 1$

(2.11) $F = Pe^{rN}$

(2.12) $P = Fe^{-rN}$

F. Continuous Compounding - Continuous Cash Flow

(2.13) $P = \bar{F}\left\{\left[\dfrac{i}{ln(1+i)}\right]\cdot\left[\dfrac{1}{(1+i)^N}\right]\right\} = \bar{F}(\overline{CPW}-i\%-N)$

(2.14) $P = \bar{A}\left\{\left[\dfrac{i}{ln(1+i)}\right]\cdot\left[\dfrac{(1+i)^N-1}{i(1+i)^N}\right]\right\} = \bar{A}(\overline{CSPW}-i\%-N)$

---

significant. In general these differences will increase as the nominal rate gets larger and as the number of compoundings increases.

Compound interest factors have been developed under two separate sets of assumptions: (*a*) receipts or disbursements take place only once during the interest period — at the end of the period — and the interest calculation takes place at that time, or (*b*) the cash flows continuously and uniformly throughout the interest period and interest is compounded continuously. The appropriate assumptions for any given analysis should be those which best approximate the specific conditions at hand.

PROBLEMS

(Unless directed otherwise, assume end-of-period compounding and effective interest rates.)

1. In the spring of 1965 Mr. Norton Simon purchased Rembrandt's painting of his son Titus, for $2,234,400. This famous portrait, painted about 1650, was purchased from Sir Francis and Lady Cook whose family acquired the portrait in 1915.

   It is frequently said that "art is a good investment." Ignoring for the moment all consideration of aesthetics, and assuming that the painting was purchased for, say, $100,000 in 1915, decide whether or not this was a "good investment." Why? Based upon this simple but dramatic example, what may be said about investments in art (or real estate, or common stock, or antique furniture, or rare coins)?

2. Determine the following assuming an interest rate of 5% per annum:
   a) The present investment required to yield an income of $60 per year beginning in 7 years and continuing forever. (Hint: determine the uniform series present worth factor for $N = \infty$.)
   b) The value at the end of 35 years of a fund created by the year-end investments of $X in year 1, $2X in year 2, $3X in year 3, and so on for 35 years.
   c) The amount which must be deposited at the *beginning* of each year for 10 years in order to provide a fund of $10,000 at the end of the 10th year.

3. Determine the present worth of the following cash flow sequence if interest is compounded at 8% per annum:

End of Period	Positive Cash Flow (in millions of pesos)
1	300
2	400
3	500
4	600
5	600
6	600
7	600

4. You are able to secure a $1,000 loan from the Happy Home Finance Company, the interest rate being stated as 2% quarterly. (Interest is compounded every 3 months.) What are the nominal and effective annual rates?

5. Consider a project having a first cost of $1,000, a life of 10 years, and no salvage value. Labor expenses during each year of operation are estimated to be $100. A major overhaul will be required beginning 5 years after the project starts, will last for one year, and will cost a total of $500. (Of course, the project will not be in operation during the overhaul period.) Using the "continuous compounding — continuous cash flow" convention for labor and overhaul expenses, what is the total cost of the project in present dollars if interest is at 6%?

6. What effective interest rate per annum corresponds to a nominal rate of 10% per annum:
   (a) Compounded semi-annually?
   (b) Compounded continuously?

7. Using an interest rate of 7%, determine the present value of the following cash flow sequence:

End of Period	Cash Flow (in thousands of bolivars)
0	−100
1-5	+ 20
6	+ 18
7	+ 16
8	+ 14
9	+ 12
10	+ 10

(It is possible, of course, to "discount" each of the cash flows one by one. However, use of other appropriate factors will greatly simplify the calculations.)

8. What annual effective interest rate should be charged in order to receive $200 at the end of 5 years for a $100 loan?

9. With interest at 20% per annum, how long will it take to recover an initial investment of $10,000 if the investor receives $2,000 annually?

10. On July 1, 1966, $1,000 is deposited in a fund drawing 4% interest. Another $1,000 will be deposited on each July 1 up to and including July 1, 1976. It is required that the fund provide a series of uniform annual withdrawals starting July 1, 1981, and that the final withdrawal on July 1, 1985, exhaust the fund. How much will be withdrawn at the end of each year during the withdrawal sequence?

3

EQUIVALENT METHODS FOR SELECTING FROM AMONG ALTERNATIVES

As noted in the preceding chapter, the time value of money must be considered when selecting from among alternatives requiring capital outlays. Any methodology used in the budgeting process necessarily includes (*a*) the amount and (*b*) the timing of cash flows for each of the alternatives as well as (*c*) a measure of the minimum return which could be received should the available funds be invested elsewhere. (The manner in which the "minimum attractive rate of return" is determined is beyond the scope of this chapter; it is discussed at some length in Chapter 10. Here, we simply consider this value as given.)

Several methods may be described for alternative selection in the capital budgeting process. Each of these methods is *equivalent* in the sense that, properly applied, they lead to identical solutions (decisions). In the following sections we explain how these methods are correctly used and, where appropriate, the equivalence of the methods is emphasized.

THE ANNUAL COST METHOD

Basic Methodology

Alternatives cannot be compared unless their respective money consequences are first translated to comparable points in time by use of an appropriate interest rate. The annual cost method translates all cash flows to an equivalent uniform series. The method is also referred to as the "net annual benefit method" since the relative economic desirability of each alternative is a direct function of the amount by which (equivalent) end-of-period positive cash flows exceed (equivalent) end-of-period negative cash flows. A period is generally one year, so the method results in computed values for net *annual benefits* or, alternatively, for *annual cost*.

The choice of a *uniform* series as a time reference has considerable appeal. Many costs and revenues actually occur on an annual or period-by-period basis. For example, there are "rental costs of $200 per month," "property taxes of $500 per year," "interest income of $100 per quarter," and so on. Moreover, even if cash flows do not (or will not) follow a uniform series, it is frequently convenient to refer to them as though they do (or will). Budget planning and control, profit determination, and accounting for operations are examples of activities wherein forecasts are generally stated in the form of uniform period results.

Example: Suppose two manufacturing processes are being compared, the first of which requires annual direct material costs of $1,000 and annual direct labor cost of $2,000. The corresponding values for the second alternative are $1,200 and $1,500. The total annual cost for the two alternatives is:

	ALTERNATIVE A	ALTERNATIVE B	DIFFERENCE (B) − (A)
Direct material	$1,000	$1,200	$200
Direct labor	2,000	1,500	−500
Total	$3,000	$2,700	−$300

Clearly, the total annual costs for ALTERNATIVES A and B are $3,000 and $2,700, respectively. What is more important for our purposes, however, is the fact that A is $300 per year more costly than B. When alternatives are mutually exclusive — that is, when the selection of one automatically precludes selection of one or more of the others — *only differences between alternatives are relevant.*

ANNUAL COST ASSUMING CAPITAL EXPENDITURE. Suppose that we are considering a proposed capital expenditure (ALTERNATIVE C) requiring an initial outlay of $10,000 and estimated annual operating costs of $1,500 per year during the life of the project. Assume that the project is to be abandoned at the end of six years. If our money is "worth" 12% per annum, the expected total annual cost for the project is:

$$\begin{aligned}\text{Annual cost} &= (\text{capital recovery}) + (\text{operating costs})\\ &= \$10{,}000(CR - 12\% - 6) + \$1{,}500\\ &= \$10{,}000(0.24323) + \$1{,}500\\ &= \$3{,}932\end{aligned}$$

Note that, in the absence of any other information, the end-of-period convention has been used here. Unless otherwise indicated, this convention will be used throughout the text. Further, "*annual cost*" is an abbreviation for "*equivalent uniform annual cost*" since all cash flows have been converted to an equivalent uniform series. Finally, note the use of the term *capital recovery* to designate the annualized equivalent value of the initial investment. This explains the choice of name for the capital recovery factor.

ASSUMING NET SALVAGE VALUES. Consider ALTERNATIVE D with the following characteristics:

First cost (C)	\$12,000
Life of project (N)	6 years
Net salvage value at end of project life (L)	\$3,000
Annual operating costs (A)	\$1,600
Minimum attractive rate of return (i)	12%

This case differs from the preceding one in that here we assume a residual value for the asset at the end of its useful life. Following the corresponding cash flow diagram shown in Figure 3-1a, the total annual cost for ALTERNATIVE D is:

$$\begin{aligned}\text{Annual cost} &= C(CR - 12\% - 6) - L(SF - 12\% - 6) + A\\ &= \$12{,}000(0.24323) - \$3{,}000(0.12323) + \$1{,}600\\ &= \$2{,}919 - \$370 + \$1{,}600\\ &= \$2{,}549 + \$1{,}600\\ &= \$4{,}149\end{aligned}$$

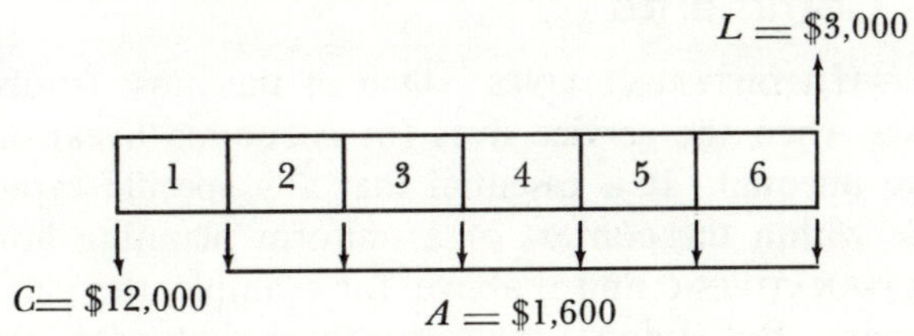

Note: As a matter of convention, downward arrows indicate negative cash flows, such as initial cost of asset and annual operating costs. Upward arrows indicate positive cash flows, such as sales revenues and positive salvage values.

Fig. 3-1a. Cash flow diagram for ALTERNATIVE D.

UNIVERSITY OF BRISTOL LIBRARY W.M.L.

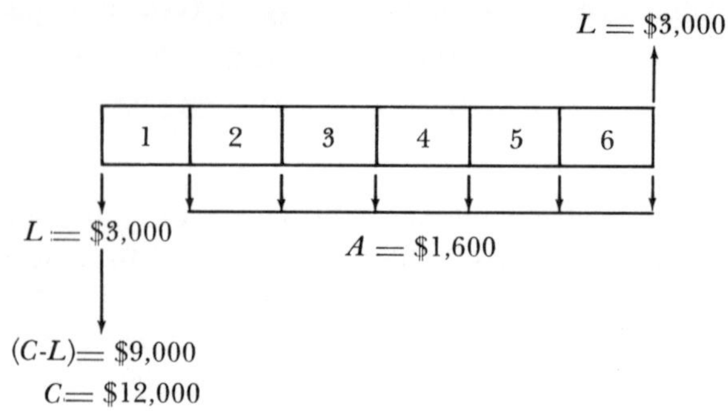

Fig. 3-1b. Cash flow diagram for ALTERNATIVE D illustrating basis for simplified capital recovery equation.

A "short cut" equation is frequently used for computing capital recovery when there exists a net salvage value. Referring to Figure 3-1b, the solution may be restated in its equivalent form:

$$\text{Annual cost} = (C - L)(CR - i\% - N) + Li + A \tag{3.1}$$

This is to say that capital recovery is equal to $(C - L)(CR - i\% - N) + Li$, thereby requiring the use of only one compound interest factor. This simplification may be demonstrated mathematically, but it is also evident from the fact that capital recovery is derived from the loss in value of the asset $(C - L)$ plus interest foregone on that portion (L) which is not "lost." In terms of the example:

$$\begin{aligned} \text{Capital recovery} &= (C - L)(CR - 12\% - 6) + Li \\ &= (\$12{,}000 - \$3{,}000)(0.24323) + (\$3{,}000)(0.12) \\ &= \$2{,}189 + \$360 \\ &= \$2{,}549 \end{aligned}$$

Additional Comments

ALTERNATIVES WITH DIFFERENT LIVES. One of the most troublesome complications arises when the service lives (or economic lives) of the various alternatives are unequal. It is essential that any specific capital allocation study be made within the context of a uniform planning horizon. When considering ALTERNATIVES C and D above, for example, the planning horizon is clearly six years. But suppose there is a third contender, ALTERNATIVE E, whose expected service life is twelve years. Assuming that only one of these three alternatives may be accepted, what is the appropriate planning horizon, and, given this, how ought the analysis to be conducted?

These questions may first be answered by assuming an estimated *duration of need* which the alternatives are expected to fulfill. For example, it may be nine years, twenty years, a very long time (approximately infinity), and so on. Then, given the duration of the need, it is necessary to make some reasonable assumptions about the *consequences of replacement assets.* To illustrate, suppose we consider ALTERNATIVE E with first cost of \$20,000, estimated salvage value of \$2,000 at the end of twelve years, and expected operating costs of \$900 per year. Assuming an interest rate of 12%, the total annual cost is:

$$\begin{aligned} \text{Annual cost} &= (\$20{,}000 - \$2{,}000)(CR - 12\% - 12) + (\$2{,}000)(0.12) + \$900 \\ &= \$18{,}000(0.16144) + \$240 + \$900 \\ &= \$3{,}146 + \$900 \\ &= \$4{,}046 \end{aligned}$$

This calculation assumes, of course, that the life of the need is at least twelve years. Shorter durations would require appropriate modification of the capital recovery cost.

Now suppose there is reason to believe that the need will continue indefinitely, that is, that the planning horizon is approximately infinite. Further, assume that replacements have the same first costs, lives, salvage values, and annual operating costs as the current alternatives. These assumptions lead to a series of cash flows as outlined in Table 3-1. Under these assumptions it is

Table 3-1

Cash Flows for ALTERNATIVES C, D, and E Assuming Infinite Planning Horizon and Identical Replacements

End of Year	ALTERNATIVE C	ALTERNATIVE D	ALTERNATIVE E
	\$	\$	\$
0	−10,000	−12,000	−20,000
1–6	−1,500	−1,600	−900
6	−10,000	−12,000 + 3,000	—
7–12	−1,500	−1,600	−900
12	−10,000	−12,000 + 3,000	−20,000 + 2,000
13–18	−1,500	−1,600	−900
18	−10,000	−12,000 + 3,000	—
19–24	−1,500	−1,600	−900
24		+3,000	+2,000
	.	.	.
	.	.	.
	.	.	.

clear that the total annual costs as previously determined remain applicable and, moreover, the same values are applicable if the planning horizon is any number of periods which is a common multiple of the lives of each of the alternatives. This is to say that, since

- the total annual cost for ALTERNATIVE C is \$3,932,
- the total annual cost for ALTERNATIVE D is \$4,149, and
- the total annual cost for ALTERNATIVE E is \$4,046,

then ALTERNATIVE C is economically superior to the other two.

Although these assumptions allow us to use the original solutions for annual cost without modification, one should resist the temptation to use them, explicitly or implicitly, without carefully considering likely future consequences. If annual costs are compared without considering differences in project lives, the solutions imply identical repetition and a planning horizon equal to a common multiple of project lives. These assumptions should always be questioned in real situations.

ALTERNATIVES WITH PERPETUAL LIVES. In certain cases the expected life of the proposal is extremely long. It may be reasonable in such cases to assume perpetual life, that is, $N = \infty$. To solve these problems it is only necessary to observe that $(CR - i\% - \infty) = i$. This result may be shown algebraically, but it is also evident from the fact that the only way in which an initial sum (C) can yield a uniform annual series of payments (A) indefinitely is to have the annual payment exactly equal to the period interest. That is, $A = iC$. To illustrate, consider ALTERNATIVE F:

First cost (C)	\$30,000
Life of project (N)	Infinite
Annual operating costs (A)	\$600
Minimum attractive rate of return (i)	12%

Then: Annual cost $= iC + A$

$$= (0.12)(\$30{,}000) + \$600$$
$$= \$4{,}200$$

CASH FLOWS FOLLOWING A UNIFORM GRADIENT. Certain expenses and revenues increase (or decrease) in an arithmetic progression. For example, we may expect wages to be \$5,000 during the first year of the project, \$5,500 in the second year, \$6,000 in the third year, and to increase by \$500 each and every year over a period of six years. Because gradient series, either precisely or approximately, frequently occur, a special compound interest factor has been derived to convert the gradient series to equivalent uniform annual series (Eq. 2.7). Use of the factor ($GUS - i\% - N$) may be illustrated using the data given in Table 3-2. Assuming an interest rate of 10%,

$$\text{Equivalent annual cost of } \textit{positive gradient} = A + G(GUS - 10\% - 6)$$
$$= \$5{,}000 + \$500(2.22)$$
$$= \$6{,}110$$

$$\text{Equivalent annual cost of } \textit{negative gradient} = A + (-G)(GUS - 10\% - 6)$$
$$= \$7{,}500 - \$500(2.22)$$
$$= \$6{,}390$$

Table 3-2

Cash Flows Illustrating Gradient Series

Interest rate: 10%

End of Year	Positive Gradient	Negative Gradient
1	$5,000	$7,500
2	5,500	7,000
3	6,000	6,500
4	6,500	6,000
5	7,000	5,500
6	7,500	5,000
Total :	$37,500	$37,500
Basic amount A :	5,000	7,500
Gradient G :	+ 500	− 500

Parenthetically, note that the total cash flows for the two gradient series are equal, yet the equivalent annual costs are different. Why? The answer, of course, lies in their *timing*. In the case of the negative gradient, the heavier cash flows occur in the earlier years.

IRREGULAR CASH FLOWS. When period-by-period cash flows follow no regular pattern, their conversion to an equivalent uniform annual series may be effected by first finding their equivalent present worth, summing all values, and then multiplying the total by the appropriate capital recovery factor. For example, assuming an interest rate of 6%:

Table 3-3

End of Period j	Cash Flow C_j	Discount Factor $(PW-6\%-j)$	Present Worth P_j
1	\$100	0.9434	\$94.34
2	50	0.8900	44.50
3	80	0.8396	67.17
4	30	0.7921	23.76
			P = \$229.77

$$\begin{aligned}\text{Thus: Annual Cost} &= P(CR\text{-}6\%\text{-}4)\\ &= \$229.77(0.28859)\\ &= \$66.31\end{aligned}$$

AN ALTERNATIVE METHOD FOR COMPUTING CAPITAL RECOVERY. Based upon the equation previously determined for computing capital recovery, another form may be derived:

$$\text{Capital recovery} = (C - L)(CR - i\% - N) + Li \tag{3.2}$$

$$= (C - L)\frac{i(1 + i)^N}{(1 + i)^N - 1} + Li$$

$$= \frac{Ci(1 + i)^N - Li(1 + i)^N + Li(1 + i)^N - Li + Ci - Ci}{(1 + i)^N - 1}$$

$$= \frac{Ci - Li}{(1 + i)^N - 1} + \frac{Ci(1 + i)^N - Ci}{(1 + i)^N - 1}$$

$$= (C - L)\frac{i}{(1 + i)^N - 1} + Ci$$

$$= (C - L)(SF - i\% - N) + Ci \tag{3.3}$$

Thus, $(C - L)(CR - i\% - N) + Li$ is equal to $(C - L)(SF - i\% - N) + Ci$. This alternative form is occasionally found in the public utility industry, although its use is extremely limited. When capital recovery is computed in this manner it is generally described as *sinking fund depreciation plus interest on first cost.*

THE PRESENT WORTH (OR PRESENT VALUE) METHOD

Basic Methodology

The essential feature of the present worth method is the *discounting to present value* of all cash flows expected to result from an investment decision. That is, in order to satisfy the basic requirement that alternatives be compared only if money consequences are measured at a common point in time, the "present date" is arbitrarily selected as the point of reference. (In practice, the "present date" is determined relative to the particular problem of interest. It is generally defined as the time at which the project life begins.) The net discounted value of all prospective cash flows is a direct measure of the relative economic attractiveness of the proposed investment.

ALTERNATIVE C (described in the preceding section) provides the data for a simple example. The cash flow diagram, illustrated in Figure 3-2, indicates the following values:

First cost (C)	\$10,000
Life of project (N)	6 years
Annual operating costs (A)	\$1,500
Minimum attractive rate of return (i)	12%

The net present worth (PW) may now be determined by discounting all cash flows which are not already occurring at "time zero" and then summing. Thus:

$$\begin{aligned} PW &= -C - A(SPW - 12\% - 6) \\ &= -\$10{,}000 - \$1{,}500(4.111) \\ &= -\$16{,}166 \end{aligned}$$

Of course, at zero interest rate, that is, if money has *no* value over time, the net present worth would be:

$$-\$10{,}000 - \$1{,}500(6) = -\$19{,}000.$$

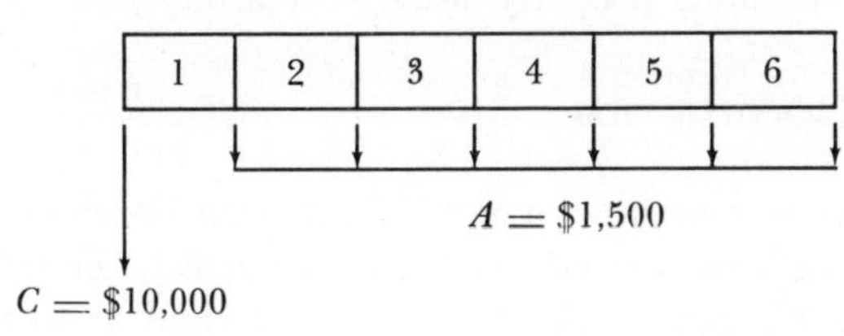

Fig. 3-2. Cash flow diagram for ALTERNATIVE C.

If the interest rate is greater than 12% the *absolute value* (unsigned number) of the present worth will be smaller than $16,166. The reason for this should be obvious: the present absolute value of future cash flows is inversely related to the interest rate.

The utility of the derived present values may be illustrated by reference to ALTERNATIVE D which was previously discussed. Recall:

First cost (C)	$12,000
Life of project (N)	6 years
Net salvage value at end of project life (L)	$3,000
Annual operating costs (A)	$1,600
Minimum attractive rate of return (i)	12%

As before, the net present worth (PW) may be determined:

$$\begin{aligned} PW &= -\ C - A(SPW - 12\% - 6) + L(PW - 12\% - 6) \\ &= -\ \$12{,}000 - \$1{,}600(4.111) + \$3{,}000(0.5066) \\ &= -\ \$12{,}000 - \$6{,}577.6 + \$1{,}519.8 \\ &= -\ \$17{,}058 \end{aligned}$$

Now suppose ALTERNATIVES C and D are mutually exclusive in the sense that selection of one precludes selection of the other. Assuming no other differences between alternatives, the computed present worths indicate that ALTERNATIVE C is less costly (hence more desirable) than ALTERNATIVE D.

The equivalence of the annual cost and present worth methods may be easily verified. As determined in the preceding section, the resulting total annual costs were $3,932 and $4,149 for ALTERNATIVES C and D, respectively. Converting these results to their equivalent present values by multiplying by ($PW - 12\% - 6$):

$$PW(\text{C}) = -\ \$3{,}932(4.111) = -\ \$16{,}165$$

and

$$PW(\text{D}) = -\ \$4{,}149(4.111) = -\ \$17{,}057$$

Allowing for error due to rounding, these are precisely the same values as those computed directly when determining net present value. The two methods are equivalent and, properly used, will always give identical results.

Additional Comments

ALTERNATIVES WITH DIFFERENT LIVES. Failure to consider equal planning horizons for the various alternatives leads to incorrect, and frequently absurd, solutions. With reference to the annual cost method, this error may not be obvious since the resulting solutions *imply* identical repetition of proposals. This is not the case with the present worth method, however. Here the implication is that there are no consequences (that is, no cash flows) after disposal of the shorter-lived asset. Figure 3-3 illustrates this situation using the data previously provided for ALTERNATIVES D and E. *Incorrect* values for the net present worths of the two proposals are found as follows:

$$PW(\text{D}) = -\$12{,}000 - \$1{,}600(SPW - 12\% - 6) + \$3{,}000(PW - 12\% - 6)$$
$$= -\$12{,}000 - \$1{,}600(0.5066) + \$3{,}000(1.974)$$
$$= -\$17{,}058$$
$$PW(\text{E}) = -\$20{,}000 - \$900(SPW - 12\% - 12) + \$2{,}000(PW - 12\% - 12)$$
$$= -\$20{,}000 - \$900(6.194) + \$2{,}000(0.2567)$$
$$= -\$25{,}061$$

These results indicate that ALTERNATIVE D is less costly than ALTERNATIVE E, a conclusion opposite to that obtained when using the annual cost method.

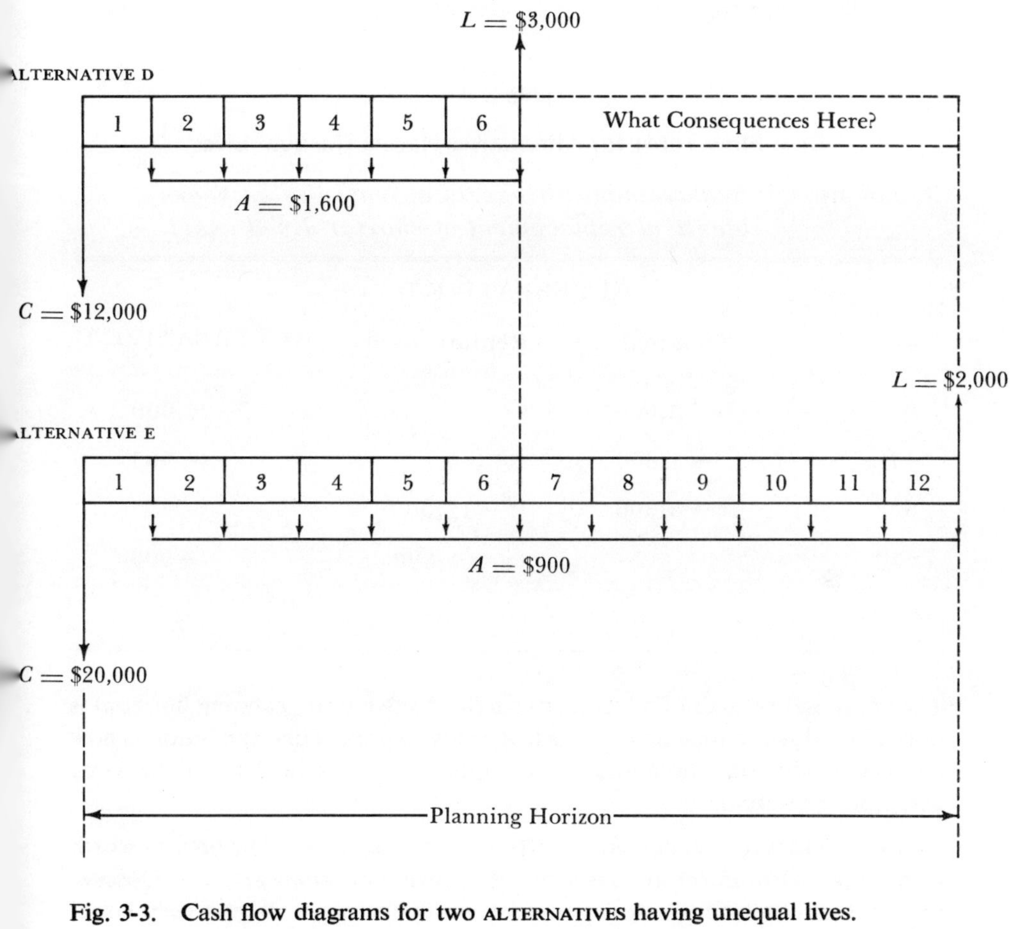

Fig. 3-3. Cash flow diagrams for two ALTERNATIVES having unequal lives.

The error occurs from failure to account for the difference in lives of the proposals.

Valid solution of this problem requires that all consequences of alternatives be accounted for over the common planning horizon. Suppose, for example, it is assumed that ALTERNATIVE D may be replaced at the end of six years with an identical replacement. The resulting cash flows for a planning horizon of twelve years are shown in Table 3-4. Based upon these assumptions, the appropriate net present worths of the two proposals, *D* and its successor, are:

$$\begin{aligned} PW(\text{D}) &= -C - A(SPW - 12\% - 12) - (C - L)(PW - 12\% - 6) + \\ &\quad L(PW - 12\% - 12) \\ &= -\$12{,}000 - \$1{,}600(6.194) - \$9{,}000(0.5066) + \$3{,}000(0.2567) \\ &= -\$12{,}000 - \$9{,}910.4 - \$4{,}559.4 + \$770.1 \\ &= -\$25{,}700 \end{aligned}$$

Table 3-4

Cash Flow Table for Alternatives Having Unequal Lives

Assumptions: Requirement for assets at least twelve years
Identical replacement of shorter-lived asset

End of Year	ALTERNATIVE D Original	ALTERNATIVE D Replacement	ALTERNATIVE E
0	$ −12,000		$ −20,000
1–6	−1,600		−900
6	+3,000	$ −12,000	
7–12		−1,600	−900
12		+3,000	+2,000

The net present worth of ALTERNATIVE E (for twelve-year planning horizon) is only $25,061, so it appears that E is less costly than D. This conclusion is now consistent with that obtained by the annual cost method when the same assumptions were used.

ALTERNATIVES WITH PERPETUAL LIVES (CAPITALIZED COST). The present worth of a perpetual uniform annual series is known as *capitalized cost.* Observe the limit of the uniform series present worth factor as *N* gets very large:

$$\lim_{N\to\infty} (SPW - i\% - N) = \lim_{N\to\infty} \frac{(1+i)^N - 1}{i(1+i)^N}$$

$$= \lim_{N\to\infty} \frac{1}{i}\left[\frac{(1+i)^N - 1}{(1+i)^N}\right]$$

$$= \frac{1}{i}$$

Thus capitalized costs are annual costs, stated as a uniform series, divided by the interest rate.

Recall the data given for ALTERNATIVE F:

First cost (C)	\$30,000
Life of project (N)	Infinite
Annual operating costs (A)	\$600
Minimum attractive rate of return (i)	12%

The capitalized cost of this proposal is its net present value:

$$\text{Capitalized cost} = C + \frac{A}{i}$$

$$= \$30{,}000 + \frac{\$600}{0.12}$$

$$= \$35{,}000$$

GRADIENT CASH FLOWS. The gradient series (arithmetic progression) of cash flows is a relatively common phenomenon. Revenues, labor expenses, raw material costs, etc., may either approximate or follow this pattern of uniform increase or decrease. Where the gradient series does occur, it is helpful to use the special gradient present worth factor (Eq. 2.8) which was derived in the preceding chapter. To illustrate, consider the following present worth calculations for the two gradient series shown in Table 3-2:

$$PW(\text{positive gradient}) = A(SPW - 10\% - 6) - G(GPW - 10\% - 6)$$

$$= \$5{,}000(4.355) + \$500(9.68)$$

$$= \$26{,}615$$

$$PW(\text{negative gradient}) = A(SPW - 10\% - 6) - G(GPW - 10\% - 6)$$

$$= \$7{,}500(4.355) - \$500(9.68)$$

$$= \$27{,}823$$

In this example, although the totals of the undiscounted cash flows are equal, the negative gradient results in the larger present value since its heavier cash flows take place earlier in time.

IRREGULAR CASH FLOWS. Period-by-period cash flows may be neither constant nor uniformly increasing or decreasing. When these irregular cash flows occur, it is necessary to discount each of them individually and then sum the results. That is:

$$PW = \sum_{j=0}^{N} C_j(1 + i)^{-j} \tag{3.4a}$$

where C_j is the cash flow taking place in the jth period. One illustration has been given in the preceding section. As another example, consider ALTERNATIVE G and assume an interest rate of 6% per period.

Table 3-5

Present Worth Solution for ALTERNATIVE G

End of Period j	Cash Flow C_j	Discount Function $(1+i)^{-j}$	Present Worth P_j
0	\$ −1,000	1.0000	\$ −1,000.00
1	+600	0.9434	+566.04
2	+500	0.8900	+445.00
3	−500	0.8396	−419.80
4	+400	0.7921	+316.84
5	+1,000	0.7473	+747.30
		Total *PW*:	\$655.38

THE RATE OF RETURN METHOD

Basic Methodology

The *rate of return* of a given investment proposal is the interest rate (per interest period) at which the present worth of receipts resulting from the project is exactly equal to the present worth of disbursements. Stated somewhat differently, it is the interest rate at which the net present worth of all receipts and disbursements is equal to zero, where receipts and disbursements are treated as positive and negative cash flows, respectively. Mathematically, it is that value of i which satisfies the equation:

$$0 = \sum_{j=0}^{N} C_j(1 + i)^{-j} \tag{3.4b}$$

assuming end-of-period cash flows and end-of-period compounding, or:

$$0 = \sum_{j=0}^{N} C_j \frac{i}{ln(1 + i)} (1 + i)^{-j} \tag{3.5}$$

assuming uniform and continuous cash flows during each period and continuous compounding of interest.

The rate of return computed in this manner takes into consideration the amount as well as the timing of expected costs and revenues. It is, in a sense, a measure of profitability of the project. In order for the project to be acceptable, however, the rate of return must then be compared to some minimum attractive rate which could be earned if the proposed project were rejected and the capital invested elsewhere. These two steps taken together — determination of the project rate of return and comparison to the minimum attractive rate of return — are the essential features of the rate of return method.

A variety of names has been given to the method of calculation described above. The most prominent among these includes the "interest rate of return," "Profitability Index," "Investor's Method," and the "discounted cash flow method." These methods are equivalent and, when properly applied, will produce precisely the same solutions as those resulting from the annual cost method or the present worth method.

To illustrate determination of the rate of return, consider the cash flows given in Column (b) of Table 3-6 for ALTERNATIVE H. Assuming end-of-

Table 3-6

Rate of Return Solution for ALTERNATIVE H

End of Period	Cash Flow	(*PW*–12%–*j*)	*PW* at 12%	(*PW*–15%–*j*)	*PW* at 15%
(a)	(b)	(c)	(d)	(e)	(f)
0	\$–1,000	1.0000	\$–1,000	1.0000	\$–1,000
1	200	0.9091	179	0.8696	174
2	200	0.8264	159	0.7561	151
3	400	0.7513	285	0.6575	263
4	600	0.6830	381	0.5718	343
Total:	\$ 400		\$ 4		\$ –69

period compounding, the rate of return is that value of i which satisfies the equation:

$$\begin{aligned} O &= \sum_{j=0}^{4} C_j(1+i)^{-j} \\ &= -\$1{,}000 + \$200(1+i)^{-1} + \$200(1+i)^{-2} + \$400(1+i)^{-3} \\ &\quad + \$600\,(1+i)^{-4} \end{aligned}$$

There is no simple algebraic solution to this equation, so a trial-and-error approach is necessary. Referring to Table 3-6, the present worth of the cash flows is $+4$ when $i = 12\%$; it is $-\$69$ when an interest rate of 15% is assumed. Since the solving interest rate should result in zero present worth, it is clear that we have bracketed the solution within the limits of the tables available in the Appendix. Thus, using straight-line interpolation:

$$\begin{aligned} i &= 12\% + (15\% - 12\%)\frac{4}{4-(-69)} \\ &= 12\% + 3\%\frac{4}{73} \\ &= 12.2\% \end{aligned}$$

Additional Comments

SHORT-CUT SOLUTIONS. In certain instances the pattern of cash flows is such that solutions may be directly determined; that is, the cumbersome trial-and-error approach may be avoided or simplified. For example, suppose it is desired to determine the prospective rate of return from an initial investment of \$100,000, which results in net revenues of \$40,000 per year for four years. The equation which, when solved, gives the prospective rate of return is:

$$\begin{aligned} O &= \sum_{j=0}^{4} C_j(1+i)^{j} \\ &= -\$100{,}000 + \$40{,}000\sum_{j=1}^{4}(1+i)^{j} \\ &= -\$100{,}000 + \$40{,}000(SPW - i\% - 4) \end{aligned}$$

This result also follows from $P = A(SPW - i\% - N)$. Thus:

$$(SPW - i\% - 4) = \frac{\$100{,}000}{\$40{,}000} = 2.5$$

From the compound interest tables, it is found that $(SPW - 20\% - 4) = 2.589$ and $(SPW - 25\% - 4) = 2.362$. Using linear interpolation, the proposed rate of return is determined to be 21.9%.

The factors for the uniform series and gradient series should be used whenever possible to simplify calculations. Again, to illustrate, consider the following pattern of cash flows:

End of Period	Cash Flow
0	$ − 850
1–20	48
20	1,000

The *solution equation*, that is, the equation which, when solved, yields the prospective rate of return, is:

$$O = -\ \$850 + \$48(SPW - i\% - 20) + \$1{,}000(PW - i\% - 20)$$

A trial-and-error approach is required here since there is more than one factor in the solution equation. However, use of the uniform series present worth factor does simplify the problem since twenty separate factors are avoided. The solution is as follows:

PW at 6% = − \$850 + \$48(11.470) + \$1,000(0.3118) = + \$12
PW at 7% = − \$850 + \$48(10.594) + \$1,000(0.2584) = − \$84
Interpolating, i = 6.125%

GUESSING THE RATE OF RETURN. When trial-and-error calculations are required, it is obviously quite helpful if initial trials can result from an "educated guess" rather than from a "shot in the dark." There are several ways in which estimates might be improved.

First, examination of the cash flow table should indicate whether the solving rate of return is low or high — or, for that matter, whether there *is* a meaningful solution. Consider the following three examples:

End of Period	Cash Flow I	Cash Flow II	Cash Flow III
0	$ − 100	$ − 100	$ − 100
1	20	30	10
2	30	60	30
3	40	40	30
4	20	70	20
Total	$ 10	$ 100	$ − 10

With an original investment of \$100, Project I results in a net gain of \$10 after four years, Project II yields a net gain of \$100, and Project III results in a net loss. It follows that the rate of return will be low for I, relatively high for II, and of course there is no meaningful rate of return for III. (There *will* be a solution to the present worth equation for Project III. What is its meaning? If the cash flows as shown represent those of the lender, then the solution rate of return is that obtained by the borrower. The lender's profit is negative in this case.)

Second, an irregular series of cash flows may be approximated by a uniform series. Returning to ALTERNATIVE H:

Table 3-7

End of Period	Actual Cash Flow	Approximate Cash Flow
0	\$ − 1,000	\$ − 1,000
1	200	350
2	200	350
3	400	350
4	600	350
Total:	\$400	\$400

The approximate rate of return may now be found:

$$O = -\ \$1{,}000 + \$350(SPW - i\% - 4)$$

$$(SPW - i\% - 4) = 2.857,$$

but $(SPW - 15\% - 4) = 2.855$, and thus i is approximately 15%.

Third, in conjunction with the result of the uniform series approximation, note the location of the largest cash flows. The largest cash flows associated with ALTERNATIVE H, for example, occur near the end of the project life, that is, during the third and fourth years. Thus the actual rate of return should be something less than 15%, and our first trial might be 12%. (As determined earlier, the solution is 12.2%.)

MULTIPLE INTEREST RATE SOLUTIONS. Although, when properly applied, the rate of return method yields the same solutions as those obtained from the annual cost and present worth methods, the algebraic structure is such that analysts may be led to incorrect solutions. This does not mean that the rate of return method is inherently incorrect — rather, it is to say that the analyst should be aware of errors which may result from certain situations. One of these, the "ranking error," is discussed later. Our discussion at this point centers upon the problem known as "the multiple interest rate solution." Consider the usual solution equation for the rate of return:

$$O = \sum_{j=0}^{N} C_j(1 + i)^{-j}$$

Theoretically, there are many solutions for i. In fact, from algebra, Descartes' Rule of Signs states that there may be as many positive roots (solutions) as there are changes in direction of sign of the C_j values.

In most problems there is only one change in sign. That is, the initial investment (negative cash flow) generally results in a sequence of net revenues or cost savings (positive cash flows). This situation normally leads to a unique solution. On the other hand, consider the following sequence of cash flows:[1]

End of Period	Cash Flow
0	\$ 1,600
1	−10,000
2	10,000

Ordinarily, the rate of return is that value of i which satisfies the equation:

$$O = +\$1{,}600 - \$10{,}000(1 + i)^{-1} + \$10{,}000(1 + i)^{-2}$$

There are two solutions: $i = 25\%$ and $i = 400\%$. Neither of these answers is correct, however.

The appropriate resolution of this problem requires consideration of an *auxiliary interest rate* represented by the return available from reinvested capital. The positive cash flow at zero date, \$1,600, may be reinvested at the minimum attractive rate of return, say, 20%. Thus its value at the end of the first period will be \$1,920(= \$1,600 + 320), and the *net* cash flow at the end of the first period is − \$8,080(= − \$10,000 + \$1,920). The revised problem has only one variation in sign:

$$O = -\$8{,}080 + \$10{,}000(1 + i)^{-1}$$

This has for its solution $i = 23.8\%$. The auxiliary interest rate has been used to determine the "value" of receiving \$1,600 one year prior to investment in the project. If money is worth 20 per cent, this preinvestment return has value \$1,920 at the time of investment. The revised question is: "What is the prospective return for a project which costs \$8,080 and yields \$10,000 one year later?"

[1] This cash flow sequence is based on an example provided by Professor Ezra Solomon, "The Arithmetic of Capital Budgeting Decisions," *Journal of Business*, Vol. XXIX (1956), p. 124.

SUMMARY

The annual cost method, the present worth method, and the rate of return method are three valid techniques which may be used for evaluating proposed investment opportunities or auditing past decisions. Each of these methods considers the amount and timing of cash flows; they differ only with respect to the reference time used.

The annual cost method requires that all cash flows be transcribed to a uniform series by use of appropriate compound interest factors. Alternatives may be compared directly if annual costs (or net annual benefits) have been "spread" uniformly over common time periods.

In the present worth method all cash flows are discounted to date zero, that is, an equivalent present value is obtained. Again, it is essential that planning horizons for each alternative be of equal length.

The rate of return method is, in a sense, the inverse of the present worth method in that the rate of return for a project is that value of *i* which satisfies the present worth equation when set equal to zero. (Of course, the rate of return may also be found from an equation which sets the sum of the annualized costs and benefits equal to zero, but the present worth format is the usual case.) This method is equivalent to the annual cost and present worth methods when properly used.

PROBLEMS

(Unless directed otherwise, assume end-of-period compounding and effective interest rates.)

1. A new warehouse will cost $150,000 and will have an expected life of 12 years with $3,000 net salvage value at the end of that time. Annual disbursements for maintenance, heating, taxes, etc., are estimated to be $2,500 the first year, $3,000 the second year, and to continue to increase at the rate of $500 per year throughout its life. If the minimum attractive rate of return is 15% before taxes, determine the equivalent total annual cost of this proposed investment.

2. A certain operation can be performed satisfactorily by either Machine X or Machine Y. Pertinent data for the two alternatives are as follows:

	Machine X	Machine Y
First cost	$6,000	$14,000
Salvage value	-0-	20% of first cost
Service life in years	12	18
Annual disbursements	$4,000	$2,400

Compare the equivalent total annual costs assuming a minimum attractive rate of return of 12% before taxes. Specify all assumptions.

3. The Black Company is considering two alternative plans for erecting a fence around its new Central City plant. *Galvanized steel* "chicken wire" fencing requires a first cost of $35,000 and estimated annual upkeep costs of $300. The expected life is 25 years. A *concrete block* wall requires a first cost of only $20,000, but it will need minor repairs every 5 years at a cost of $1,000 and major repairs every 10 years at a cost of $5,000. Assuming an interest rate of 10% before taxes and a perpetual (continuing) need, determine the equivalent total annual costs for the two plans. Specify all other assumptions.

4. A specialized vending machine may be purchased for $20,000. The expected excess of receipts over disbursements is $4,000 a year for the first four years and $3,000 in the fifth year. It is expected that the machine will be sold at the end of the fifth year for $12,000. Treat the annual receipts and disbursements using the *uniform flow, continuous compounding* convention. If the effective interest rate is 10% per annum before taxes, what is the net present worth of this series of cash flows?

5. Consider a prospective investment in a warehouse having a first cost of $300,000, operating and maintenance costs of $35,000 per year, and an estimated net disposal value of $50,000 at the end of 60 years. Assume an interest rate of 8%.
   (a) What is the present value of this investment if the planning horizon is 60 years?
   (b) If replacement structures will have the same first cost, life, salvage value, and operating and maintenance costs as the original building, what is the capitalized cost of perpetual service? What is the difference between sixty-year and "infinite" life?

6. Two types of conveyor systems are being considered by the Blue Corporation:

	System X	System Y
Initial investment	$5,000	$12,000
Net salvage value	$1,000	-0-
Annual disbursements	$900	$600
Estimated life	10 years	15 years

Assuming a pre-tax interest rate of 20%, which system appears to be the better investment, everything else being equal? State all necessary assumptions.

7. Two years ago the White Trucking Company leased a terminal site from the Eastern Pacific Railroad and prepaid the rent for a period of 5 years. The total prepaid rent was $60,000. The terms of the lease permit the Company to continue to rent the site for a period of five additional years by payment of $10,000 at the beginning of each year of the second 5-year period.

   The Railroad has now decided that it is in need of funds to finance legal action in connection with a possible merger. The Railroad has proposed to the Company that it now prepay the rental that was to have been paid year-by-year in the second 5-year period. Assuming interest at 8% per annum, what is a fair payment to be made now in lieu of the five annual payments?

8. In order to raise capital for acquisition purposes, the Brown Company sells 4% bonds to an investment banking firm for $2,800,000. The face value of these bonds is $3,000,000, and they will mature in 25 years. Dividend payments will be made semi-annually. Initial disbursements in connection with the bond issue are $150,000, and each year additional expenses (for example, trustee and registrar fees) are expected to be $25,000. Expressed as an interest rate, what is the actual cost of this borrowed money?

9. The data for ALTERNATIVES C and D in the text are repeated as follows:

	ALT. C	ALT. D
First cost	$10,000	$12,000
Expected life	6 years	6 years
Net salvage value	-0-	$3,000
Annual operating costs	$1,500	$1,600

   Suppose our problem is such that either C *or* D must be selected.
   (a) What is the expected rate of return on the additional (incremental) $2,000 investment in ALTERNATIVE D?
   (b) If the minimum attractive rate of return for the Company is 12% before taxes, is the additional investment justified?
   (c) Which alternative should be selected? Is this the same solution as that obtained from the annual cost and present worth methods?
   (d) At what interest rate(s), if any, would D be less costly than C?

10. The Green Corporation is considering installation of a semi-automatic freight conveyor requiring $300,000 immediate investment. It is estimated that, if the conveyor is purchased, it will be kept for 10 years and

then sold for $12,000. It is further believed that this will result in cost savings as follows:

Year	Net Savings	Year	Net Savings
1	$60,000	6	$55,000
2	60,000	7	50,000
3	60,000	8	45,000
4	60,000	9	40,000
5	60,000	10	35,000

Determine the prospective rate of return before taxes of this investment.

Note to instructor: Digital or analog computers may be used effectively to determine the rate of return solutions to several of the problems of this chapter. At least some of the problems should be solved manually, however, in order to improve understanding of the underlying procedures.

4

SOME INCORRECT AND/OR APPROXIMATE METHODS

Although the capital allocation techniques discussed in the preceding chapter are demonstrably valid, they are left generally unused by a large percentage of the business community. Significant evidence exists to indicate that proper capital budgeting methods are not yet widely used by industrial enterprises.

There are a number of reasons for this unhappy state of affairs. First, introduction of these techniques into college curricula is a relatively recent development. (By contrast, academic institutions have long taught the principles of double-entry accounting.) Second, in many cases businessmen call upon their "golden nugget of experience" to make decisions pertaining to the allocation of limited capital. Differences among alternatives may appear to be sufficiently large that the appropriate course of action is either immediately obvious or follows from a very few preliminary calculations. In any event, the businessman's intuition, based upon accumulated experience, frequently leads to the decision. Finally, certain incorrect and/or approximate methods are frequently used to select from among alternatives in the mistaken view that these are valid. Unfortunately, these methods have been institutionalized by extensive historical usage because of their apparent simplicity. The purpose of the following discussion is to present the most common of these methods in order to establish their advantages and disadvantages when employed in the capital budgeting process.

THE PAYBACK METHOD

Theory

The payback (or payout) method is widely used in American industry to determine the relative attractiveness of investment proposals. The essence of this technique is (*a*) determination of the *number of periods required to recover initial investment costs* and, once this has been done for each of the alternatives under consideration, (*b*) comparison of alternatives on the basis of their respective payback periods.

To illustrate, consider a proposal having a first cost of \$10,000 and net revenues (excess of receipts over disbursements) of \$2,000 per year for each year over a period of ten years. In this case the payout period is:

$$\text{Payout Period} = \frac{\$10{,}000}{\$2{,}000/\text{year}} = 5 \text{ years}$$

Now consider another project having a first cost of \$9,000 and net revenues of \$1,500 per year for seven years. The payout period for this proposal is \$9,000/\$1,500 = 6 years. According to the payback method, the first alternative is superior since its initial cost will be recovered more quickly.

Theoretical Errors

There are a number of objections to the payback method, resulting primarily from its disregard of the consequences of the investment beyond the end of the payback period. For example, consider the cash flow sequences for ALTERNATIVES P and Q shown in Table 4-1. It takes exactly 4.0 periods to

Table 4-1

Payback and Present Worth Solutions for ALTERNATIVES P and Q
(assumed interest rate: i = 15%)

		ALTERNATIVE P		ALTERNATIVE Q	
End of Period *j*	(PW - 15% - *j*)	Cash Flow	Present Worth @ 15%	Cash Flow	Present Worth @ 15%
0	1.0000	\$ −1,000	\$ −1,000.000	\$ −1,000	\$ −1,000.00
1	0.8696	100	86.96	600	521.76
2	0.7561	200	151.32	100	75.61
3	0.6575	300	197.25	100	65.75
4	0.5718	400	228.72	100	57.18
5	0.4972	500	248.60	600	298.32
Net Present Worth at 15%:			− \$ 87.15		\$ 18.62
Payback Period:		4.00		4.17	

recover the initial outlay of \$1,000 for ALTERNATIVE P; it takes slightly longer, 4.17 periods, to recover the initial outlay for ALTERNATIVE Q. Thus it would appear that P is superior to Q since it requires a lesser number of periods to "pay back" the initial investment. A proper present worth analysis, on the other hand, indicates the contrary: Q is better than P since it has the larger net present value. In fact, the calculations of Table 4-1 show that ALTERNATIVE P is economically undesirable if an effective interest rate of 15% is assumed. The error is largely due to the difference in timing of the cash flows during the first four years.

Now consider an additional proposal, ALTERNATIVE R, which has an initial cost of \$10,000 and is expected to yield net returns of \$1,000 each year for six years. The resulting payback solution, ten years, is meaningless since the expected life of the proposal is less than the total number of periods required for payback.

Still another error can be illustrated by the following example. Let ALTERNATIVE S be described by an initial cost of \$8,000, annual net revenues of \$4,000 each year for five years, and no terminal salvage value. Thus two years are required for payback. Now consider ALTERNATIVE T with initial cost of \$9,000, annual net revenues of \$3,000 each year for five years, and an expected salvage value of \$8,000 at the end of the fifth year. Since *three years* are required for T to recover the initial \$9,000 investment, it appears as though S is superior to T. This solution is incorrect, however, as may be shown by the following calculations of present worth:

$$\begin{aligned}\text{Present Worth}\\ (\text{ALTERNATIVE S}) &= -\$8{,}000 + \$4{,}000(SPW - 10\% - 5)\\ &= -\$8{,}000 + \$4{,}000(3.791)\\ &= \$7{,}164\end{aligned}$$

$$\begin{aligned}\text{Present Worth}\\ (\text{ALTERNATIVE T}) &= -\$9{,}000 + \$3{,}000(SPW - 10\% - 5) +\\ &\quad \$8{,}000(PW - 10\% - 5)\\ &= -\$9{,}000 + \$3{,}000(3.791) + \$8{,}000(0.6209)\\ &= \$7{,}337\end{aligned}$$

ALTERNATIVE T is clearly superior to S by this method. Why the inconsistency? Because the payback method ignores consequences beyond the end of the payback periods. In this example the \$8,000 salvage value at the end of five years for ALTERNATIVE T proved to be decisive.

Possible Usefulness

The payback method *may* be useful under very special conditions: when the lives of the alternatives are equal and, other than the initial investment, there is a uniform pattern of annual cash flows. However, even the existence of these conditions may lead to spurious results. To illustrate, consider ALTERNATIVE U with initial investment of \$100 and net annual receipts of \$20 each year for ten years. The initial cost of ALTERNATIVE V is \$80, and it is expected to produce net receipts of \$10 each year for ten years. The payback periods are clearly five years for U and eight years for V, thus indicating that U is superior to V. This solution may be shown to be dependent upon the relevant interest rate, that is, the minimum attractive rate of return. Observe that, under these conditions, the number of payback periods is equal to the uniform series present worth factor:

$$\text{Payback Periods} = \frac{\text{Initial Investment}}{\text{Net Annual Receipts}} = \frac{C}{A} = (SPW - i\% - N)$$

Using the data from the example:

$$\begin{array}{l}\text{Payback Periods} \\ \text{(ALTERNATIVE U)}\end{array} = \frac{\$100}{\$20} = 5.0 = (SPW - i\% - 10)$$

$$\begin{array}{l}\text{Payback Periods} \\ \text{(ALTERNATIVE V)}\end{array} = \frac{\$80}{\$10} = 8.0 = (SPW - i\% - 10)$$

From the compound interest tables we now determine that the solving rates of return are approximately 16% for ALTERNATIVE U and 4% for ALTERNATIVE V. Despite resulting payback periods shorter than project lives, (a) *neither* alternative is desirable if the minimum attractive rate of return is greater than 16%; (b) if it is between 4% and 16%, ALTERNATIVE U should be accepted and V rejected; (c) if the minimum attractive rate of return is less than 4%, then, although both alternatives are acceptable, U is superior to V. Only solutions (b) and (c) are the same as that given by the payback method.

Now, let us suppose that one or the other of the alternatives *must* be selected. In this event, we note that if U is selected and V rejected the following cash flows are expected to result:

End of Period	ALTERNATIVE U	ALTERNATIVE V	DIFFERENCE U − V
0	−100	−80	−20
1−10	+20	+10	+10

From this it is clear that $(SPW - i\% - 10) = 20/10 = 2.0$, and reference to the compound interest tables indicates that the incremental rate of return of U over V is approximately 49%. It is to be concluded, therefore, that, if either U or V *must* be selected, then U should be chosen for all values of the minimum attractive rate of return less than 49%; V should be chosen for values greater than 49%. These conditions are illustrated in Figure 4-1.

Since the payback method is a measure of the rapidity with which original investments are repaid, it yields information which may be of considerable interest to analysts. When future consequences of a prospective investment are highly uncertain, for example, management may desire to alleviate the dangers inherent in uncertainty by recovering the initial cost as quickly as possible. Under these conditions, payback period computations provide an index of one aspect of a proposed investment.

Another possible use of the payback method occurs when a firm's current capital is extremely limited and, further, cash flow estimates indicate similar limitations during the next few budgeting periods. If the firm also expects

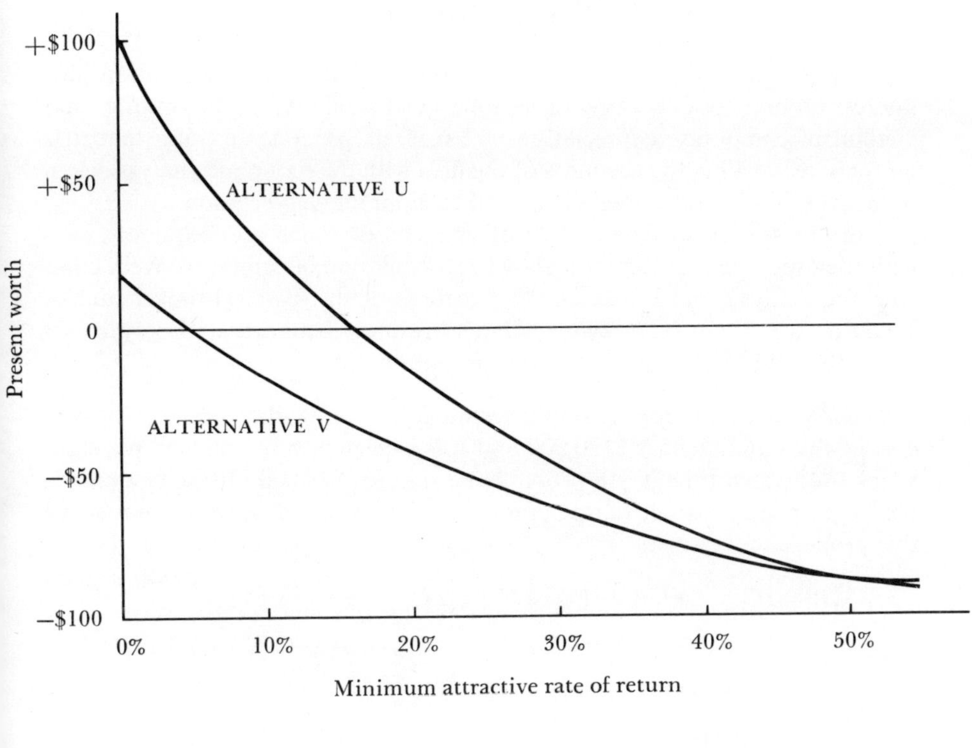

Fig. 4-1. Present worths of ALTERNATIVES U and V as functions of the minimum attractive rate of return.

unusually profitable investment opportunities to arise in the near future, then it is desirable to recover capital as quickly as possible in order to take advantage of these potential reinvestments. Information provided by the payback method should be useful under these conditions. In any case, this method should only be used to provide information *in addition* to that given by correct methods such as those discussed in the preceding chapter.

APPROXIMATE METHODS FOR COMPUTING CAPITAL RECOVERY

In our discussion of the annual cost method in Chapter 3, we derived the following expression for computing the cost of capital recovery (*CR*):

$$CR = (C - L)(CR - i\% - N) + Li \qquad (3.2)$$

where C is the first cost, L is the net salvage value, N is the life of the proposal, and i is the minimum attractive rate of return. Moreover, an alternative expression for computation of the capital recovery cost was shown to be:

$$CR = (C - L)(SF - i\% - N) + Ci \qquad (3.3)$$

This second equation is generally known as "sinking fund depreciation plus interest on first cost" because of its superficial similarity to the sinking fund method of computing depreciation.[1] That is, its proponents claim that it is useful in reconciling the accounts of the firm with the economic analysis when in fact the sinking fund method is used to compute depreciation.

In this section we discuss two other methods which are frequently used with the rationale that their use allows reconciliation of capital recovery costs with the analysis and the accounting records of the firm. However, unlike Equation 3.3, these other two methods are incorrect in that they will not generally yield results consistent with Equation 3.2.

Example: A firm is considering investment in a heavy-duty crane. The first cost of this equipment is $120,000 and it is expected to be retained for eight years after which time it will probably be sold for $20,000. If the company's pre-tax minimum attractive rate of return is 10%, the capital recovery cost for this proposed investment is:

$$\begin{aligned} CR &= (C - L)(CR - i\% - N) + Li \\ &= (\$120{,}000 - \$20{,}000)(CR - 10\% - 8) + (\$20{,}000)(0.10) \\ &= (\$100{,}000)(0.18744) + \$2{,}000 \\ &= \$20{,}744 \end{aligned}$$

[1] Sinking fund depreciation, as well as other depreciation methods, will be discussed at length in Chapter 6.

Verifying this solution using Equation 3.3:

$$\begin{aligned} CR &= (C - L)(SF - i\% - N) + Ci \\ &= (\$120{,}000 - \$20{,}000)(SF - 10\% - 8) + (\$120{,}000)(0.10) \\ &= (\$100{,}000)(0.08744) + \$12{,}000 \\ &= \$20{,}744 \end{aligned}$$

Straight Line Depreciation Plus Interest on First Cost

This method is frequently recommended for its intuitive appeal as well as for its similarity to accounting results where straight line depreciation is actually being used for the asset in question. The annual *depreciation* charge is found from:

$$\begin{aligned} \text{Annual Depreciation} &= \frac{(\textit{First Cost}) - (\textit{Salvage Value})}{(\textit{Expected Life})} \\ &= \frac{C - L}{N} \end{aligned} \tag{4.1}$$

Thus, it is argued, the annual *capital recovery* cost should be the annual (straight line) depreciation charge plus the interest foregone on the original investment. That is:

$$CR = \frac{C - L}{N} + Ci \tag{4.2}$$

Using the data from the example:

$$\begin{aligned} CR &= \frac{\$120{,}000 - \$20{,}000}{8} + (\$120{,}000)(0.10) \\ &= \$12{,}500 + \$12{,}000 \\ &= \$24{,}500 \end{aligned}$$

The solution is somewhat larger than the correct answer, \$20,744. This will always be the case unless the expected salvage value is equal to or greater than the first cost.

Straight Line Depreciation Plus Average Interest

It may be argued that the preceding method is incorrect since a portion of the capital recovery cost results from interest on the initial investment.

But, since the "value" of the asset is declining from year to year (as measured by the straight line depreciation), the interest should be *averaged* over the life of the asset. In tabular form:

	Value of Asset at Start of Period		
Period	Diminishing Portion	Non-Diminishing Portion	Interest on Value of Asset at Start of Period
1	$(C-L)$	L	$i(C-L)+Li$
2	$(C-L)\left(1-\frac{1}{N}\right)$	L	$i(C-L)\left(1-\frac{1}{N}\right)+Li$
⋮	⋮	⋮	⋮
N	$(C-L)\left(\frac{1}{N}\right)$	L	$i(C-L)\left(\frac{1}{N}\right)+Li$

Total Interest : $i(C-L)\dfrac{N+1}{2}+NLi$

Average Interest : $i(C-L)\dfrac{N+1}{2N}+Li$

The expression for capital recovery now becomes:

$$CR=\frac{C-L}{N}+i(C-L)\frac{N+1}{2N}+Li \qquad (4.3)$$

The expression for capital recovery now becomes:

$$CR=\frac{C-L}{N}+i\left(C-L\right)\frac{N+1}{2N}+Li \qquad (4.3)$$

Again, using the data from the example:

$$CR=\frac{\$120{,}000-\$20{,}000}{8}+(0.10)(\$120{,}000-\$20{,}000)\frac{8+1}{2(8)}+$$

$$(\$20{,}000)(0.10)$$

$$=\$12{,}500+\$5{,}625+\$2{,}000$$

$$=\$20{,}125$$

Although much closer, this result is lower than the correct solution, \$20,744. The essential difference is that this method results in an *average* rather than an *equivalent* annual cost.

RATE OF RETURN IMPROPERLY COMPUTED

Example: Consider *Alternatives X* and *Y* with the following cash flows:

End of Period	Cash Flows Before Taxes ALT. Y	ALT. Z
0	\$ −50,000	\$ − 50,000
1	+ 5,000	+ 14,000
2	+ 10,000	+ 14,000
3	+ 15,000	+ 14,000
4	+ 20,000	+ 14,000
5	+ 25,000	+ 14,000
	\$ + 25,000	\$ + 20,000

The rate of return for ALTERNATIVE Y is found as follows:

$$PW(\text{Y}) = 0 = -\$50{,}000 + \$5{,}000(SPW - i\% - 5) + \$5{,}000(GPW - i\% - 5)$$

$$PW@10\% = -\$50{,}000 + \$5{,}000(3.791) + \$5{,}000(6.862) = +3.265$$

$$PW@12\% = -\$50{,}000 + \$5{,}000(3.605) + \$5{,}000(6.397) = -10$$

Thus the solving rate of return for Y is approximately 12.0%.

The rate of return for ALTERNATIVE Z is found as follows:

$$PW(\text{Z}) = 0 = -\$50{,}000 + \$14{,}000(SPW - i\% - 5)$$

$$(PW - i\% - 5) = \frac{50{,}000}{14{,}000} = 3.571$$

$$(PW - 12\% - 5) = 3.605$$

$$(PW - 15\% - 5) = 3.352$$

Thus the solving rate of return for Z is approximately 12.4%.

(As a note of caution, it should be emphasized at this point that Z is not necessarily better than Y even though it has the higher rate of return. Project superiority depends upon the minimum attractive rate of return. For example, at 0% interest rate Y is superior to Z; the superiority is reversed if the minimum attractive rate of return is, say, 15%.[2] This issue is discussed at length in the next chapter.)

Original Book Method[3]

The project rate of return as computed by the original book method is found by dividing the average annual accounting profit (excess of receipts over cash disbursements and depreciation) by the original book value (first cost) of the asset. Using the data from the example and assuming that the company uses straight line depreciation in its accounts, the annual book profits are shown in Table 4-2.

Table 4-2

Determination of Annual Accounting Profits for Two Alternatives

(*Assumption: Straight line depreciation for both assets.*)

	ALTERNATIVE Y			ALTERNATIVE Z		
Year	Cash Flow	Less Depreciation	Profit	Cash Flow	Less Depreciation	Profit
1	$ 5,000	$ −10,000	$ −5,000	$ 14,000	$ −10,000	$ 4,000
2	10,000	−10,000	-0-	14,000	−10,000	4,000
3	15,000	−10,000	5,000	14,000	−10,000	4,000
4	20,000	−10,000	10,000	14,000	−10,000	4,000
5	25,000	−10,000	15,000	14,000	−10,000	4,000
Total:	$ 75,000	$ −50,000	$ 25,000	$ 70,000	$ −50,000	$ 20,000
Average Annual Profit:			$ 5,000			$ 4,000

$$\text{Rate of Return (Y)} = \frac{\text{Average Annual Profit (Y)}}{\text{First Cost (Y)}} \qquad (4.4)$$

$$= \frac{\$5{,}000}{\$50{,}000}$$

$$= 10\%$$

[2] It may be shown that Y is superior to Z for all values of the minimum attractive rate of return less than 10.6%; Z is superior for larger values.

[3] The related concepts of depreciation and book value are discussed in Chapter 6. Thus it is suggested that the material there be reviewed prior to study of this section.

$$\text{Rate of Return (z)} = \frac{\text{Average Annual Profit (z)}}{\text{First Cost (z)}}$$

$$= \frac{\$4{,}000}{\$50{,}000}$$

$$= 8\%$$

Compared to the correct values of 12% and 12.4% for Y and Z, respectively, this method understates the true rates of return (and, incidentally, reverses their relative position).

Average Book Method[4]

It may be argued that the value of the investment is reduced from year to year, and thus the rate of return should be based on the average book value. In the case of straight line depreciation, the average book value is simply one-half the difference between the first cost and the expected salvage value. Referring to the example:

$$\text{Rate of Return (Y)} = \frac{\text{Average Annual Profit (Y)}}{\text{Average Book Value (Y)}} \tag{4.5}$$

$$= \frac{\$5{,}000}{(\$50{,}000 - 0)/2}$$

$$= 20\%$$

$$\text{Rate of Return (z)} = \frac{\text{Average Annual Profit (z)}}{\text{Average Book Value (z)}}$$

$$= \frac{\$4{,}000}{(\$50{,}000 - 0)/2}$$

$$= 16\%$$

Comparing these results with those found by the original book method, we note that the differences arise entirely from the values in the denominators. Moreover, these figures are considerably higher (for this example) than those obtained by using proper compound interest methods.

Year-by-Year Book Method[5]

Still another method is based upon year-by-year ratios of profit after depreciation to book value at the start of the year. To illustrate, refer to ALTERNATIVE Y:

[4] See footnote 3.
[5] See footnote 3.

Year	Profit After Depreciation	Book Value at Start of Year	"Rate of Return"
1	$– 5,000	$50,000	loss
2	0	40,000	0
3	5,000	30,000	17%
4	10,000	20,000	50%
5	15,000	10,000	150%

A major problem here is the difficulty in applying the results in any useful way. What is the meaning of these values? Perhaps the analyst could average the year-by-year rates to compare alternatives, but this strategy leads to some obvious additional problems.

Each of the three preceding methods used to compute rates of return share a common disadvantage: they are all dependent upon book values which in turn are functions of the depreciation schedules used by the firm. Although there is a certain inherent appeal in using methods based upon book values — there appears to be, in general, a greater understanding of basic accounting methods than of compound interest calculations — rate of return solutions should not be influenced by an arbitrary (or otherwise motivated) allocation of the investment over accounting periods.

Hoskold's Method

This method assumes that uniform annual deposits are made into a sinking fund that is conservatively invested to earn interest at a relatively low rate. The value of the fund at the end of the life of the asset should be just enough for identical replacement. The rate of return is then determined as the ratio of the amount remaining after the sinking fund deposit to the initial investment. In the mining industry, this approach has traditionally been known as Hoskold's Method.

To illustrate, refer to ALTERNATIVE Z previously discussed and assume annual investment is a 5% sinking fund. The project rate of return is determined as follows:

$$\text{Amount required at end of 5 years} = \$50{,}000$$

$$\begin{aligned}\text{Annual sinking fund deposit} &= \$50{,}000(SF - 5\% - 5)\\ &= \$50{,}000(0.18097)\\ &= \$9{,}049\end{aligned}$$

$$\begin{aligned}\text{Cash remaining after sinking fund deposit} &= \$14{,}000 - \$9{,}049\\ &= \$4{,}951\end{aligned}$$

$$\text{Rate of Return} = \frac{\$4{,}951}{\$50{,}000} = 9.9\%$$

This solution is somewhat less than the correct value, 12.4%, because it is an averaging of two investments, one returning 12.4% and the other returning 5%. If investment in ALTERNATIVE Z actually requires annual deposits into a sinking fund earning 5%, then determination of the rate of return should consider both investments. Otherwise, the merits of the investment (a) ALTERNATIVE Z, and (b) the sinking fund should be determined independently. For example, suppose the minimum attractive rate of return for the firm is 11%. If a sinking fund is *not* required, ALTERNATIVE Z is economically desirable since it has an expected return of 12.4%; if the sinking fund *is* required along with the investment in Z, then the proposal should be rejected since its return is only 9.9%.

SUMMARY

Unfortunately, approximate or incorrect methods are frequently used in industry to select from among alternative investment opportunities. Principal among these is the payback (or payout method) which measures the number of periods necessary to recover the initial investment. The payback method does provide some valuable information under certain circumstances, but it should never be used as the sole criterion.

There are several methods used for evaluating capital recovery cost, two of which have been discussed in this chapter. When interest on first cost is added to straight line depreciation, the resulting capital recovery cost will give too high a result (except when the salvage value is 100% or more). On the other hand, when average interest is added to straight line depreciation, the capital recovery cost will be too low (except when the salvage value is 100% or more). Errors arising from this latter method are largely due to the fact that it is an averaging process rather than an equivalence calculation.

A number of methods based upon asset book values have been used to determine project rates of return. Each of these methods is fundamentally incorrect in that the rate of return is considered a function of an accounting device for allocating first cost (less salvage value, if any) over the life of the asset. Thus it is possible to alter apparent profitability by changing the depreciation schedule for the asset in question. (It is true that depreciation schedules can affect profitability, but only because of the effect on cash flows for taxes. This matter is discussed in Chapters 6 and 7.)

Rate of return computations may be erroneous if sinking fund deposits are included when in fact these sinking funds are not essential to the proposal being evaluated. In such cases the resulting project rate of return is an average of the correct rate of return and the earning rate of the sinking fund.

PROBLEMS

1. Proposal I has a first cost of $40,000, expected excess of receipts over disbursements of $10,000 each year for 7 years, and zero salvage value at the end of that time. Proposal II has a first cost of $30,000, net revenues of $6,000 per year for 7 years, and is expected to be sold for 100% of the first cost at the end of the seventh year.
   (a) Assuming an interest rate of 5%, use the present worth method to determine the most economically desirable alternative.
   (b) Solve the same problem by the payback method.
   (c) Comment on the results of (a) and (b).

2. Mister Miser is considering investing $10,000 in one of two alternatives. (It is assumed that he has other investment opportunities elsewhere which, with similar risk, will return at least 10%.) His first alternative requires an initial cost of $10,000 and requires additional annual expenditures of $3,000. However, the investment is expected to yield revenues of $6,000 per year for 5 years, at the end of which time it will be sold for net salvage value of $100.

   The second alternative requires an original investment of $10,000 also, but there are no other cash flow consequences until the twentieth year, at which time it is expected that the asset will be sold for $60,000.
   (a) Use the present worth or rate of return method to determine which of the alternatives, if any, is most desirable. Assume that replacements for the first alternative will be made with identical assets.
   (b) Which alternative is indicated by the payback method?
   (c) Comment on the results of (a) and (b). In particular, discuss the effects of the replacement assumption in (a).

3. Consider the problem presented by the following table of cash flows for alternatives Alpha and Beta:

End of Period	Alpha	Beta
0	$-100	$-220
1	50	100
2	50	100
3	50	100

   (a) Determine the best alternative by the payback method.
   (b) Assuming a minimum attractive rate of return of 15%, determine the best alternative by either the present worth or the annual cost method.

(c) The payback method is independent of the interest rate. However, what must be the value of the minimum attractive rate of return in order to reverse the decision in (b)?

4. The payback method may be modified by subtracting annual straight line depreciation from the annual cash flows before income taxes. For the alternatives of Problem 3, determine the payback period after depreciation. What may be said about the double-counting of depreciation?

5. Consider the following alternative materials-handling systems:

	Semi-automatic	Fully Automatic
Original cost	$24,000	$40,000
Expected salvage value	0	10,000
Annual operating costs	8,000	6,000

Whichever system is selected will be kept for a period of 12 years.
(a) Assuming a minimum attractive rate of return of 10% before income taxes, determine the equivalent net annual costs of the two plans using correct methods.
(b) Using the method of "straight line depreciation plus interest on first cost" to compute capital recovery, determine the net annual costs of the two plans.

6. Use the method of "straight line depreciation plus average interest" to determine the equivalent net annual costs of the two alternatives of Problem 5.

7. A company is considering investment in certain depreciable property. Estimates for the two alternatives under consideration are as follows:

	Location M	Location N
First cost of property	$1,000,000	$1,400,000
Salvage value	200,000	200,000
Annual cash revenues (net)	120,000	160,000
Useful life	25 years	25 years

(a) Determine the correct rates of return for each of the two proposals.
(b) If the minimum attractive rate of return for the company is 9%

before income taxes, are either or both of the alternatives economically acceptable?

(c) Using a minimum attractive rate of return of 9%, determine whether the extra investment in Location N ($400,000 increment) is justified. That is, find the rate of return on the incremental investment and compare it to the minimum attractive rate of return.

(d) Determine the rates of return for Locations M and N using the "original book method." Compare your results with a minimum attractive rate of return of 9%.

8. Solve Problem 7(d) using the "average book method."

9. Solve Problem 7(d) by using the average of the year-by-year rates of return as measured by the ratio of profit after depreciation to book value at start of year. Assume straight line depreciation.

10. Determine the rates of return for Locations M and N described in Problem 7 if the firm uses Haskold's method with a 4% sinking fund.

5

MULTIPLE ALTERNATIVES[1]

TWO OR MORE MUTUALLY EXCLUSIVE ALTERNATIVES

Much of our earlier discussion was related to determining the economic acceptability of a single proposal. However, the capital budgeting problem is more generally concerned with selecting one or more alternatives from among a larger number of contenders for limited capital. Thus we now extend our discussion to include multiple (two or more) alternatives.

Before proceeding, it is helpful first to establish the concept of *mutual exclusiveness* in two contexts. First, we may be dealing with alternatives which are mutually exclusive in the sense that only one of several available alternatives is necessary to fill a given function, all others being superfluous. The second type of mutual exclusiveness refers to the case in which one or more of the alternatives may be acceptable, but, due to limitations of capital, not all the alternatives can be accepted. We will refer to the former case as "technical" and to the latter as "financial" mutual exclusiveness.

As examples, a firm may wish to invest in a new warehouse *and* install a computer facility in its central accounting office. If sufficient capital is available for one but not both of these projects, they are *financially mutually*

[1] Much of the material appearing in this chapter is based upon an earlier paper published by the author: "Two Principal Problems Associated with the Rate of Return Method: The 'Ranking Problem' and the 'Preselection Problem'," *Journal of Industrial Engineering*, XVII, No. 4 (April 1966), 202–08.

exclusive. On the other hand, suppose the firm is considering building the new warehouse with either a one-story or two-story configuration. These latter alternatives are clearly *technically mutually exclusive*.

This notion of financial mutual exclusiveness is readily apparent when only two alternatives are considered. When dealing with an array of three or more proposals, however, this concept must be revised somewhat in order to consider alternatives which are *financially mutually exclusive at the margin*. This is to say that the last alternative acceptable, i.e., the marginal alternative, automatically excludes all other alternatives for which adequate financing is not available. Several of the examples presented in this chapter have been designed to amplify this concept and demonstrate correct methods of solution.

DIRECT SOLUTIONS BY RANKING ALTERNATIVES

Both the annual cost method and the present worth method are particularly useful when considering multiple alternatives since, unlike the rate of return method, alternatives may be *ranked* in descending order of present value or annual benefits, and the ranked order may be interpreted as a priority schedule.

The Annual Cost (or Net Annual Benefits) Method of Solution

Consider the following estimates for three alternatives which are being considered for a new boiler system to be installed in the central steam plant:

	Types of Boiler System		
	Alpha	Beta	Chi
Initial Cost	$50,000	$70,000	$100,000
Annual operating costs	7,000	3,500	2,000
Annual maintenance costs	2,000	1,500	1,000
Net salvage value	0	10,000	30,000
Expected service life (years)	20	20	20

These proposals are technically mutually exclusive since each will accomplish the same function. (In some instances another alternative is implied: rather than purchase one of the defined proposals, invest the funds elsewhere at an assumed return defined by the minimum attractive rate of return. In this particular example, however, it is assumed that one of the three boiler systems must be installed; failure to do so will result in an unacceptable loss to the firm.)

Using the given input data, the equivalent uniform annual costs (or net annual benefits) are determined for each of the alternatives, and that alternative with the smallest equivalent uniform annual cost (or largest net annual benefit) is selected. Assuming an interest rate of 10% before taxes, this procedure may be illustrated from the example:

[Equivalent Uniform Annual Cost

= (Capital Recovery Cost) + (Annual Costs of Operation and Maintenance)]

Thus: $EUAC$ (Alpha) = \$50,000(CR – 10% – 20) + \$7,000 + \$2,000

= \$50,000(0.11746) + \$9,000

= \$14,873

$EUAC$ (Beta) = (\$70,000 – \$10,000)(CR – 10% – 20)+ \$10,000(0.10) + \$3,500 + \$1,500

= \$60,000(0.11746) + \$1,000 + \$5,000

= \$13,048

$EUAC$ (Chi) = (\$100,000 – \$30,000)(CR – 10% – 20) + \$30,000(0.10) + \$2,000 + \$1,000

= \$70,000(0.11746) + \$3,000 + \$3,000

= \$14,222

Clearly the Beta system is least expensive since it has the smallest equivalent uniform annual cost.

The Present Worth Method of Solution

The present worth method of solution may be used to select from among mutually exclusive alternatives in a manner analogous to that of the annual cost method. That is, the net present worths of each of the alternatives are computed, and that alternative with the largest present value is selected.[2]

To illustrate this technique, consider two plans which have been suggested to local management for funding. The first involves installation of an overhead conveyor in the shipping department to reduce handling costs; the second calls for purchase of a special fixture and microscope which may be

[2] It is necessary, of course, that the planning horizons for all alternatives be equal.

used to reduce inspection costs. Estimates concerning these proposals are as follows:

	Overhead Conveyor	Fixture and Microscope
Initial Cost	$50,000	$30,000
Annual reductions for disbursements	20,000	15,000
Net salvage value	10,000	20,000
Expected service life[a] (years)	10	10

[a] The expected lives for the alternatives are assumed equal to avoid the complications arising from unequal lives (Chapter 3). Here, assume that each of the alternatives is associated with a common product, and the product will be discontinued after ten years.

If only $50,000 is available to management for allocation at the time these proposals are presented, the alternatives are clearly financially mutually exclusive. Assuming an interest rate of 20% before taxes, equivalent present worths (*PW*) of the alternatives are now determined:

$$PW = (\text{Initial Cost}) + (\text{Present Value of Future Consequences})$$

$$\begin{aligned} PW\ (\text{Conveyor}) &= -\ \$50{,}000 + \$20{,}000(SPW - 20\% - 10) + \$10{,}000(PW - 20\% - 10) \\ &= -\ \$50{,}000 + \$20{,}000(4.192) + \$10{,}000(0.1615) \\ &= \$35{,}455 \end{aligned}$$

$$\begin{aligned} PW\ (\text{Fixture \& 'scope}) &= -\ \$30{,}000 + \$15{,}000(SPW - 20\% - 10) + \$20{,}000(PW - 20\% - 10) \\ &= -\ \$30{,}000 + \$15{,}000(4.192) + \$20{,}000(0.1615) \\ &= \$36{,}110 \end{aligned}$$

This analysis indicates that both proposals are superior to the implied third alternative, that is, to invest the entire $50,000 elsewhere at a minimum expected return of 20% before taxes. Of the two, however, investment in the fixture and microscope appears to offer the greater return since it has the larger present worth. That is, it is preferable to invest $30,000 in the fixture and microscope and $20,000 elsewhere at 20% than it is to invest the entire $50,000 in the overhead conveyor.

SOLUTIONS REQUIRING INCREMENTAL ANALYSIS

Review of the Rate of Return Calculation

Recall from Chapter 3, that the rate of return of a given proposal is defined as the interest rate (per interest period) at which the present worth of receipts resulting from the project is exactly equal to the present worth of disbursements. Stated somewhat differently, it is the interest rate at which the present worth of all receipts and disbursements is equal to zero, where receipts and disbursements are treated as positive and negative cash flows respectively. Mathematically, it is that value of i which satisfies the equation:

$$0 = \sum_{j=0}^{N} C_j \frac{1}{(1+i)^j} \tag{3.4}$$

where C_j is the cash flow which takes place at the end of the jth interest period, N is the total number of interest periods over which the cash flow takes place, and i is the rate of return. (This equation represents the assumption that cash flows take place, and interest is compounded, at the *end* of each interest period. If these assumptions are not valid for any given case, the basic present worth equation may be modified by using the appropriate factors as developed in Chapter 2.) In order for the project to be acceptable, the solving rate of return must then be compared to some minimum attractive rate which could be earned if the project were rejected and the capital invested elsewhere. These two steps taken together, (a) determination of the project rate of return and (b) comparison to the minimum attractive rate of return, are the essential features of the rate of return method.

Consideration of Two Alternatives

Selection of one proposal from among two mutually exclusive alternatives represents the simplest case involving multiple alternatives. To illustrate the proper use of the rate of return method in this instance, consider the two alternatives described in Table 5-1. ALTERNATIVES A and B each have useful lives of ten years and zero salvage values. The minimum attractive rate of return is assumed to be 6%, and the total capital available for investment is $25,000. The required initial investments are $10,000 and $20,000 for A and B, respectively, and hence only one of the two alternatives may be accepted. The two proposals are financially mutually exclusive since insufficient funds are available for acceptance of both.

The rates of return for the two alternatives as shown in Column (e) of

Table 5-1

Financially Mutually Exclusive Alternatives

(*Assumptions*: *Expected life of each proposal is 10 years. Expected salvage value of each proposal is zero. Minimum attractive rate of return is 6%. Total capital available for investment is $25,000.*)

Alter- native (a)	Initial Invest- ment (b)	Net Annual Benefits (c)	($SPW - i\% - 10$) (d) = (b)/(c)	Project Rate of Return (e)	Present Worth of Net Annual Benefits (f)	Net Present Worth (g) = (f) – (b)
A	$10,000	$1,628	6.143	10%	$11,982	$1,982
B	20,000	3,116	6.418	9%	22,934	2,934

Table 5-1 are the solutions of the following general equation:

$$\text{Present Worth } (PW) = 0 = -C + A(SPW - i\% - 10)$$
$$(SPW - i\% - 10) = C/A$$

where C is the initial investment and A represents the net annual benefits. This follows directly from Equation 3.4 when the C_j are uniform for $j = 1, 2, \cdots, N$. That is, rather than use a series of single payment present worth factors, the uniform series present worth factors may be employed to simplify the calculations.

The project rates of return are shown in Table 5-1 as 10% and 9% for ALTERNATIVES A and B, respectively. But, since only $25,000 is available for investment, does this mean that A should be accepted and B rejected? No. The *rates of return* given in Column (e) of Table 5-1 *do not necessarily indicate the superiority of one proposal over the other.* In fact, a correct analysis of these alternatives indicates that B is preferable to A.

Parenthetically, as discussed earlier in this chapter, the present worth method may be used to determine the relative attractiveness of the alternatives. Column (f) of Table 5-1 summarizes the present worth of the net annual benefits as shown in Column (c), and Column (g) is the sum of *all* the cash flows incurred by the proposal. The mathematical statement of these calculations is:

$$PW = A(SPW - 6\% - 10) - C$$

where

$$(SPW - 6\% - 10) = 7.360$$

Since the resulting net present worth of ALTERNATIVE A is less than that of B, present worth analysis indicates that the latter proposal is superior.

Proper application of the rate of return method also indicates that B is superior to A. The original investment of $10,000 in ALTERNATIVE A yields a rate of return of 10%, which is greater than the minimum attractive rate required, 6%. In order to determine if B is superior to A, it is now necessary to compute the return on the *incremental* investment required by selecting B rather than A. Clearly, the incremental investment of $10,000 (= $20,000 − $10,000) produces incremental net annual benefits of $1,488 (= $3,116 − $1,628) at the end of each year for a period of ten years. Thus the $(SPW - i\% - 10)$ is 6.72 (= $10,000/$1,488), and reference to compound interest tables indicates that the incremental rate of return is about 8%. Since this is greater than the minimum attractive rate of return, we conclude that the additional investment in B is justified and that A should be rejected in favor of B. It is demonstrably incorrect to rank two alternatives in descending order of rates of return and to conclude that that alternative having the higher rate is economically superior. Rates of return are *not* indices of desirability.

Correct application of the rate of return method requires determination of the prospective return on the incremental investment, but this assumes that irrelevant increments are avoided. In the example, B is compared to A only because A was found to be preferable to "doing nothing." In the event that the rate of return for A would have been, say, 4%, then B would be compared to "doing nothing" without further reference to A. That is, if the rate of return for any project is less than the minimum attractive rate of return, that project is removed from the list of prospective alternatives.

Consideration of More than Two Alternatives

The data summarized in Table 5-2 is the result of adding one more proposal, ALTERNATIVE C, to A and B previously discussed. All assumptions pertaining to project lives, salvage values, and minimum attractive rate of return are unchanged, except that the capital available for investment is now $75,000. All calculations have been made as in the preceding section.

TECHNICALLY MUTUALLY EXCLUSIVE PROPOSALS. Assume that alternatives A, B, and C are equivalent methods for performing a given function, i.e., only one of the three need be accepted. As indicated by Column (g) of Table 5-2, present worth is maximized if C is selected to the exclusion of A and B.

Although Column (e) indicates that A has the highest project rate of return, *correct* use of the rate of return method yields the proper solution, ALTERNATIVE C. First, ALTERNATIVE A is acceptable (as compared to "doing nothing") since its project rate of return, 10%, is greater than the minimum attractive rate of return. Second, B is compared to A and, as was determined in the previous section, B is found to be preferable to A since the incremental rate of return is greater than 6%. Third, C is compared to B:

Incremental investment = \$50,000 − \$20,000 = \$30,000

Incremental net annual benefits = \$7,450 − \$3,116 = \$4,334

$$\text{Incremental present worth} = -\$30{,}000 + \$4{,}334(SPW - i\% - 10)$$

$$(SPW - i\% - 10) = \$30{,}000/\$4{,}334 = 6.922$$

Consulting the compound interest tables for this value of the uniform series present worth factor, we find that the incremental rate of return is greater than the minimum attractive rate of return, and thus C is preferable to B (which is preferable to A, which is preferable to "doing nothing"). Hence, as was indicated by the present worth method, C is the best alternative of those offered.

FINANCIALLY MUTUALLY EXCLUSIVE PROPOSALS. Suppose that *one or more* of the proposals shown in Table 5-2 may be accepted because they are not technically equivalent, that is, each performs a different function. The rates of return in Column (e) are each greater than the minimum attractive rate of return, indicating that all these proposals are desirable. However, since the total initial investment of all three ($80,000) exceeds the limit of available

Table 5-2

Three Mutually Exclusive Alternatives

(*Assumptions*: *Expected life of each proposal is 10 years. Expected salvage value of each proposal is zero. Minimum attractive rate of return is 6%. Total capital available for investment is $75,000.*)

Alternative (a)	Initial Investment (b)	Net Annual Benefits (c)	($SPW - i\% - 10$) (d)	Project Rate of Return (e)	Present Worth of Net Annual Benefits (f)	Net Present Worth (g)
A	$10,000	$1,628	6.143	10%	$11,982	$1,982
B	20,000	3,116	6.418	9%	22,934	2,934
C	50,000	7,450	6.711	8%	54,832	4,832

capital, the problem is one of determining which of the alternatives must be excluded from the final capital budget.

Initially, there are eight possible alternatives:

I	Do nothing, that is, invest all funds elsewhere at the minimum attractive rate of return, 6%.	
II	Select ALTERNATIVE A only	(P = \$10,000).
III	Select ALTERNATIVE B only	(P = \$20,000).
IV	Select ALTERNATIVE C only	(P = \$50,000).
V	Select ALTERNATIVES A and B	(P = \$30,000).
VI	Select ALTERNATIVES A and C	(P = \$60,000).
VII	Select ALTERNATIVES B and C	(P = \$70,000).
VIII	Select ALTERNATIVES A, B, and C	(P = \$80,000).

Each of these possibilities is considered to be a "budget package," that is, the possibilities have now been defined as mutually exclusive investment strategies.

The *net* present worth of investing all funds elsewhere at the minimum attractive rate of return is, of course, zero. The net present worth of the next three packages — A, B, or C considered independently — is shown in the last column of Table 5-2. Finally, the net present worth of the last four packages is computed in Table 5-3 and shown in Column (f). Since the present worth

Table 5-3

Present Worth Solution Based Upon Budget Packages

Package[a] (a)	Alter- natives (b)	Initial Invest- ment (c)	Net Annual Benefits (d)	Present Worth of Net Annual Benefits (e)	Net Present Worth (f)
V	A and B	\$30,000	\$ 4,744	\$34,916	\$4,916
VI	A and C	60,000	9,078	66,814	6,814
VII	B and C	70,000	10,566	77,766	7,766
VIII	A, B and C	80,000 . . . . not financially feasible (only \$75,000 available).			

[a]There are, of course, three other possible packages: A, B, or C taken alone. See Table 5-2.

is maximized by selecting package VII (ALTERNATIVES B and C), it follows that the alternative to be rejected is A.

This is not the same solution which would have been obtained by simply ranking the alternatives in descending order of rates of return and selecting those proposals with the higher values. This present worth solution clearly illustrates the error which may result from assuming that rates of return strictly correspond to economic utility.

To illustrate that the rate of return method gives the identical solution, refer to the calculations shown in Table 5-4. The procedure for selecting the

Table 5-4

Rate of Return Solution Based Upon Budget Packages

Compare Packages (a)	Incremental Initial Investment (b)	Incremental Net Annual Benefits (c)	(SPW - i%- 10) (d)	Incremental Package Rate of Return (e)	Accept (f)
II with I	$10,000	$1,628	6.143	10.0%	II
III with II	10,000	1,488	6.720	8.0%	III
IV with III	30,000	4,334	6.922	7.3%	IV
V with IV	0	410	0	∞	V
VI with V	30,000	4,334	6.922	7.3%	VI
VII with VI	10,000	1,488	6.720	8.0%	VII
VIII with VII	. . . not financially feasible (only $75,000 available)				

optimum package is precisely the same as that given in connection with the previous problem. The packages are arrayed in ascending order of initial investment — an initial condition which is computationally helpful but not otherwise necessary — and each increment of investment is examined to determine whether the annual benefits which result from the added investment produce a rate of return greater than the required minimum. For example, total initial investment of $30,000 in package V will produce total net annual benefits of $4,744 each year for ten years, and the corresponding figures for package VI are $60,000 and $9,078. If VI is chosen rather than V, the additional investment of $30,000 will produce additional annual benefits of $4,334. The incremental rate of return is 7.3%, and, since this is greater than the required minimum, the additional investment in VI is justified.

The end result of the iterative procedure indicates that package VII is superior to all others. This is, of course, precisely the same solution as that obtained by the present worth method and different than the solution resulting from a simple ranking of the alternatives in descending order of rates of return.

THE PROBLEM OF PRELIMINARY SELECTION

A problem closely associated with the "ranking error" arises when there is some form of selection of alternatives preliminary to preparation of the final capital budget. This case generally occurs in one of two situations. First, some sort of screening may take place at organizational levels subordinate to (or other than) the senior executive level at which the final budget is structured. Second, a proposal may be selected from among two or more alternatives, each of which is mutually exclusive for *technical* reasons, prior to consideration as a contender for limited capital funds.

Example: A company is considering four alternatives, shown in Table 5-5. As in the previous examples, it is assumed that each proposal has an expected life of ten years and zero salvage value, and the pre-tax minimum attractive rate of return is 6%. Total capital available for investment is $30,000. The two proposals, D1 and D2, represent alternative inspection devices specially designed to reduce scrap associated with a particular production operation. Since selection of one precludes the other, they are technically mutually exclusive.

The first question to be resolved is the selection of either D1 or D2. In Table 5-5 the prospective rate of return for ALTERNATIVE D1 is shown to be 9%, and since this is greater than the required minimum of 6%, D1 is acceptable. Further, the incremental return on the extra investment is also greater than 6%, indicating that we are justified in selecting D2 rather than D1. That is, if D2 is selected rather than D1:

$$\text{Incremental investment} = \$20{,}000 - \$10{,}000 = \$10{,}000$$

$$\text{Incremental net annual benefits} = \$2{,}981 - \$1{,}558 = \$1{,}423$$

$$\text{Incremental present worth} = \$10{,}000 + \$1{,}423(SPW - i\% - 10)$$

$$(SPW - i\% - 10) = \$10{,}000/\$1{,}423 = 7.027$$

Thus, from compound interest tables, the incremental rate of return is 7%.

Having selected D2 as the most desirable of the two technically mutually exclusive alternatives, we now consider A, D2, and E as candidates for the $30,000 available for investment. Since these three proposals require a total first cost of $40,000, however, it is clear that one must be excluded from the final budget. But which one? If the alternatives are ranked in descending order of rates of return — as they are in Table 5-5 — that alternative having the lowest rate is E, and it might be concluded that the budget should therefore include only A and D2. But this is the "ranking error," and the conclusion is quite incorrect.

Table 5-5

Illustration of Ranking Error with Preliminary Selection

Assumptions: *Expected life of each proposal is 10 years. Expected salvage value of each proposal is zero. Minimum attractive rate of return is 6%. Total capital available for investment is $30,000.*

Alternative (a)	Initial Investment (b)	Net Annual Benefits (c)	(SPW-i%-10) (d)	Project Rate of Return (e)	Present Worth of Net Annual Benefits (f)	Net Present Worth (g)
A	$10,000	$1,628	6.143	10%	$11,982	$1,982
D1	10,000	1,558	6.418	9%	11,467	1,467
D2	20,000	2,981	6.709	8%	21,940	1,940
E	10,000	1,457	6.863	7.5%	10,724	724

The proper decision may be obtained by first considering the various packages (alternative budgets) which are available. There are twelve of these: the always possible decision to invest all the funds elsewhere at the minimum attractive rate of return, investment in either A, D1, D2, or E, considered independently, and investment in any one of the seven packages arrayed in Table 5-6. Excluding package VII because of insufficient funds, we see that net present worth is maximized if VI is accepted as the optimum package.

Table 5-6

Present Worth Solution Based Upon Budget Packages

Package[a] (a)	Alternatives (b)	Initial Investment (in M) (c)	Net Annual Benefits (d)	Present Worth of Net Annual Benefits (e)	Net Present Worth (f)
I	A and D1	$20	$3,186	$23,449	$3,449
II	A and E	20	3,085	22,706	2,706
III	D1 and E	20	3,015	22,190	2,190
IV	A and D2	30	4,609	33,922	3,922
V	D2 and E	30	4,438	32,664	2,664
VI	A, D1 and E	30	4,643	34,172	4,172
VII	A, D2 and E	40	not financially feasible (only $30,000 available).		

[a] The four additional packages, A, D1, D2 and E taken alone, are shown in Table 5-5.

Application of the present worth method indicates that acceptance of A, D1, and E is the best possible decision under the circumstances. (The rate of return method gives the same results if the packages are analyzed using the incremental technique previously discussed.) Preliminary selection from among technically mutually exclusive alternatives, coupled with the "ranking error," yields an incorrect solution because it assumes that the excluded ALTERNATIVE D1 should not be considered further. This assumption is valid, however, only if unlimited capital is available for investment. If *all* possible alternatives are not considered, including those which may be mutually exclusive for technical reasons, there is no assurance that the final capital budget represents the optimum employment of limited funds. Moreover, even properly applied procedures will give incorrect results under these circumstances, as may be seen by reviewing Table 5-6. If ALTERNATIVE D1 were eliminated from consideration by virtue of the fact that D2 is superior to it, packages I, III, and VI would not be considered. Of the remaining packages, present worth is maximized by the selection of IV, indicating that A and D2 should be accepted in the final budget. A better alternative will have been overlooked.

SUMMARY

Two or more investment proposals may each be capable of fulfilling a given function. These alternatives are then said to be mutually exclusive for technical reasons. Further, proposals may be mutually exclusive due to limitations of capital. When insufficient funds are available for the financing of all desirable alternatives, the selection of the last (marginal) project precludes selection of one or more of the others.

Regardless of whether alternatives are mutually exclusive for technical or financial reasons, valid techniques must be employed for selection of the most economical project(s) from among all contenders. When using the annual cost method, the equivalent uniform annual cost (or net annual benefits) of each of the alternatives is determined and the most desirable projects are directly indicated by the results. The present worth method is analogous in that the best projects are selected by examining net present values of the cash flows for all alternatives.

Although there is a one-to-one correspondence between a ranked order of annual costs (or present worths) and relative economic attractiveness, alternatives should *not* be compared on the basis of their respective rates of return. That is, projects having higher rates of return are not necessarily superior to those yielding smaller rates of return. The rate of return method requires that incremental rates of return be calculated by successively comparing increments of investment with incremental cash flows resulting from those investments. This procedure is iterative, but care should be taken to insure that comparisons are not made between alternatives, one of which has been proven uneconomic by a prior calculation.

In the event that financially mutually exclusive alternatives are being considered, correct analysis must be based upon the definition of alternative capital budget packages, each of which is mutually exclusive. Once all the packages have been completely described, the optimum package may be selected by any one of the several methods commonly used in economic analysis which takes into account the amount and timing of cash flows and the time value of money. Again, if the rate of return method is used, it is essential that the optimum package be chosen by an iterative technique in which successive increments of investment are examined to determine if they yield incremental rates of return in excess of the required minimum. (Caution: acceptance of that package having the highest rate of return is simply a repetition of the ranking error.)

It should be noted that the "budget package" formulation relates entirely to the use of the rate of return method. The incremental approach is relatively inefficient, but fortunately other procedures for solution of the capital budgeting problem are available.[4] However, these techniques generally depend upon net present worths or other hierarchical measures as the appropriate figure of merit.

The last example in this chapter illustrates the problem which arises when selection of alternatives takes place prior to determination of the final capital budget. If investment funds are limited, it may be better to accept the inferior of two or more technically mutually exclusive alternatives in order to "free" capital for investment in one or more other projects. (In the example, D1 and E together were superior to D2 alone.) The budgeting procedures of most firms are such that it may be extremely difficult, if not impossible, to avoid preselection of alternatives. Nevertheless, it may be possible to take some reasonable steps to guard against this error, particularly with respect to those proposals requiring large capital outlays.

PROBLEMS

1. The Comma Corporation is considering relocation of its western processing plant. Six alternatives are presently under consideration by management:

Alternative	Required Initial Investment	Annual Reduction in Disbursements as Compared to Existing Location
I	$1,300,000	$ 300,000
II	1,600,000	500,000
III	2,400,000	820,000
IV	2,600,000	840,000
V	3,600,000	1,200,000
VI	5,000,000	1,520,000

It is assumed that the relocated plant will be used for fifty years. Regardless which alternative is selected, it is expected that the plant will have a

[4] Our capital budgeting problem described in this chapter is occasionally referred to as the *Lorie-Savage Problem* after an earlier article: Lorie, J. H., and L. J. Savage, "Three Problems in Rationing Capital," *Journal of Business*, XXVIII, No. 4 (October 1955), pp. 229–39. Several mathematical programming methods have been proposed for the determination of the optimal "portfolio" (set of alternatives to be selected), e.g., Lagrangian multipliers, dynamic programming, linear programming, and integer programming. Discussion of these techniques is beyond the scope of this text, but, for the reader interested in additional references, we especially recommend: Weingartner, H. Martin, "Capital Budgeting of Interrelated Projects," *Management Science*, XII, No. 7 (March 1966), pp. 485–516.

net salvage value of approximately zero at the end of the fifty years. The pre-tax minimum attractive rate of return used by the Corporation is 25%.

Use the *annual cost method* to determine which alternative, if any, should be selected.

2. Use the *present worth method* to select from among the alternatives described in Problem 1.
3. Use the *rate of return method* to select from among the alternatives described in Problem 1.
4. The Asterisk Association is considering purchase of a small computer for its Research Department. Several mutually exclusive alternatives are being considered. Estimates relative to each are as follows:

Computer	First Cost of Computer	Estimated Salvage Value 10 Years Hence	Net Annual Savings Resulting from New Computer vs. Existing Conditions
A	$280,000	$240,000	$46,000
B	340,000	280,000	56,000
C	380,000	310,000	62,000
D	440,000	350,000	72,000

The company plans to keep the computer for ten years, at which time it will sell it. If the pre-tax minimum attractive rate of return is 15%, use the *present worth method* or the *annual cost method* to determine which alternative, if any, should be selected.

5. Use the *rate of return method* to select from among the alternatives described in Problem 4.
6. A Current Lighting System is presently installed at the executive headquarters of the Certain Corporation. Two other systems are under consideration, each of which is more costly initially but will increase the time between replacements. Estimates for the proposals are as follows:

	Lighting System		
	Current	Lumenite	Wattsnu
Time between replacements	2 years	3 years	6 years
Initial Cost	$20,000	$30,000	$50,000
Annual Operating Costs	$ 3,000	$ 3,500	$ 2,500
Net Salvage Value	$ 4,000	$ 5,000	$10,000

Assuming a minimum attractive rate of return of 12% before taxes, use the *present worth method* or the *annual cost method* to determine whether the Current System should be retained or replaced.

7. Use the *rate of return method* to select from among the alternatives described in Problem 6.

8.[5] The Budget Committee of a manufacturing firm has approved the expenditure of $80,000 for improvement of its manufacturing facilities. The plant manager has received proposals for cost reduction programs from four department managers. These are:

Department A: Four mutually exclusive proposals for improvement of the receiving department:

Proposal	Initial Investment	Net Annual Savings in Disbursements
A1	$10,000	$2,000
A2	15,000	5,000
A3	25,000	7,800
A4	30,000	9,500

Department B: Three mutually exclusive proposals for improvement in assembly:

B1	$10,000	$ 4,100
B2	20,000	7,800
B3	30,000	10,000

Department C: Three mutually exclusive proposals for improvement in inspection:

C1	$10,000	$4,000
C2	15,000	5,000
C3	20,000	7,500

Department D: One proposal for a new forklift truck:

D1	$15,000	$4,600

It is assumed that each proposal will have a five-year life and zero salvage value. The Budget Committee requires that each alternative must earn

[5] Based on a problem first appearing in *Principles of Engineering Economy* (4th Ed.), E. L. Grant and W. G. Ireson, The Ronald Press Company, 1960.

at least 15% before taxes. Use the *annual cost method* or the *present worth method* to determine which alternatives should be recommended.

9. Use the *rate of return method* to select from among the alternatives described in Problem 8.

10. A comptroller is considering the following investment proposals which have been received from the (E) production, (F) quality control, and (G) shipping departments:

Alternative	Initial Investment	Annual Excess of Receipts over Disbursements
E1	$2,000	$ 275
E2	4,000	770
F1	4,000	1,075
F2	8,000	1,750
G1	4,000	1,100

Alternatives E1 and E2 are mutually exclusive for technical reasons; F1 and F2 are also mutually exclusive. Each of the alternatives has an expected life of ten years, and zero salvage values are assumed. A minimum attractive rate of return of 10% is used by the firm.

(a) Which proposals should be recommended if investment funds are essentially unlimited?

(b) Which proposals should be recommended if only $14,000 are available for new investments?

6

EFFECTS OF DEPRECIATION ON TAXABLE INCOME

In order that the relative economic desirability of investment opportunities may be determined, it is first necessary to establish (or estimate) the amounts and timing of *all* cash flows expected to arise as consequences of the decisions. With the exception of certain charitable institutions, religious groups, philanthropic foundations, and other specially defined non-profit organizations, individuals and business firms are subject to the tax laws of local, state, and federal governments. The amounts and timing of tax payments are important cash flow considerations, and the capital budgeting process is not complete unless these cash flows are formally considered in the analysis.

Determination of cash flows for taxes is discussed in Chapters 6 and 7. In this chapter, several methods are presented which illustrate the effect of capital investment on *taxable income*; the objective of the next chapter is to combine taxable income with appropriate tax rates to produce *tax payments.*

It is important to note at this point that determination of taxable income and tax payments is largely specified by legislation and/or regulations of appropriate government agencies. Since the material presented in Chapters 6 and 7 is necessarily abbreviated, and since laws and regulations are subject to change, our primary emphasis in these two chapters is limited to the presentation of general principles. The material presented is governed by the laws and regulations in effect at the time of preparation of the text. When dealing with specific real world cases, the analyst is always well advised to consult current, informed opinion.[1]

TERMINOLOGY AND CONCEPTS

A great deal of difficulty arises from confusion as to the meaning of *depreciation*. In our discussion we use the accounting concept as defined in a report of the Committee on Terminology of the American Institute of Certified Public Accountants:[2]

> Depreciation accounting is a system of accounting which aims to distribute the cost or other basic value of tangible capital assets, less salvage (if any), over the estimated useful life of the unit (which may be a group of assets) in a systematic and rational manner. It is a process of allocation, not of valuation. Depreciation for the year is the portion of the total charge under such a system that is allocated to the year.

According to relevant federal laws and regulations of the Internal Revenue Service, the cost or other basic value of machinery, equipment, buildings, trucks, office furniture, and certain other property with useful life of more than one year is a *capital expenditure*, and may not be deducted as an expense in the year of purchase. However, depreciation may be deducted for exhaustion, wear and tear, and obsolescence of property *used in the trade or business* or *held for the production of income*. Land is not depreciable, since its life is indeterminable.

Usually, the *cost* of the property is its *basis*, but this value may be increased by such items as purchase commissions and cost of improvements having a life of more than one year. The estimated *salvage value* is the amount which is expected to be realized, by sale or other dispositions, when the asset is retired from service. An asset may not be depreciated below its expected salvage value.

The estimated *useful life* used in computing depreciation depends upon such factors as its age when acquired, maintenance policy, and conditions of use. It is that period over which the asset may reasonably be expected to be used in the trade or business. As is demonstrated, it is generally to the firm's advantage (and the Government's disadvantage) to depreciate the asset as rapidly as possible. The Internal Revenue Service has therefore established,

[1] A number of useful, inexpensive pamphlets are available from the Superintendent of Documents, U.S. Government Printing Office, Washington, D.C. Especially interesting are: *Regulations Relating to Depreciation, Treasury Decision No. 6182*, Internal Revenue Service Publication No. 311 (Rev. 12–57); *Depreciation — Guidelines and Rules, Revenue Procedure 62–21*, I.R.S. Publication No. 456 (Rev. 8–64); *Your Federal Income Tax — for Individuals*, I.R.S. Publication No. 17 (revised each year); *Tax Guide for Small Business*, I.R.S. Publication No. 334 (revised each year); *Depreciation, Investment Credit, Amortization, Depletion*, I.R.S. Document No. 5050.

[2] American Institute of Certified Public Accountants, *Accounting Research Bulletin 22*, 1944.

for various classes of assets, minimum lives which may be used when computing depreciation.[3] These are guidelines only, however, and shorter lives may be used if it can be proved that such estimates are warranted for the particular firm.

METHODS OF COMPUTING DEPRECIATION

Straight Line Method

Under the straight line method, the estimated salvage value is subtracted from the original cost (or other basis) of the property. This depreciable amount is then divided by the estimated useful life, and the resulting value is the depreciation charge to be used each year. In symbols:

$$d = \frac{C - L}{N} \tag{6.1}$$

where d is the annual depreciation charge, C is the original cost (or other basis), L is the estimated salvage value and N is the expected useful life of the asset used for depreciation purposes.

To illustrate, consider an asset whose initial cost is \$40,000, estimated salvage value is \$4,000, and expected useful life is eight years. The annual depreciation charge is:

$$d = \frac{\$40,000 - \$4,000}{8 \text{ years}} = \$4,500 \text{ per year}$$

(*N.B.*: The depreciation methods presented in this chapter are illustrated by examples presuming *item accounting*, that is, each individual asset is treated as a separate account. *Group*, *classified*, or *composite* accounting is frequently used to combine two or more assets in a single account. These differences are mentioned here only to correct the impression that the straight line method of depreciation accounting is easily applied. Such *is* the case when dealing with item accounts, but the straight line method creates certain numerical difficulties when multiple-asset accounting is used.)

Book value is defined as the difference between the original cost (or other basis) and the accumulated depreciation to date. Referring to the example, the book value b of the asset immediately after the depreciation charge for the sixth year has been made is:

$$b_6 = \$40,000 - 6(\$4,500) = \$13,000$$

[3] *Depreciation Guidelines and Rules, Revenue Procedure 62–21*, Internal Revenue Service Publication No. 456 (Rev. 8–64).

It should be emphasized that book value and market value at any point in time need not necessarily be the same; in fact, they rarely are. This is to be expected since depreciation accounting is a method of allocation, not valuation.

Declining Balance Method

Whereas the straight line method results in a constant depreciation charge each year, the declining balance method applies a constant *rate* each year to the book value of the asset at the beginning of the year. Any declining balance rate may be used insofar as it does not exceed twice the straight line rate excluding salvage value. Thus the maximum allowable rate is $(2)(100\%/N)$. The maximum rate is almost always used, and this application is known as the double declining balance (*DDB*) method of depreciation. (This method may not be used when N equals 1 or 2 for obvious reasons.)

From the example, the double declining balance rate is 2.00/8, or 25%. The book value at the beginning of the first year is $40,000, and the depreciation charge for the first year is therefore 25% of $40,000, or $10,000. The book value at the beginning of the second year is now $30,000, and the depreciation charge for the second year is 25% of $30,000, or $7,500. And so on. Calculations for each of the eight years are given in Table 6-1.

Table 6-1

Double Declining Balance Depreciation For Asset Having First Cost of $40,000 and Estimated Useful Life of 8 Years

Year j	Book Value at Start of Year b_{j-1}	Depreciation Charge for Year d_j	Book Value at End of Year b_j
1	$40,000.00	$10,000.00	$30,000.00
2	30,000.00	7,500.00	22,500.00
3	22,500.00	5,625.00	16,875.00
4	16,875.00	4,218.75	12,656.25
5	12,656.25	3,164.06	9,492.19
6	9,492.19	2,373.05	7,120.14
7	7,120.14	1,780.04	5,340.10
8	5,340.10	1,335.03	4,005.07

Even though the declining balance method *appears* to ignore salvage value, the user must be alert to the restriction that an asset is not allowed to be depreciated below salvage value. This constraint is met in the example, but suppose that salvage value is, say, \$4,500 rather than \$4,000 assumed above. In this event, the depreciation charge in the eighth year is limited to \$840.10, and the book value at the end of the eighth year is exactly \$4,500.

In certain rare instances it may be desirable to select a declining balance rate which will cause the book value at the end of year N to be exactly equal to the expected salvage value L. This value may be determined by observing that the declining balance method causes the book value to decrease at a decreasing rate. Specifically:

$$b_j = C(1 - a)^j \tag{6.2}$$

where a is the declining balance rate and b_j is the book value at the end of the year j. Thus, since $b_N = L$, the rate which equates the expected salvage value to the book value at the end of year N is:

$$a = 1 - \sqrt[N]{\frac{L}{C}} \tag{6.3}$$

The resulting value of a must, of course, be equal to or less than $2/N$ in order to be acceptable. Also, note that a is undetermined if the expected salvage value is zero.

From Table 6-1, the book value at the end of the fourth year is \$12,656, or approximately 32% of the initial value of the asset. This coincides with a useful rule of thumb: the double declining balance method "writes off" (depreciates) about two-thirds of the cost of the asset in the first one-half of its useful life.

Sum of the Years Digits Method (Applied to a Single Asset)

The sum of the years digits (SYD) method also causes the book value of the asset to decrease at a decreasing rate. Here the annual depreciation charges are computed by applying changing fractions to the cost (or other basis) reduced by the estimated salvage value. The numerator of the fraction is the number of years of useful life remaining (including the year for which the depreciation is being computed), and the denominator is the sum of all the years digits corresponding to the estimated useful life of the asset. In general:

$$\begin{aligned}
d_1 &= \frac{N}{(\text{SYD})}(C - L) \\
d_2 &= \frac{N - 1}{(\text{SYD})}(C - L) \\
&\;\;\vdots \\
d_N &= \frac{1}{(\text{SYD})}(C - L)
\end{aligned} \tag{6.4}$$

where

$$\text{SYD} = \sum_{j=1}^{N} j = \frac{N(N+1)}{2} \tag{6.5}$$

Referring to the example, the amount to be depreciated is \$40,000 − \$4,000, or \$36,000, and the sum of years digits is $(8 \times 9)/2$, or 36. Thus the depreciation charge the first year is 8/36 of \$36,000, the depreciation charge the second year is 7/36 of \$36,000, and so on. Depreciation calculations for all years are summarized in Table 6-2. (Note that depreciation allowance is reduced each year by a constant amount, 1/(SYD). As is demonstrated in the following chapter, this uniform decrease frequently leads to opportunities to use the gradient factors developed previously.)

Table 6-2

Sum of the Years Digits Depreciation for Asset Having First Cost of \$40,000, Estimated Useful Life of 8 Years, and Expected Salvage Value of \$4,000

Year j	Depreciation Rate for Year a_j	Amount to be Depreciated $C - L$	Depreciation Charge for Year d_j
1	8/36	\$36,000	\$8,000
2	7/36	36,000	7,000
3	6/36	36,000	6,000
4	5/36	36,000	5,000
5	4/36	36,000	4,000
6	3/36	36,000	3,000
7	2/36	36,000	2,000
8	1/36	36,000	1,000
Total:	1.00		\$36,000

It may be shown that the book value at the end of year j is:

$$b_j = C - \frac{(C - L)}{(\text{SYD})} \sum_{k=1}^{j} (N + 1 - k) \tag{6.6}$$

where b_j is the book value at the end of the year after the depreciation charge for that year has been made. To illustrate, consider the book value at the end of the fourth year:

$$b_4 = \$40{,}000 - \frac{\$36{,}000}{36} \sum_{k=1}^{4} (8 + 1 - k)$$
$$= \$40{,}000 - \$1{,}000\,(8 + 7 + 6 + 5)$$
$$= \$14{,}000$$

Referring to Table 6-2, note that a total of \$26,000 has been depreciated during the first four years, or approximately 72% of the total amount to be depreciated, \$36,000. This coincides with a useful rule of thumb for the sum of the years digits method: about three-fourths of the amount to be depreciated will be written off during the first half of the expected useful life.

Sinking Fund Method of Depreciation Accounting

Whereas both the declining balance and sum of the years digits methods decrease the book value of the asset at a *decreasing* rate, the sinking fund method of depreciation accounting results in an *increasing* rate of writeoff over time. Here an imaginary sinking fund is established so that the "value" of this imaginary fund at the end of the expected useful life of the asset is exactly equal to the first cost minus the salvage value, that is, the amount to be depreciated. An imaginary uniform deposit is made into the sinking fund at the end of each year, and this deposit, added to the accumulated interest on the fund up to that point, represents the depreciation charge for that particular year.

Although the rate at which the imaginary sinking fund earns interest is generally in the range of 3% to 7%, it is arbitrarily established and may take on any value. There is an inverse relationship between the interest rate and the rate at which the book value of the asset decreases. The asset is depreciated very slowly at high interest rates; the sinking fund method yields the same results as the straight line method if a rate of 0% is used.

Again referring to the example, the amount to be depreciated $(C - L)$ is \$36,000 over an expected useful life of eight years. Assuming an interest rate of 5%, the annual sinking fund deposit is $(C - L)(SF - 5\% - 8)$, or \$36,000 (0.10472) = \$3,770. Calculations for determining the year-by-year depreciation charges are summarized in Table 6-3. It will be observed that the depreciation charge in the year j is:

$$d_j = (C - L)(SF - i\% - N) + i \sum_{k=0}^{j-1} D_k, \qquad \text{where } d_0 = 0 \quad (6.7)$$

For any interest rate greater than 0%, the book values using sinking fund depreciation are always greater than those for the straight line method. The difference increases with the interest rate and with asset life.

Table 6-3

**Illustration of Sinking Fund Depreciation Method
Allocation of $36,000 over 8-Year Period
Using 5% Sinking Fund Rate**

Year	Amount in Imaginary Sinking Fund at Start of Year (a)	Interest on Amount in Fund (b) = i(a)	Sinking Fund Deposit (c)	Depreciation Charge for Year (d) = (b) + (c)
1	0	0	$3,770	$3,770
2	$ 3,770	$ 189	3,770	3,959
3	7,729	386	3,770	4,156
4	11,885	594	3,770	4,364
5	16,249	812	3,770	4,582
6	20,831	1,042	3,770	4,812
7	25,643	1,282	3,770	5,052
8	30,695	1,535	3,770	5,305
			Total:	$36,000

The Reverse Sum of Years Digits Method

When using the sum of years digits method for determining depreciation allowances, a constantly *diminishing* fraction is applied each year to the amount to be depreciated ($C - L$), with the result that the book value is decreased at a *decreasing* rate. It is possible to decrease book value at an *increasing* rate through the simple device of multiplying the amount to be depreciated by a constantly *increasing* fraction.

From the example, the amount to be depreciated is $36,000. Further, the sum of years digits is $1 + 2 + \cdots + 8$, or 36. The fraction to be written off is 1/36 the first year, 2/36 the second year, and so on until 8/36 is depreciated in the eighth and final year. Thus:

$$D_1 = \frac{1}{36}(\$36{,}000) = \$1{,}000$$

$$D_2 = \frac{2}{36}(\$36{,}000) = \$2{,}000$$

$$\vdots$$

$$D_8 = \frac{8}{36}(\$36{,}000) = \$8{,}000$$

The Service Output Method

In some instances it may be most reasonable to associate decrease in value with productive output of the asset. This will occur in those cases where depreciation is more directly related to "wear and tear" than, say, style obsolescence.

The amount to be depreciated ($C - L$) is divided by the number of units of output expected to be produced over the useful life of the asset. This value, the *depreciation rate*, is then multiplied by the actual number of units produced in any given year to determine the depreciation charge for that year. To illustrate from the example, suppose that the asset in question is expected to have a useful life of 20,000 hours of operation and, further, assume that reduction in asset value is directly related to the number of hours of operation. Since the amount to be depreciated is $36,000, the depreciation rate is $36,000/20,000, or $1.80 per hour of operation. If the asset is operated for 2,500 hours during the first year of ownership, for example, the depreciation charge in the first year will be 2,500 hrs × $1.80/hr, or $4,500.

The depreciation charge each year is computed by multiplying the depreciation rate by the number of units of service output for that year. The asset may not be depreciated below expected salvage value, however, where salvage value is predetermined as in the other methods.

DEPLETION

Owners of certain mineral deposits, standing timber, or oil and gas wells are allowed to "deplete," rather than depreciate, these assets over time. As in the case of depreciation, certain rules have been established for determination of allowable depletion deductions. Depletion for mineral deposits and oil and gas wells may be determined by either the cost depletion or the percentage depletion method. That method which yields the greatest deduction will normally be used.

When using the *cost depletion method*, the first cost or adjusted basis of the resource is determined and the total number of remaining recoverable units is estimated. The adjusted basis refers to the original cost less the accumulated depletion to date; it can never be less than zero. The allowable cost depletion for the tax year is the product of the depletion unit times the number of units produced (or sold) in the year, where the depletion unit is the ratio of the cost basis to the number of remaining recoverable units. That is:

$$\text{Depletion for year} = \begin{pmatrix}\text{Units produced or}\\ \text{sold during year}\end{pmatrix} \cdot \left(\frac{\text{Cost basis}}{\text{Total recoverable units}}\right)$$

Percentage depletion takes a predetermined percentage of the gross depletable income from the property during the tax year, but the allowable deduction must not be greater than 50% of the net taxable income from the property before the depletion deduction. Depletion percentages are set by law. Some of the more common values are:

Clay used to make brick and tile	5%
Coal and sodium chloride	10%
Metallic and most other minerals	15%
Lead and zinc (from U.S. deposits)	23%
Oil and Gas	$27\frac{1}{2}$%

It is interesting to note that percentage depletion may continue to be taken as long as the property continues to produce, even though the adjusted basis is zero. Thus, in this particular instance, it is possible to write off more than the original cost or other basis of the property.

To illustrate the determination of the depletion allowances for oil, gas, or mineral properties, consider a mine producing a certain metallic mineral qualifying for the 15% depletion percentage. Suppose that the mine was purchased for $4 million and, at that time, 400,000 tons of ore were believed to be producible. Further, suppose that 30,000 tons are produced during the tax year and sold at $100 per ton; the total deductible operating expenses (other than depletion) are $1.6 million. The cost depletion allowance for the year is determined as follows:

$$\text{Cost depletion} = (30{,}000 \text{ tons}) \frac{\$4{,}000{,}000}{400{,}000 \text{ tons}}$$
$$= \$300{,}000$$

The percentage depletion is 15% of the gross depletable income from the property, or:

$$\text{Percentage depletion} = 0.15\,(\$100 \times 30{,}000 \text{ tons})$$
$$= \$450{,}000$$

The net taxable income before depletion is $3 million less $1.6 million, or $1.4 million. The percentage depletion determined above is not greater than 50% of this value, or $700,000, and hence the full $450,000 is allowable. The depletion used to determine taxable income is that resulting from the percentage depletion method since this results in lower taxable income, hence lower income taxes.

A summary of the income statement for the tax year is as follows:

Gross revenue (30,000 tons @ $100/ton)		$3,000,000
Deductible operating expenses	$1,600,000	
Depletion (percentage method)	450,000	2,050,000
Taxable income		$ 950,000

Percentage depletion cannot be used for timber. Rather, the cost depletion method must be used in which the depletion unit is the cost (or adjusted basis) of the timber on hand divided by the total depletable units. The cost basis refers to the timber only, not the land.

SOME ADDITIONAL RULES FOR DEPRECIABLE PROPERTY

Additional First Year Depreciation

Accelerated write-off of certain qualifying property is allowed by the United States Government in the form of a special "one-shot" deduction of 20% of the cost of the property (ignoring salvage value) in the year in which the asset is purchased. "Qualifying property" is tangible personal property, other than land or buildings, having a remaining useful life of at least six years at the time of purchase. The property may be new or used, but the deduction may only be taken in the first tax year for which a depreciation deduction is allowable. The additional allowance is limited to the first $10,000 of property reported purchased on an individual tax return, or to the first $20,000 for a joint return.

To illustrate, suppose that Mr. Jones purchased a second-hand commercial cleaning and pressing machine for his chain of cleaning plants. The machine cost $14,300, it has a remaining useful life of seven years at the time of acquisition, and it will probably be sold at the end of that time for a net salvage value of $1,800. Mr. Jones uses straight line depreciation and he files an individual return. Assuming that he has not purchased any other qualifying property during the year, and further assuming that the machine was purchased at the beginning of the tax year, the depreciation allowance for each of the five years is determined as follows:

$$\text{Initial cost} = \$14{,}300$$

$$\text{Limitation (individual return)} = \$10{,}000$$

$$\text{Additional first year depreciation} = (0.20)(\$10{,}000) = \$2{,}000$$

$$\text{Revised basis for depreciation} = \$14{,}300 - \$2{,}000 = \$12{,}300$$

$$\text{Amount to be depreciated} = \$12{,}300 - \$1{,}800 = \$10{,}500$$

$$\text{Annual depreciation allowance} = \$10{,}500/7 \text{ yrs.} = \$1{,}500$$

Thus the total depreciation allowance in the first year is $3,500 and the charge for years two through seven is $1,500 per year.

Investment Credit

As is demonstrated in the following chapter, the relative attractiveness of prospective investment can be directly affected by the depreciation method to be used. Thus, if government prescribes depreciation practice through laws and regulations, business activity can be influenced to a significant degree. The *investment credit*, although having no direct effect on the depreciation schedule, is also a powerful encouragement to new investment. The investment credit is an initial tax reduction equal to 7% of "qualified investment" in certain new and used depreciable property (other than buildings and their structural components). The tax credit percentage is only 3% for public utilities. The amount of qualified investment for new property is dependent upon the expected remaining useful life of the asset at the time of acquisition; the entire investment is qualified if the life of the asset is eight years or more, only two-thirds of the investment is qualified if the expected useful life is six or seven years, only one-third of the investment is qualified if the life is four or five years, and there is no qualified investment if the life is less than four years. The qualified investment in *used* property cannot exceed $50,000. To illustrate:

Asset	Useful Life (yrs)	Initial Cost	Qualified Investment
New Vehicle W	4	$ 4,200	$ 1,400
New Instrument X	7	1,800	1,200
Used Equipment Y	10	80,000	50,000
New Machine Z	9	7,500	7,500
Total qualified investment:			$60,100
Investment Credit (at 7% of qualified investment) :			$ 4,207

The investment credit is *not* a deduction from taxable income as is the depreciation expense. Rather, it is deducted directly from the tax liability of the firm and consequently cannot exceed the tax liability in the tax year in which computed. The investment credit is also limited in that, if the tax liability exceeds $25,000, the credit is limited to $25,000 plus one-fourth of the excess above $25,000. Unused credits are not lost however. They may be carried back three years and the balance which is still unused may be carried forward to the next five tax years. Unlike the extra first-year depreciation, the investment credit has *no effect* on the cost basis of the property.

SOME EFFECTS OF DEPRECIATION ACCOUNTING

The *balance sheet* and *profit and loss statement* are the two principal financial documents of any firm. The former records (or summarizes) the financial health of the enterprise, as measured by its assets and liabilities, at a particular point in time, whereas the latter is a statement of the financial success of the enterprise, as measured by its income and expenses, over a specified period of time.

As illustrated by the four depreciation methods shown in Table 6-4, both the balance sheet and profit and loss statement are affected by the depreciation

Table 6-4

Summary of Depreciation Charges and Book Values Using Four Different Depreciation Methods

(*Assumptions*: *First cost of $40,000. Expected salvage value of $4,000. Expected life of 8 years.*)

	DEPRECIATION EXPENSE FOR YEAR				BOOK VALUE AT END OF YEAR			
Year	Straight Line	Declining Balance	Sum of the Years Digits	Sinking Fund	Straight Line	Declining Balance	Sum of the Years Digits	Sinking Fund
0	—	—	—	—	$40,000	$40,000	$40,000	$40,000
1	$4,500	$10,000	$8,000	$3,770	35,500	30,000	32,000	36,230
2	4,500	7,500	7,000	3,959	31,000	22,500	25,000	32,272
3	4,500	5,625	6,000	4,156	26,500	16,875	19,000	28,115
4	4,500	4,219	5,000	4,364	22,000	12,656	14,000	23,751
5	4,500	3,164	4,000	4,582	17,500	9,492	10,000	19,169
6	4,500	2,373	3,000	4,812	13,000	7,120	7,000	14,357
7	4,500	1,780	2,000	5,052	8,500	5,340	5,000	9,305
8	4,500	1,335	1,000	5,305	4,000	4,005	4,000	4,000

schedule used by the firm for an asset (or group of assets). A large depreciation expense for the tax year will reduce reported pre-tax profits (taxable income), and the tax liability for that year will be reduced accordingly. For example, in comparing the declining balance method to the straight line method, it becomes obvious that the former results in smaller taxable income in the earlier years but larger taxable income in the later years. The effect on the balance sheet, on the other hand, is reversed. So-called *accelerated* depreciation schedules such as the declining balance or sum of the years digits methods tend to produce lower book values in the early years than do, say, the straight line or sinking fund methods.

SUMMARY

A number of alternative depreciation methods have been presented: the straight line method depreciates the asset at a uniform rate over time, the declining balance and sum of years digits methods decrease the book value of the asset at a decreasing rate, the sinking fund and "reverse" sum of years digits methods decrease the book value at an increasing rate, and the service output method writes off the asset in direct proportion to the percentage of potential output produced during each tax year. With the possible exception of the declining balance method, each of the schedules results in the same *total* depreciation over the service life of the asset. (Since the declining balance method initially ignores salvage value except as a lower bound, it is quite possible that this method will write off the asset to some value larger than the expected salvage value.) As illustrated by the generalizations of Figure 6-1, the primary difference between depreciation methods is the *timing* of the depreciation expense and, by extension, the effect on taxable incomes and cash flows for taxes.

In a sense, depletion is a form of depreciation especially applicable to mineral deposits, oil and gas wells, or standing timber. Both cost depletion and percentage depletion should be computed for oil, gas, and mineral resources, and that method which yields the largest deduction should be used. Only cost depletion may be used for timber deposits.

Both the 20% extra first year depreciation and the new investment credit have been discussed as "tax incentives" whereby potential investment in capital assets is made to appear more attractive by changing the amount or the timing of cash flows for taxes. The extra first year allowance is limited to the first $10,000 of qualifying tangible personal property ($20,000 on a joint return), and the cost basis of the asset is reduced by the amount of the extra allowance. Its over-all effect is rather limited. On the other hand, the import of the new investment credit is significant in our context, especially

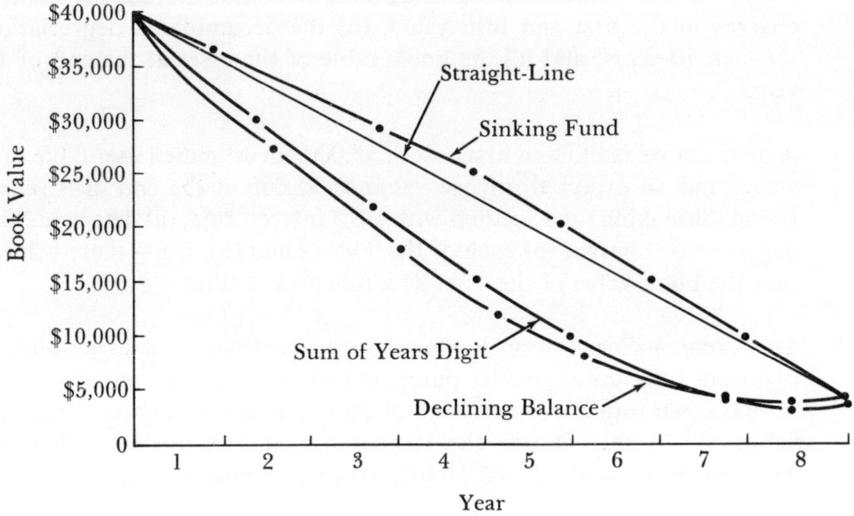

Fig. 6-1. Book value as function of time.

with respect to long-lived capital assets. The credit is applied directly to the firm's tax liability, and the cost basis of the asset is not affected.

The primary emphasis in this chapter has been the amount and timing of depreciation charges and consequent effects on taxable income. In the following chapter, we trace the effects on cash flows for taxes and, when the amounts and timing of these cash flows have been determined, the effect on investment decisions is illustrated.

PROBLEMS

1. A depreciable asset has a first cost of $11,000, an estimated useful life of 12 years, and an expected salvage value of $1,400 at the end of 12 years. Using the straight line method of depreciation, determine (a) the annual depreciation charge, (b) the accumulated depreciation through 4 years, and (c) the book value of the asset at the end of 8 years.

2. A depreciable asset has a first cost of $100,000, an estimated useful life of 10 years, and an expected salvage value of $25,000 at the end of 10 years. Using the double declining balance method, (a) determine the depreciation charges for each of the 10 years and (b) using these values, plot the book value of the asset as a function of time.

3. A depreciable asset has a first cost of $30,000, an estimated useful life of 15 years, and an expected salvage value of $6,000 at the end of 15 years.

Using the sum of the years digits method, determine (a) the depreciation charges in the first and fifth years, (b) the accumulated depreciation through 10 years, and (c) the book value of the asset at the end of 15 years.

4. A depreciable asset has a first cost of \$5,000, an estimated useful life of 9 years, and an expected salvage value of \$1,000 at the end of 9 years. Using the sinking fund method with a 5% interest rate, (a) determine the depreciation charges for each of the 9 years and (b), using these values, plot the book value of the asset as a function of time.

5. The Comma Corporation is planning the purchase of a high-volume, overhead bulk conveyor. If purchased, it will have an initial cost of \$100,000, an estimated useful life of 10 years, and an expected salvage value of \$20,000. During the 10-year period it is predicted that the conveyor will handle a total of 400,000 tons of bulk raw materials:

Year	Tons Handled	Year	Tons Handled
1	20,000	6	60,000
2	30,000	7	50,000
3	40,000	8	40,000
4	50,000	9	30,000
5	60,000	10	20,000

(a) With the above projections, determine the expected depreciation charges for each of the 10 years if the service output method is used.
(b) What is the depreciation charge in the third year if only 35,000 tons are actually handled?

6. Current federal tax laws state that any consistent method of computing depreciation may be used, provided depreciation allowances computed by these methods do not result in accumulated allowances at the end of any year greater than the total of accumulated allowances which could have resulted from the use of the double declining balance method. This limitation applies only during the first two-thirds of the useful life of the property.

Consider a depreciable asset with first cost of \$10,000, estimated useful life of 6 years, and an expected salvage value of \$1,800. Determine the maximum accumulated depreciation (a) through 3 years, (b) through 4 years, (c) through 5 years, and (d) through 6 years.

7. A small company plans to purchase the following assets during the next tax year:

Asset	Estimated Useful Life (years)	Initial Cost
Automobile	3	$ 3,000
Truck	5	9,000
Office machine	7	12,000
Plant equipment	12	15,000

(a) What is the limit on new investment credit if the company's expected tax liability next year is $28,000?
(b) If the above assets are purchased, what is the new investment credit?

8. The Green Corporation purchased the following assets during the current tax year:

Asset	Estimated Useful Life (years)	Initial Cost	Expected Salvage Value
One-half acre of land and small buildings	20	$30,000	$10,000
Room air conditioners (new)	6	1,800	300
Company bus (used)	9	6,000	1,000
Office equipment (new)	5	5,000	500

Determine the allowable "additional first-year depreciation" as the result of the purchase of these assets.

9. The Gusher Corporation is planning to purchase an oil property for $500,000. Initial engineering estimates indicate that the property is capable of producing 1,000,000 bbls of oil, and a preliminary cost study indicates that deductible operating expenses (other than depletion) will be about $1.60 per bbl. If 100,000 bbls are expected to be sold at $2.25 per bbl during the first year of operation, what will be the depletion deduction?

10. The Dunn Mining Company owns a small mine which produces a certain metallic mineral. The mine, now ending its third year of operation, was originally purchased for \$200,000. A total of \$20,000 has been charged as depletion expense for the first two years. At the beginning of the third year it was estimated that 8,000 tons of ore were still available in the mine. During the third year 2,000 tons are sold at an average price of \$155 per ton, and \$230,000 in deductible operating expenses (other than depletion) are incurred. Determine the depletion deduction and taxable income for the third year of operation.

7

TAXES AND PROFITABILITY

The primary discussion of the preceding chapter centered upon the ways in which new capital investments affect taxable income during the life of the assets as well as in the year in which the assets are acquired. In this chapter we relate taxable income to cash flows for taxes by examining the principal features of current (1969) federal tax regulations. The effect of cash flows for taxes on relative attractiveness of investment proposals is also demonstrated.

INCOME AND DISPOSAL TAXES FOR CORPORATIONS[1]

Tax Rates on Corporate Income[2]

Corporations are taxed at a "normal" rate of 22% on all taxable income, and at a "surtax" rate of 26% of all taxable income beyond $25,000. Thus the incremental corporate income tax rates are 22% for the first $25,000 of taxable income and 48% on all taxable income in excess of $25,000. (In some instances corporations which are members of a "controlled group"

[1] Our discussion of income taxes is limited here to incorporated business enterprises. An excellent reference for single proprietorships or partnerships is Internal Revenue Service Publication No. 334, *Tax Guide for Small Business*, available from the U.S. Government Printing Office, Washington, D.C. 20402.

[2] As this text is being published (March 1969), the U.S. federal government is imposing a 10% tax surcharge for individuals and corporations. Since the government tells us that the surcharge is intended to be only "temporary," however, we have included its mention in this text only in the form of a footnote. We trust that future events will justify our optimism.

may elect to pay a 6% penalty tax on the first \$25,000 of taxable income in order to minimize total federal income taxes paid.)

In addition to income taxes levied by the federal government, taxes are also levied by many states on corporate income. State income taxes are frequently deductible (as a business expense) on federal returns, but federal income taxes are rarely deductible on state returns. In the more usual case, then, the *combined incremental tax rate* may be determined from:

$$t = s + (1 - s)f$$

where s is the appropriate state tax rate and f is the appropriate federal tax rate. The combined incremental tax rate is simply $s + f$ in the event that neither federal nor state taxes are deductible on state or federal tax returns, respectively.

The appropriate corporate income tax rate applicable to an analysis of a given investment proposal should be that rate which is applicable to the *incremental* amount of taxable income. For example, suppose that the Comma Corporation is considering a proposal which, if accepted, will have the effect of increasing taxable income from \$29,000 to \$30,000 in the first year. Assuming no state taxes paid on corporate income, the *average* federal income tax rate paid will be 26.3% if the new asset is purchased:

$$\textit{Average}\text{ tax rate} = \frac{0.22(\$30{,}000) + 0.26(\$30{,}000 - 25{,}000)}{\$30{,}000} = \frac{\$7{,}900}{\$30{,}000} = 26.3\%$$

The tax rate which should be used in the analysis is 48%, however, since each dollar of taxable income beyond \$25,000 will be taxed at that rate. The Comma Corporation must pay a federal income tax of \$7,420 if the new asset *is not* purchased:

$$0.22(\$29{,}000) + 0.26(\$29{,}000 - \$25{,}000) = \$7{,}420.$$

But the tax will be \$7,900 if the asset *is* purchased, and thus the incremental tax of \$480 represents an incremental rate of 48% on the \$1,000 increase in taxable income.

Determination of the appropriate incremental tax rate is made considerably more complicated if personal income tax rates are also considered. Federal tax laws require stockholders to report dividends paid to them by corporations (and real estate investment trusts). Since these dividends result from profits which were initially taxed as corporate income and, further, since these dividends must also be taxed as individual income, every dollar of pre-tax earnings of the corporation is taxed twice. In order to mitigate the effect of "double taxation," federal tax law currently (1969) allows the individual taxpayer to exclude the first $100 of ordinary dividends received from taxable domestic corporations. Nevertheless, as illustrated in the following example, incremental tax rates may be quite high when both corporate and personal tax rates are considered.

Suppose that ownership of the Comma Corporation is represented by one hundred shares of common stock and, further, suppose that Mr. Master owns ten of these shares. If Mr. Master's personal incremental income tax rate is 25%, the after-tax profit resulting from the proposal discussed above is as follows:

Increment in corporate taxable income		$1,000
Corporate income tax		480
After-tax corporate income		$ 520
After-tax corporate income per share (paid out as dividends)	$5.20	
Increase in Mr. Master's personal taxable income (10 shares)		$52
Increase in personal income tax		13
Increase in Mr. Master's after-tax income		$39

Assuming that Mr. Master has at least $100 in "qualifying" dividends from other sources, the incremental effect of the investment from Mr. Master's point of view is to increase his wealth by $39. Thus, since his share of the pre-tax corporate income was $100, the correct combined incremental tax rate, strictly speaking, should be 61%.

If each of the stockholders in the example share the same incremental personal income tax rate, or if there are very few stockholders, then determination of the combined incremental tax rate is relatively straightforward. Whenever this situation occurs (or can be approximated), the compound personal and corporate incremental rate is to be used since decisions should be made from the point of view of the *owners* of the enterprise. However, as is usually the case with publicly held corporations, the number and diversity of stockholders is such that determination of any meaningful incremental personal income tax rate for the stockholders as a group is virtually impossible. In these instances it is advisable to consider only corporate taxes, bearing in mind that after-tax corporate profits must eventually be distributed to stockholders, at which time there will be an additional tax effect.

Timing of Tax Payments

In general, income taxes resulting from wages and salaries paid to *individuals* are collected by the federal government during the tax year. Estimated income taxes are withheld at the time of payment of wages and salaries — usually weekly, bi-weekly, or monthly — and the difference between estimated taxes and computed taxes is paid on or before the fifteenth day of the fourth month after the close of the tax year. If the amount withheld during the tax year exceeds the computed tax, the overpayment will be remitted upon receipt of the individual's tax return and processing by the Internal Revenue Service. State and local governments requiring income tax payments differ in their policies; some have instituted withholding plans whereas others require payment within a few months after the end of the tax year. In general, however, individual income taxes are paid at approximately the same time as individual income is received.

Corporations with federal income taxes of *$100,000 or less* are required to file tax returns and pay these taxes in two equal installments during the first half of the tax year following the tax year in which the income was earned. In this case, the tax consequence of an investment decision may lag the decision by as much as fifteen months.

There is a definite advantage to the firm, of course, in postponing negative cash flows for taxes as long as possible. But there is a corresponding disadvantage to the government. Not only does the government wish to collect its tax obligations when incurred, but it also desires relatively uniform cash receipts in order to minimize its own cash budgeting problems. Thus the government has established a different set of regulations for those corporations with income tax liabilities *in excess of $100,000* per year. Throughout the 1960's, the percentage of the tax liability paid during the year in which the liability is incurred has steadily increased. In 1959 for example, corporations were required to pay 50% of the estimated tax in excess of $100,000 in the year in which the income was earned; by 1965 this percentage had increased to 58% (4% in each of the first two quarters and 25% in each of the last two quarters of the year). The percentage is expected to increase each year until, by 1970, corporations will pay 25% of the estimated total tax in excess of $100,000 during each quarter of the tax year. The remaining tax liability is to be paid in two equal installments during the first half of the following year. A graphic presentation of this situation, as well as the case in which estimated tax liability is not greater than $100,000 is presented in Figure 7-1 (where t is the actual tax and t' is the estimated tax).

To illustrate the more complex case, suppose that the Comma Corporation expects to pay federal income taxes in the amount of $260,000 as the result of operations during 1970. (We assume that the Corporation's fiscal year coincides with the calender year.) Of this amount, $160,000 must be paid during 1970 at the rate of $40,000 during each of the four quarters of the year. Now suppose that, at the end of the year, it is determined that the actual tax burden for 1970 is $274,000. Since $160,000 has already been paid during 1970, $57,000 will be paid during each of the first two quarters of 1971.

The timing of income tax payments is relevant to capital budgeting

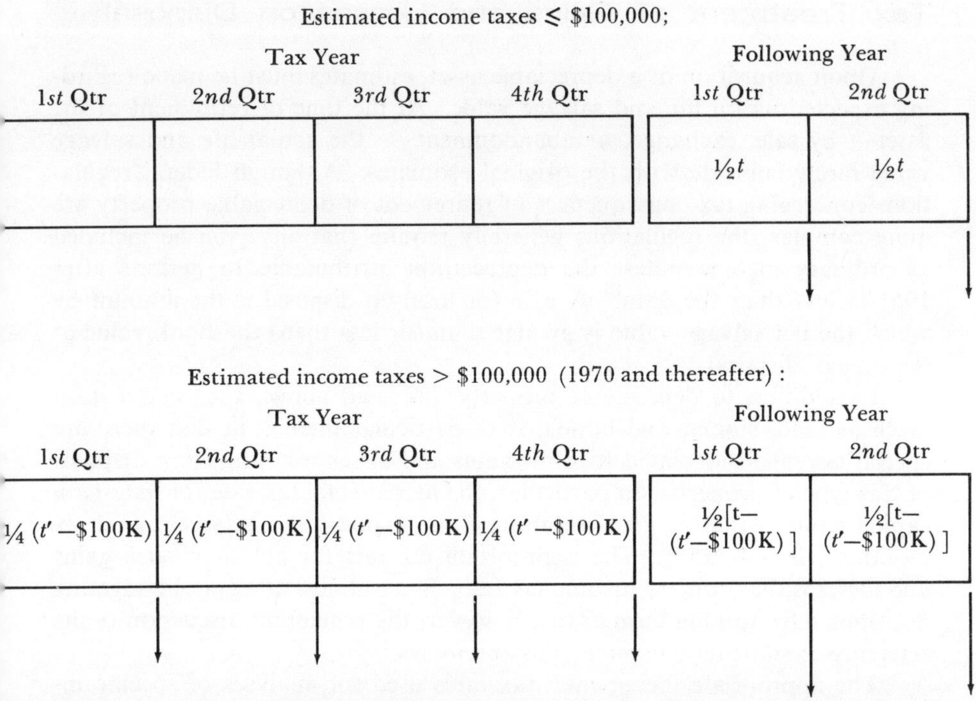

Fig. 7-1. Timing of tax payments.

questions for two very important reasons. First, firms must be able to predict amounts and timing of cash flows with reasonable accuracy to insure that short-term cash commitments — for example, payrolls, operating supplies — are met. Second, the timing of cash flows for taxes directly affects the relative economic attractiveness of an investment proposal. Postponement of negative cash flows has the effect of increasing apparent profitability. Despite these obvious considerations, however, the time lag between the investment (or direct consequence of the investment) and the cash flow for income taxes is generally ignored in economic analyses on the grounds that the time lag is so short as to be relatively inconsequential. For individuals and corporations paying income taxes in excess of $100,000 per year, this simplifying assumption seems reasonable. Further, even for those corporations with income taxes less than $100,000 per year, the assumption may not be unreasonable in that the average time lag is about ten or eleven months.

Unless specifically instructed otherwise, throughout the remainder of this text we assume no time lag between cash flows before taxes and the resulting cash flows for taxes. This assumption should not be blindly repeated, however, since specific investment decisions may be sensitive to precise determination of timing of all cash flows.

Tax Treatment of Gains and Losses on Disposal

Upon acquisition of a depreciable asset, estimates must be made regarding expected useful life and salvage value. At the time of retirement of the asset — by sale, exchange, or abandonment — the actual life and salvage value rarely coincide with the original estimates. Although federal regulations concerning tax consequences of retirement of depreciable property are quite complex, the regulations generally require that any *gain* be included as ordinary income unless the depreciation attributable to periods after 1961 is less than the gain.[3] A gain (or loss) on disposal is the amount by which the net salvage value is greater than (or less than) the book value at the time of disposal.

In addition to depreciable property discussed above, the *capital asset* (such as land, stocks, and bonds) is of particular interest in that there are special tax rates associated with the gains and losses resulting from disposal of this type of property. In particular, the incremental tax rate for *long-term* capital gains — that is, gains resulting from disposal of assets held over six months — is only 25%. The appropriate tax rate for net *short-term* gains and losses is the ordinary income tax rate. Since almost all capital budgeting decisions refer to long-term assets, however, the remaining discussion omits reference to short-term capital gains and losses.

The appropriate incremental tax rates used for analyses of specific investment proposals are, in general, determined by noting whether or not the property is to be treated as a capital asset. In general, gains and losses on disposal of depreciable assets are treated as ordinary income and hence the appropriate rate is the incremental tax rate pertaining to ordinary income.

Recapture Rule for Investment Credit

If an asset is sold or otherwise disposed of prior to expiration of the "useful life" on which the investment credit was initially determined, the amount of the investment subject to the credit must be recomputed using the shorter life. For example, consider New Machine Z discussed in the preceding chapter. The expected useful life at time of purchase was nine years, and consequently the entire first cost of \$7,500 qualified for the credit:

$$0.07(\$7,500) = \$525$$

Now suppose that Machine Y is sold at the end of seven years. Had this been known at the time of acquisition, only two-thirds of the investment would qualify, and the credit would have been only:

$$0.07(2/3)(\$7,500) = \$350$$

[3] In the event that depreciation attributable to periods after 1961 is less than the gain, the amount by which the gain exceeds the post-1961 depreciation is considered to be a capital gain. The amount equal to post-1961 depreciation is treated as ordinary income.

The difference between the investment credit (a) as initially computed and (b) as determined in retrospect is added to the tax liability in the year in which disposal takes place. In the example, the firm's tax liability would increase by $175 as the result of this transaction.

EFFECT OF TAXES ON PROFITABILITY

The prospective rate of return, equivalent uniform annual cost, net present worth, etc., of an investment proposal are affected by the amounts and timing of *all* cash flows resulting from the investment. For most investment proposals contemplated by firms subject to income taxes, tax payments and receipts are important considerations which have direct effect upon these measures of economic attractiveness. (In this context a tax "receipt" results from a reduction in the tax liability of the firm). In this section we demonstrate a procedure for determining net cash flows after taxes and, further, the effect of changes in tax payments on rate of return is illustrated for a project with a given series of before-tax cash flows.

Determining After-Tax Rate of Return

Consider an asset which may be purchased for $10,000 and is to be retained for five years, at the end of which time it will be sold with zero net salvage value. If the asset is expected to result in net operating savings of, say, $3,000 each and every year during its life, the project rate of return *before taxes* is 15.3%, determined as follows:

$$0 = -\$10{,}000 + \$3{,}000(SPW - i\% - 5)$$

$$(SPW - i\% - 5) = 3.333$$

Thus: $$i = 15.3\%$$

In order to establish the rates of return *after taxes* for this proposal, it is first necessary to establish: (a) whether the asset is to be written off as a business expense in the year in which it is purchased (expensed) or, instead, is to be carried on the books of account as a capital item and written off over time (capitalized); (b) the depreciation method to be applied to the asset if capitalized; (c) the life and salvage value to be used in computing depreciation; and (d) the appropriate incremental tax rate. (It is also necessary to determine cash flows affected by "additional first year depreciation" and "new investment credit" where applicable, although these considerations are temporarily ignored in the following discussion.)

In the example, we assume that the asset is to be capitalized and that the straight line depreciation method will be used. An expected life of five years and zero salvage value are assumed when computing annual depreciation charges. The current earnings level for the firm is such that the incremental tax rate is 50%, and it is assumed that this rate remains constant over the next five years.

There is no immediate tax effect when the asset is purchased. However, income reported by the firm each year will be reduced by the depreciation charge, and there will be a corresponding effect on income taxes paid. The annual depreciation expense *d* is determined as follows:

$$d = \frac{C - L_d}{N_d} = \frac{\$10{,}000 - \$0}{5} = \$2{,}000$$

where C is the initial cost of the asset, L_d is the salvage value for depreciation purposes and N_d is the expected life for depreciation purposes. (In general L_d and N_d need not, necessarily coincide with the life N_a and salvage value L_a which are expected to actually result.) The cash flow for taxes in a given year may now be computed. In the first year, for example, acquisition of the asset is expected to result in an increase of \$3,000 in cash flows before taxes, but this increase in pre-tax profit is partially offset by the \$2,000 depreciation expense. The net effect is to increase taxable income by \$1,000, and the tax liability will increase incrementally by 50% of this amount, or \$500. Combining the \$3,000 decrease in operating expenses with the \$500 increase in taxes, the effect of the investment in the first year is a \$2,500 net increase in the firm's after-tax cash flow. (In this particular example the after-tax cash flows for all years other than year zero are identical since the pre-tax cash flows, depreciation expense, and tax rate do not change from year to year and, further, there is no tax effect upon disposal at the end of the fifth year. It should also be noted that, in this and other examples and problems, it is assumed that the asset is acquired at the beginning of the tax year and taxes are paid at the end of the tax year.)

Determination of the after-tax cash flows is simplified somewhat by use of a *cash flow table* of the type illustrated in Table 7-1. The situation described above is shown as CASE A in the Table. The after-tax rate of return, 7.9%, is determined in the usual manner:

$$0 = \$10{,}000 + \$2{,}500(SPW - i\% - 5)$$

$$(SPW - i\% - 5) = 4.000$$

Thus:

$$i = 7.9\%$$

Effect of Changes in Depreciation Method

Straight line depreciation is used in connection with CASE A as described above. Now consider the same basic situation with the exception that double declining balance depreciation is used. In this instance, shown as CASE B in

Table 7-1, the accumulated depreciation over the life of the asset is somewhat less than that of CASE A (since the declining balance method ignores salvage value), yet this disadvantage is more than offset by the fact that the larger depreciation expenses occur earlier. The book value of the asset at the end of five years will be \$777.60 and, if the asset has no salvage value upon disposal, the firm will report a loss in that amount and the tax liability will be decreased accordingly. The net effect of "accelerating" depreciation and thereby "decelerating" negative cash flows for taxes is to increase the rate of return to 8.8%. This solution is found from:

$$0 = \sum_{j=1}^{5} C_j (1 + i)^{-j}$$
$$= - \$10{,}000 + \$3{,}500(1 + i)^{-1} + \$2{,}700(1 + i)^{-2} + \cdots + \$2{,}148(1 + i)^{-5}$$

By trial-and-error and linear interpolation, the solution to this equation occurs when $i = 8.8\%$.

In general, it is possible to change from the declining balance method to the straight line method at any time during the useful life of the property without the consent of the Internal Revenue Service. CASE C, illustrated in Table 7-4, reflects the effect of such a shift at the earliest "profitable" opportunity, that is, during the fourth year. (It is left as an exercise for the reader to show that the most advantageous time for switching occurs during the fourth year.) After-tax cash flows of \$2,040 in each of the last two years — rather than \$1,932 in the fourth year and \$2,148 in the fifth year — result in a slight increase in the after-tax rate of return to 8.9%.

The effect of using the sum of years digits depreciation method is illustrated as CASE D in Table 7-1. Noting that the after-tax cash flows decrease at the rate of \$333 per year, the gradient present worth factor has been used to determine the rate of return. (Since the sum of years digits method always results in a uniform annual decrease in depreciation expense, proposals employing this form of depreciation frequently result in a uniform gradient pattern of after-tax cash flows.) The rate of return is the trial-and-error solution of:

$$0 = - \$10{,}000 + \$3{,}167(SPW - i\% - 5) - \$333(GPW - i\% - 5)$$

The resulting after-tax rate of return, 8.8%, is the same as that obtained from the declining balance method (to the nearest one-tenth of a percent) but somewhat larger than that resulting from use of the straight line method.

Effect of New Investment Credit

As mentioned earlier, the "new investment credit" provision of the United States Federal income tax regulations is intended to promote capital investment by providing a direct financial incentive. CASE E of Table 7-1

Table 7-1

Cash Flow Tables for Asset under Alternative Tax Treatments

Given: *First cost of asset is $10,000, Net operating savings before taxes are $3,000 per year for 5 years, Incremental corporate income tax rate is 50%, Additional first-year depreciation omitted from all cases, New investment credit considered only in CASE E.*

	End of Year	Effect on Cash Flow Before Taxes[a]	Depreciation Expense	Effect on Taxable Income	Effect on Cash Flow for Taxes	Effect on Cash Flow After Taxes	Rate of Return
CASE A							
Straight Line	0	−10,000				−10,000	
Depreciation	1	+3,000	−2,000	+1,000	−500	+2,500	
	2	+3,000	−2,000	+1,000	−500	+2,500	
	3	+3,000	−2,000	+1,000	−500	+2,500	$i = 7.9\%$
$N_d = N_a = 5$	4	+3,000	−2,000	+1,000	−500	+2,500	
$L_d = L_a = 0$	5	+3,000	−2,000	+1,000	−500	+2,500	
						+2,500	
CASE B							
Double Declining	0	−10,000				−10,000	
Balance Depreciation	1	+3,000	−4,000	−1,000	+500	+3,500	
	2	+3,000	−2,400	+600	−300	+2,700	
	3	+3,000	−1,400	+1,560	−780	+2,200	$i = 8.8\%$
	4	+3,000	−864	+2,136	−1,068	+1,932	
$N_d = N_a = 5$	5	+3,000	−518.40	+2,481.60	−1,240.80	+1,759.20	
$L_d = L_a = 0$	5	0	(777.60)[b]	−777.60	+388.80	+388.80	
						+2,500	

[a] Before-tax rate of return is approximately 15%.
[b] Book value

CASE C							
Double Declining	0	−10,000				−10,000	
Balance: Shift	1	+ 3,000	−4,000	−1,000	+ 500	+ 3,500	
to Straight Line	2	+ 3,000	−2,400	+ 600	− 300	+ 2,700	
	3	+ 3,000	−1,440	+1,560	− 780	+ 2,220	$i = 8.9\%$
$N_d = N_a = 5$	4	+ 3,000	−1,080	+1,920	− 960	+ 2,040	
$L_d = L_a = 0$	5	+ 3,000	−1,080	+1,920	− 960	+ 2,040	
						+ 2,500	
CASE D							
Sum of Years Digits	0	−10,000				−10,000	
Depreciation	1	+ 3,000	−3,333	− 333	+ 167	+ 3,167	
	2	+ 3,000	−2,667	+ 333	− 167	+ 2,833	
	3	+ 3,000	−2,000	+1,000	− 500	+ 2,500	$i = 8.8\%$
$N_d = N_a = 5$	4	+ 3,000	−1,333	+1,667	− 833	+ 2,167	
$L_d = L_a = 0$	5	+ 3,000	− 667	+2,333	−1,167	+ 1,833	
						+ 2,500	
CASE E							
Straight Line	0	−10,000				−10,000	
Depreciation:	1	7% ×	1/3 ×	$10,000 =	+ 233	+ 233	
New Investment	1	+ 3,000	−2,000	+1,000	− 500	+ 2,500	
Credit	2	+ 3,000	−2,000	+1,000	− 500	+ 2,500	$i = 8.8\%$
	3	+ 3,000	−2,000	+1,000	− 500	+ 2,500	
$N_d = N_a = 5$	4	+ 3,000	−2,000	+1,000	− 500	+ 2,500	
$L_d = L_a = 0$	5	+ 3,000	−2,000	+1,000	− 500	+ 2,500	
						+ 2,733	

Table 7-1 (continued)

Cash Flow Tables for Asset under Alternative Tax Treatments

	End of Year	Effect on Cash Flow Before Taxes	Depreciation Expense	Effect on Taxable Income	Effect on Cash Flow for Taxes	Effect on Cash Flow After Taxes	Rate of Return
CASE F							
Straight Line	0	− 10,000				− 10,000	
Depreciation:	1	+ 3,000	− 3,333	− 333	+ 167	+ 3,167	
Shorter "Ex-	2	+ 3,000	− 3,333	− 333	+ 167	+ 3,167	
pected Life"	3	+ 3,000	− 3,000	− 333	+ 167	+ 3,167	$i = 9.3\%$
$3 = N_d < N_a = 5$	4	+ 3,000	0	+ 3,000	− 1,500	+ 1,500	
$L_d = L_a = 0$	5	+ 3,000	0	+ 3,000	− 1,500	+ 1,500	
						+ 2,500	
CASE G							
Straight Line	0	− 10,000		− 10,000	+ 5,000	− 5,000	
Depreciation:	1	+ 3,000	0	+ 3,000	− 1,500	+ 1,500	
Asset Expensed	2	+ 3,000	0	+ 3,000	− 1,500	+ 1,500	
	3	+ 3,000	0	+ 3,000	− 1,500	+ 1,500	$i = 15.0\%$
$0 = N_d < N_a = 5$	4	+ 3,000	0	+ 3,000	− 1,500	+ 1,500	
$L_d = L_a = 0$	5	+ 3,000	0	+ 3,000	− 1,500	+ 1,500	
						+ 2,500	

CASE H							
Straight Line	0	− 10,000				− 10,000	
Depreciation:	1	+ 3,000	− 1,000	+ 2,000	− 1,000	+ 2,000	
Expected Positive	2	+ 3,000	− 1,000	+ 2,000	− 1,000	+ 2,000	
Salvage Value	3	+ 3,000	− 1,000	+ 2,000	− 1,000	+ 2,000	
	4	+ 3,000	− 1,000	+ 2,000	− 1,000	+ 2,000	$i = 12.1\%$
$N_d = N_a = 5$	5	+ 3,000	− 1,000	+ 2,000	− 1,000	+ 2,000	
$L_d = L_a = \$5,000$	5	+ 5,000	(5,000)[b]	0	0	+ 5,000	
						+ 5,000	
CASE J							
Straight Line	0	− 10,000				− 10,000	
Depreciation:	1	+ 3,000	− 2,000	+ 1,000	− 500	+ 2,500	
Gain on Disposal	2	+ 3,000	− 2,000	+ 1,000	− 500	+ 2,500	
	3	+ 3,000	− 2,000	+ 1,000	− 500	+ 2,500	$i = 13.6\%$
	4	+ 3,000	− 2,000	+ 1,000	− 500	+ 2,500	
$N_d = N_a = 5$	5	+ 3,000	− 2,000	+ 1,000	− 500	+ 2,500	
$0 = L_d < L_a = \$5,000$	5	+ 5,000	(-0-)[b]	+ 5,000	− 2,500	+ 2,500	
						+ 5,000	

summarizes the effect for the example under the assumption that straight line depreciation is used. Since the asset is expected to be held for five years, only one-third of the initial cost is applicable when determining the credit. Thus:

$$\text{Tax Credit} = 7\% \times 1/3 \times \$10{,}000 = \$233$$

This is a deduction from the firm's tax liability and, based upon our earlier assumptions concerning *timing* of the initial investment, the new investment credit has the net effect of increasing the firm's cash flow by $233 one year after the purchase of the asset.

The cost basis is not affected by the new investment credit. Thus, as in CASE A above, the depreciation charges are determined to be $2,000 per year. Referring to the table of cash flow shown as CASE E in Table 7-1, the rate of return is the solution of the equation:

$$0 = -\ \$10{,}000 + \$233(PW - i\% - 1) + \$2{,}500(SPW - i\% - 5)$$

The solution, $i = 8.8\%$, is considerably greater than that obtained in CASE A, 7.9%, in which the new investment credit was ignored. Thus, from the point of view of the firm's management, the effect of the new investment credit provision is to cause prospective investment projects to appear more profitable than would otherwise be the case.

Effect of Shortened Expected Life

CASE F illustrates the effect of using an expected life for depreciation computations L_d which is shorter than that actually expected to occur L_a. Specifically, the expected life for depreciation is only three years whereas it is assumed that the asset is used for five years. Both L_a and L_d are assumed to be zero. The after-tax cash flows, given in Table 7-1, result in a prospective rate of return of approximately 9.3% for the proposal.

Expensing an item represents, in a sense, the minimum life over which the purchase is "depreciated." In this case it is assumed that the item is consumed during the year in which it is procured. The cost of the item is considered an immediate expense and results in a deduction from taxable income in the year in which the item is procured. (Assets assumed to have useful lives of more than one year are *capitalized* and depreciated by one of the methods discussed earlier.) CASE G, illustrated in Table 7-1, describes the situation in which the initial investment of $10,000 is entirely written off (or expensed) in the first year. The after-tax rate of return is shown to be 15%.

Effect of Positive Salvage Value

Both CASES H and J consider the basic example as described above except that here it is assumed that the asset may be sold at the end of five years for $5,000. Straight line depreciation is used in both instances except that CASE

H assumes L_d is \$5,000, whereas CASE J assumes L_d will be zero. As illustrated in Table 7-1, a slight advantage results from using a minimum expected salvage value for depreciation purposes. Although a tax will ultimately be paid when a gain results from disposal of the asset, the net effect is postponement of the negative cash flow for taxes. Thus the prospective rates of return are 12.1% and 13.6% for CASES H and J, respectively.

SUMMARY

Both the absolute and relative economic attractiveness of prospective investment proposals are significantly affected by relevant federal and state tax regulations. It is essential, therefore, that analyses concerned with problems of capital budgeting take into consideration tax rates, scheduling of tax payments, and other matters which relate to amounts and timing of cash flows for income taxes. In general, the critical level of taxable corporate income is \$25,000; the incremental federal income tax rate is 22% on all taxable income below that level and 26% on all taxable income in excess of \$25,000.

Tax regulations of state governments vary from state to state and detailed discussion has consequently been avoided here. In any event, analysts should include *all* relevant taxes — federal, state, and local — when determining the appropriate tax rate applicable to incremental income to be generated by an investment proposal.

Corporate income is subject to "double taxation" in that after-tax profits, when distributed in the form of dividends, are taxed as personal income. It is extremely difficult to completely determine incremental tax rates for large, publicly held corporations but, whenever the number of owners is so small as to permit reasonably precise determination of incremental individual income tax rates, it is recommended that both tax structures be considered.

There is, in general, a substantial lag between the times at which the pre-tax cash flow resulting from the investment occurs and the time at which the associated tax effect takes place. The analyst should include these effects where timing appears to be critical with respect to a specific investment decision; otherwise, a simplifying assumption may reasonably be made.

The prospective rate of return of an investment proposal is clearly affected by tax considerations, but the relative effect is controlled to a large extent by the depreciation schedule used and/or the expected life assumed for depreciation purposes. Table 7-2 summarizes the after-tax rates of return resulting from a variety of depreciation methods used in connection with a certain investment proposal. In each instance the pre-tax cash flows were identical. In addition to the obvious value of the new investment credit, prospective after-tax rates of return are improved (a) by "accelerating" the

Table 7-2

Effects of Depreciation Schedules on Rates of Return: Summary of Results from Table 7-1

Depreciation Method	Depreciable Life		
	5 years	3 years	Expensed
Straight Line	7.9%	9.3%	15.0%
Double Declining Balance	8.8%	—	—
Double Declining Balance: Shift to Straight Line	8.9%	—	—
Sum of Years Digits	9.0%	—	—
Straight Line: New Investment Credit	8.8%	—	—

Note: Pre-tax rate of return is 15%.

rate at which depreciation expense is claimed over the expected life of the asset or (b) by using a depreciable life somewhat less than the expected useful life. The total after-tax cash flows are the same in both instances; only the timing differs.

Parenthetically, it is important to note that the federal government places limits on both the permissible depreciation method and the allowable depreciable life. In general, the rate used in the declining balance method cannot exceed twice the straight line rate (ignoring salvage value), and in no case may an asset be depreciated below its expected salvage value. The Internal Revenue Service has suggested "average useful lives" which may be used for depreciation purposes, and the "reserve ratio test"[4] has been prescribed as a technique for establishing whether a firm's retirement and replacement practices are consistent with lives used for those assets. Shorter useful lives may be used in individual cases when they can be clearly justified.

PROBLEMS

In the following problems, assume that all pre-tax cash flows except the initial investment take place at the end of the tax year. Assume that the cash flow associated with initial procurement of the asset takes place at the beginning of

[4] For additional discussion of the "reserve ratio test" and other guidelines for depreciation, see *Depreciation Guidelines and Rules*, Internal Revenue Service Publication No. 456.

the first tax year. Unless otherwise stated, assume that all cash flows for taxes take place at the end of the years in which the respective taxable incomes occur. Also assume that incremental tax rates are not expected to vary over the life of the asset. Ignore "new investment credit" and "extra first year depreciation" unless otherwise directed.

1. The White Trucking Company is a large, publicly held common carrier having an incremental tax rate of 40%. The Company is planning to purchase new truck-washing equipment for its Los Angeles maintenance base. This new equipment will cost $150,000, have an estimated life of 10 years, and is expected to have a terminal salvage value of $40,000.

   It is expected that the new equipment will cause a reduction in annual operating expenditures, other than taxes, of $30,000 each year for the 10-year period. If the equipment is to be depreciated by the sum of years digits method, what is the prospective after-tax rate of return?

2. If the relevant new investment credit and extra first year depreciation allowance are considered, what is the prospective after-tax rate of return of the asset described in Problem 1?

3. Missile and Space Electronics, Inc., has just received a four-year contract to manufacture a small, high-frequency pulse generator for the Air Force. Their manufacturing expense estimates for bidding purposes are shown below as ALTERNATIVE I. Since submitting the bid, the Company's Engineering Division has developed what is possibly a better proposal, using extensive mechanization, shown below as ALTERNATIVE II. Which of these two would you recommend be used on the basis of rate of return after income taxes? The minimum after-tax rate of return is 15%.

   For this project only, assume negligible salvage values. Capitalize the machines and tooling as one group using straight line depreciation over the project life of 4 years. Assume that all other items may be expensed in the year in which they are spent. The incremental income tax rate is 50%. Other appropriate input data are as follows:

	Alternative I	Alternative II
Initial product development	$ 50,000	$ 50,000
Preproduction engineering	90,000	122,000
Machine tools and tooling	12,000	40,000
Annual labor cost	35,000	15,000
Annual operating expenses for this contract (other than labor)	20,000	20,000
Annual sales revenue from this contract	115,000	115,000

4. The White Trucking Company is considering installation of an electronically controlled drag line in its Chicago terminal. The initial investment will be $300,000, but it will cause a reduction in annual operating disbursements of $50,000 a year for 12 years (the expected life of the equipment).

   The investment will be depreciated for income tax purposes by the straight line method using 20-year life and zero salvage value. However, the equipment will be useless to the Company at the end of 12 years and, at that time, will be disposed of at a zero net salvage value. Determine the prospective after-tax rate of return on this investment if the incremental tax rate is 40%.

5. The Brown Company is considering purchase of some special equipment costing $60,000. If purchased, it will cause an expected excess of receipts over disbursements of $16,000 a year for 5 years; at the end of that time the equipment will be worthless. It is expected that the equipment will be purchased with a down payment of $10,000, and the remainder will be paid off at the rate of $10,000 per year plus 6% on the unpaid balance. Determine the after-tax rate of return on the original investment ($10,000) assuming a 50% effective tax rate and sum of years digits depreciation based upon 5-year life and zero salvage value.

6. Determine the prospective after-tax rate of return of the proposal described in Problem 5 if the double declining balance method of depreciation is used.

7. Consider the problem described in Problem 5. Which of the following three changes in tax treatment will result in the greatest increase in prospective after-tax rate of return: reduction of allowable depreciable life to three years, permission to use *triple* declining balance method, or reduction in the incremental tax rate to 40%? Show all work.

8. A lumber mill produces 1,000 MBM (1 MBM = 1,000 board feet) of finished lumber per year at a net positive cash flow of $30,000 before depreciation charges and income tax. The nearby source of saw logs will be exhausted this year, however. Hauling logs from a more distant source will cost an additional $10 per MBM log measure. An MBM of logs will produce two-thirds of an MBM of finished lumber.

   The mill was installed 10 years ago at a cost of $120,000 on land that cost $10,000. The mill has been depreciated on a 20-year, sum of the years digits basis with salvage value originally estimated to be $15,000. The mill owner has received an offer of $40,000 for the mill — which includes its removal from the land — and a separate offer of $30,000 for the land if the mill is removed.

The mill owner is in the 40% tax bracket. Assume that the original estimate of mill life and salvage value remain unchanged and that the current offer for the land is to be used as its estimated value ten years hence.

In a sense, the owner is investing anew in his mill if he foregoes the opportunity represented by the offer. What is his prospective after-tax rate of return if he refuses to sell?

9. The Black Company is considering a proposal to manufacture a new product. The Planning Department has been asked to make an economic analysis assuming that production will begin January 3, 1972 (zero date) and terminate after 12 years. An incremental tax rate of 50% is to be used in the study.

   Original cost of machinery and equipment is $90,000. An estimated life of 12 years with $12,000 salvage value will be used for tax purposes. The sum of years digits depreciation method will be used. In addition, $30,000 of working capital will be required at zero date. It is assumed that the working capital will be fully recovered at the end of 12 years. Estimated receipts from sale of the product are $60,000 in year 1, $90,000 in year 2, and $120,000 a year from years 3 through 12. Estimated operating disbursements are $48,000 in year 1, $65,000 in year 2, and $80,000 a year from years 3 through 12.

   Determine the prospective rate of return after taxes that is indicated by the above estimates.

10. Three financing plans are available for a new truck: Plan I is a cash purchase for $2,000; Plan II requires a 20% down payment with the balance paid in three equal end-of-year payments (which include interest at 6% on the unpaid balance); Plan III is a lease with 3 equal beginning-of-year payments of $750.

    The truck will be used for 3 years. If purchased, it will be sold at that time for the expected salvage value, $200. The Company is in the 40% tax bracket and uses sum of years digits depreciation. The after-tax minimum attractive rate of return is 15%.

    Determine the equivalent uniform annual cost for each of the three plans.

8

SPECIAL PROBLEMS OF REPLACEMENT AND RETIREMENT

Physical assets are retired, with or without replacement, for several reasons, not all of which need be mutually exclusive. For example, assets physically deteriorate with age, improved alternatives become available, and there may be changes in production or service requirements. Decisions must be made by management concerning retirement and replacement prior to the point at which the asset is no longer physically capable of functioning. Since these decisions occur so frequently in industry, it is appropriate to devote this chapter to discussion of the special problems of retirement and replacement.

RETIREMENT WITHOUT REPLACEMENT

In this section we are concerned with the economic consequences of the decision to retire an asset from service at some time prior to its maximum physical life. If it is assumed that the retired asset will not be replaced, the appropriate decision rule is straightforward: *the asset should not be retired if the net present value of all prospective consequences during the remaining life is greater than zero.*

To illustrate, consider the following cost and revenue estimates concerning an asset which, at the time of the analysis, is three years old and which has a remaining physical life of two years.

Year	Expected Revenue	Expected Operating Costs	Expected End-of-Year Salvage Value
4	$1,200	$800	$300
5	1,000	900	0

Further assume that the asset may currently be sold for $600 and that the pre-tax minimum attractive rate of return for the firm is 10%.

If the asset is kept one more year, the relevant consequences are (*a*) a foregone opportunity to receive $600 "today," (*b*) net receipts of $400 during the next year, and (*c*) a salvage value of $300 at the end of the year. With our usual assumption of end-of-period cash flows and compounding, the net present worth of this policy is:

$$\begin{aligned} PW &= -\ \$600 + (\$400 + 300)(PW - 10\% - 1) \\ &= -\ \$600 + \$700(0.9091) \\ &= \$36 \end{aligned}$$

Thus the analysis indicates that the asset should *not* be immediately retired; it should be kept for *at least* one more year.

Although the retirement question has been answered for the moment, it may be of some interest to determine if, based upon current estimates, the asset should be kept for *two* years, that is, through the end of its physical life. The expected consequences are (*a*) an immediate cost (opportunity foregone) of $600, (*b*) net receipts from operations of $400 and $200 at the end of years four and five, respectively, and (*c*) zero net salvage value upon disposal. Thus:

$$\begin{aligned} PW &= -\ \$600 + \$400(PW - 10\% - 1) + \$200(PW - 10\% - 2) \\ &= -\ \$600 + \$400(0.9091) + \$200(0.8264) \\ &= -\ \$71 \end{aligned}$$

It appears at this point that, unless there are some changes in the estimates for the fifth year, the asset will be retired from service at the end of the fourth year.

RETIREMENT WITH IDENTICAL REPLACEMENT

Let us now examine the question of retirement of an asset whose replacement is identical with respect to initial cost, annual operating income and expenses, physical life, and year-by-year market values upon disposal. The appropriate procedure to be followed in this case is illustrated with reference to the following example.

Consider a \$10,000 asset with maximum physical life of six years and having the end-of-year market values as given in Column (b) of Table 8-1. A pre-tax minimum attractive rate of return of 10% is assumed.

The first step requires determination of the *economic life* of the potential replacement asset, where "economic life" is defined as that service life, equal to or less than the maximum physical life, which yields the minimum equivalent uniform annual cost. (The term "*challenger*" is generally used in the literature of replacement economy to denote the asset being considered to replace the existing asset, or "*defender*.")

In order to determine the economic life of the challenger, it is necessary to compute the equivalent uniform annual costs (*EUAC*) for all possible service lives. This may be done by repetitive use of the equation:

$$\begin{aligned} EUAC &= \text{Capital Recovery Cost} + \text{Operating Costs} \\ &= [(C - L)(CR - i\% - N) + Li] + A \end{aligned}$$

It is generally more convenient to carry out these calculations in tabular form as is illustrated in Table 8-1. The figures shown in Column (g) are $(C - L)(CR - 10\% - j) + L(0.10)$. Column (m) presents the annualized operating costs thru j years determined by discounting the year-by-year operating costs to date zero, summing, and then multiplying the sum by the appropriate capital recovery factor. This procedure may be verified by considering the equivalent uniform annual cost for a given life of, say, three years:

$$\begin{aligned} EUAC(3) &= [(C - L)(CR - 10\% - 3) + L(0.10)] \\ &\quad + [(CR - 10\% - 3) \sum_{j=1}^{3} C_j (PW - 10\% - j)] \\ &= [(\$10{,}000 - \$2{,}500)(0.40211) + \$2{,}500(0.10)] \\ &\quad + (0.40211)[\$5{,}000(0.9091) + \$5{,}600(0.8264) \\ &\quad + \$6{,}300(0.7513)] \\ &= [\$3{,}016 + \$250] + 0.40211\ [\$13{,}907] \\ &= \$8{,}858 \end{aligned}$$

The results of the calculations of Table 8-1 are shown graphically in Figure 8-1. The pattern is typical of most replacement problems; capital recovery costs tend to decrease over time whereas operating costs tend to increase. (The cost histories of most private autos are excellent examples of this characteristic.) The minimum total equivalent uniform annual cost occurs at four years, and this is therefore the economic life for the challenger[1].

[1] As shown both by column (n) of Table 8-1 and by Figure 8-1, the equivalent uniform annual costs for lives other than the economic life are relatively only slightly higher than the minimum value. Since the total cost curve is relatively flat through a wide range, this suggests that the economic life is rather sensitive to values assumed for input data. This phenomenon appears to occur quite frequently in connection with actual replacement studies.

Table 8-1

Determination of Equivalent Uniform Annual Costs for $10,000 Asset if Retained for Varying Periods from 1 thru 6 Years, with Minimum Attractive Rate of Return at 10%

Year j (a)	Salvage Value (L) at End of Year (b)	First Cost Minus Salvage Value (c) = $10,000 - (b)	Capital Recovery Factor (CR-10%-j) (d)	Recovery of Initial Cost (e) = (c) × (d)	Recovery of Salvage Value $L(0.10)$ (f)	Capital Recovery if kept thru j years (g) = (e) + (f)
1	$7,000	$ 3,000	1.10000	$3,300	$700	$4,000
2	4,500	5,500	0.57619	3,169	450	3,619
3	2,500	7,500	0.40211	3,016	250	3,266
4	1,000	9,000	0.31547	2,839	100	2,939
5	0	10,000	0.26380	2,638	0	2,638
6	0	10,000	0.22961	2,296	0	2,296

			Present Worth of Operating Costs			Equivalent Uniform Annual Costs if Retired after j Years	
Year j	Operating Costs During j^{th} Year (h)	Present Worth Factor (PW-10%-j) (i)	During j^{th} Year (j) = (h)(i)	Thru j Years (k) = Σ(j)	Capital Recovery Factor (CR-10%-j) (l)	Optg. Costs (m)	Total (n) = (g) + (m)
1	$5,000	0.9091	$4,546	$ 4,456	1.10000	$5,000	$9,000
2	5,600	0.8264	4,628	9,174	0.57619	5,286	8,905
3	6,300	0.7513	4,733	13,907	0.40211	5,592	8,858
4	7,000	0.6830	4,781	18,688	0.31547	5,896	8,835
5	8,000	0.6209	4,967	23,655	0.26380	6,240	8,878
6	9,000	0.5645	5,081	28,736	0.22961	6,598	8,894

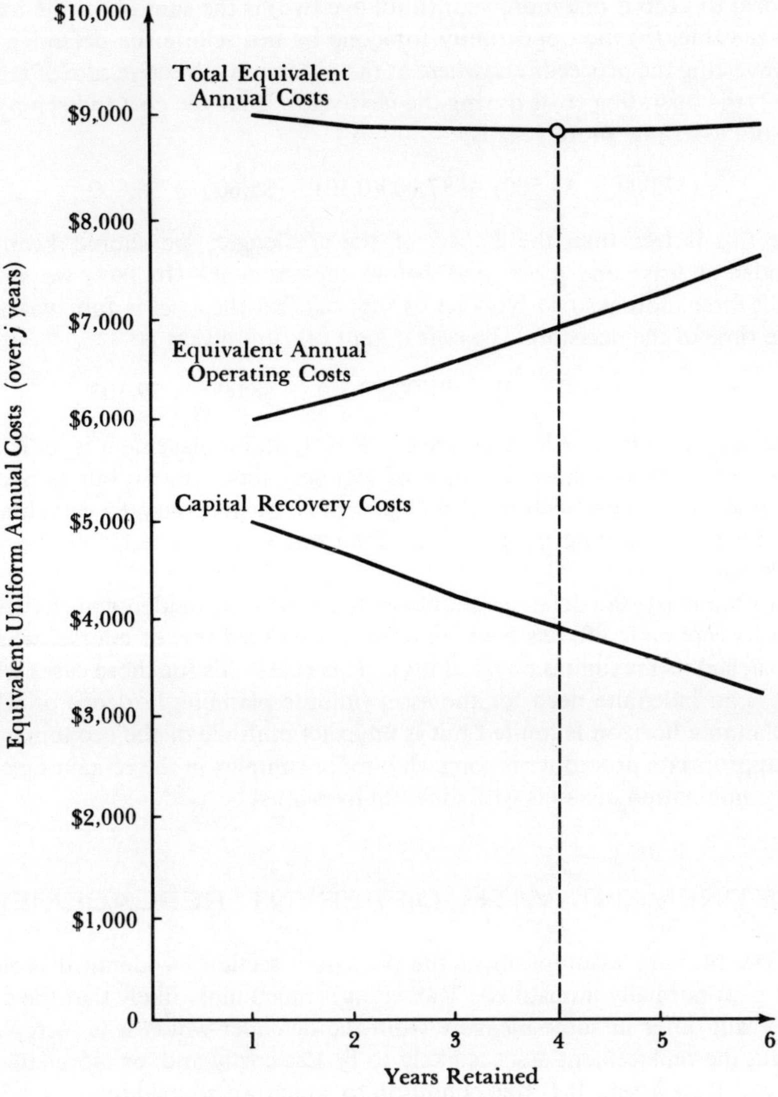

Fig. 8-1. Determination of economic life.

Moreover, since the challenger is identical to the defender, we conclude that the existing asset should not be replaced until such time as its economic life has been equaled or exceeded.

Another way of approaching this problem is to view the question as follows: "Shall we retain the asset for at least one more year (up to its physical life) or shall we replace it with the available challenger?" Referring to the example, suppose that the defender is one year old at the time of the decision.

The cost to keep it one more year (until age two) is the sum of (*a*) the loss in market value, (*b*) the opportunity foregone by not selling the defender now and investing the proceeds elsewhere at the minimum attractive rate of return, and (*c*) the operating costs during the next year. Thus the cost to keep a one-year-old asset one more year is:

$$(\$7{,}000 - \$4{,}500) + \$7{,}000(0.10) + \$5{,}600 = \$8{,}800$$

Since this is less than the *EUAC* of the challenger, we should keep the defender at least one more year before replacement. (In fact, we should keep it three more years!) Now let us suppose that the asset is four years old at the time of the decision. The cost if kept one more year is:

$$(\$1{,}000 - 0) + \$1{,}000(0.10) + \$8{,}000 = \$9{,}100$$

This is larger than the *EUAC* of the challenger, and replacement is indicated. (This conclusion is valid in the case of identical replacement, but as is demonstrated in the next section, it will generally be necessary to examine the defender for remaining lives of more than one year before forming a final conclusion.)

In summary, the defender should be replaced with an identical challenger when its economic life has been equaled or exceeded (or, of course, when it has reached its maximum physical life). This rule holds for those cases where there is an indefinite need for the asset (infinite planning horizon) or where the planning horizon is limited but is an exact multiple of the economic life. The appropriate procedure is somewhat more complex in the remaining cases since combination of assets with different lives must be used.

RETIREMENT WITH DIFFERENT REPLACEMENT

The primary assumption of the preceding section — identical replacement — is normally unjustified. Rather, it is much more likely that the challenger will differ in some measure from the defender which it is to replace. Indeed, the replacement asset is likely to be less costly and/or more efficient than the older asset. It is this condition to which we now address ourselves. *We continue to assume, however, that all future challengers do not differ significantly in any respect from the current challenger.*

The replacement problem is essentially one of comparing retention of the defender for one or more years with the best available challenger. In a sense, each possible replacement asset represents, in turn, a number of "challengers" as defined by the *various possible periods* for which the challenger will be retained. This is to say that an asset having a maximum physical life of six years may be viewed as six separate challengers: challenger with one-year life, challenger with two-year life, . . . , challenger with six-year life. There will be an equivalent uniform annual cost associated with each of these, of course, and the minimum *EUAC* will define the economic life for that asset. Thus the first step in resolving the replacement question is to determine the *EUAC* associated with the economic life for each replacement asset under consideration. That challenger-life combination having the lowest *EUAC* will be the one to be compared with the defender.

To illustrate this first step, suppose that only one challenger is physically capable of replacing the existing asset, and suppose further that this challenger is the one described by Table 8-1. Recall, this is a \$10,000 asset having maximum physical life of six years. Assuming a pre-tax minimum attractive rate of return of 10%, the economic life for the challenger was shown to be four years, and the equivalent uniform annual cost at this life is \$8,835.

Second, it is necessary to determine the cost of extending the life of the defender *one* more year. Assuming that the defender's market value is currently \$8,000, the market value will fall to \$5,000 at the end of the year and the operating costs next year are expected to be \$5,500, the cost incurred by keeping the defender one more year is:

$$
\begin{aligned}
EUAC(1) &= (\$8{,}000 - \$5{,}000)(CR - 10\% - 1) + \$5{,}000(0.10) + \$5{,}500 \\
&= \$3{,}000(1.1) + \$500 + \$5{,}500 \\
&= \$9{,}300
\end{aligned}
$$

If this value were less than the *EUAC* of the best available challenger, then retention of the defender would be indicated. If it is not — as is the case in this example — we must continue the analysis.

As a third step, the *EUAC* of the defender if kept *two* more years must now be determined. Let us assume that the net salvage value of the defender at the end of the second year is only \$4,000 and that the operating costs during the second year are expected to increase to \$6,000. Thus the *EUAC* if kept for two more years is:

$$
\begin{aligned}
EUAC(2) &= (\$8{,}000 - \$4{,}000)(CR - 10\% - 2) + \$4{,}000(0.10) \\
&\quad + (CR - 10\% - 2)[\$5{,}500(PW - 10\% - 1) \\
&\quad + \$6{,}000(PW - 10\% - 2)] \\
&= \$8{,}443
\end{aligned}
$$

This value is now less than that of the best available challenger, \$8,835, and retention is indicated. We may conclude that it is more economical to keep the defender at least two more years than to replace with the existing challenger. On the other hand, had the *EUAC* for the defender with life of two more years resulted in a value *greater* than that of the *EUAC* for the best challenger, it would be necessary to continue the analysis by examining the defender with an assumed life of three years. These steps would be continued until such time as the *EUAC* of the defender became less than that of the challenger or until the maximum physical life of the defender is reached. *Replacement should take place if there is no defender life resulting in an EUAC less than that of the best available challenger.*

It will be noted that the economic life of the defender is not necessarily determined with this procedure. In the example we observed that replacement should not take place since the *EUAC* for the defender life of two years is less than the *EUAC* of the challenger. However, it is quite possible that the *EUAC* will be still lower if the defender is kept for three more years. This additional information is irrelevant here since the question at hand deals only with current replacement, not with economic life of the defender.

The procedure outlined above is valid when the need for the service provided by the defender and/or its successive challengers is indeterminate, that is, the planning horizon is infinite. Problems specifying finite planning horizons generally result in complications beyond the scope of our present discussion.

IMPROVED FUTURE CHALLENGERS

A principal assumption implicit in each of the preceding sections is the invariability of future challengers. That is, it was assumed that the challengers which will be available in the future will in no way differ from the challenger which is presently available. This assumption is questionable, of course, since, in general, it seems much more likely that improved challengers will become available with the passage of time. In a competitive economy where so much of our productive capacity is directed to the development of more efficient and less costly products, it is to be expected that, in most cases, future challengers will be superior to those presently available in terms of initial cost, maintainability, useful physical life, and so on. Consideration of this possibility adds considerable complexity to retirement and replacement analyses.

GENERALIZED REPLACEMENT MODEL: A graphic illustration of the replacement problem in its general form is shown in Figure 8-2. Here I_k, N_k, and L_k represent the initial cost, life, and salvage value respectively of the kth replacement. No cash receipts are shown in Figure 8-2 since it is assumed that the values for C_{kn} ($n = 1,2 \ldots, N_k$) represent the total of costs minus revenues for the particular interest period. Note that N_0 is the remaining life of the asset to be replaced, the defender. Optimum replacement policy is determined by selecting those values of N_k which minimize the total expected cost of the system. Should the analysis indicate that the defender ought to be

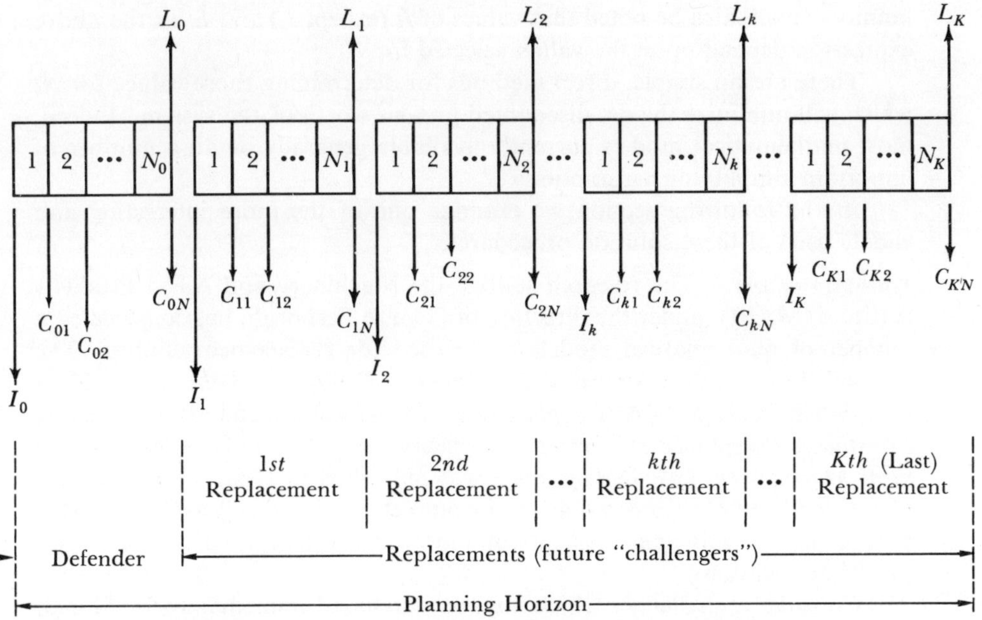

Fig. 8-2. Cash flow diagram for generalized replacement model.

replaced immediately, N_0 will be equal to zero. The set of lives ($N_0, N_1, N_2, \ldots, N_k, \ldots, N_K$) which minimizes the net present value P of all system costs over the planning horizon defines the solution.

From Figure 8-2 it can be seen that P as a function of the lives of the defender and the chain of replacements is given by:

$$
\begin{aligned}
P(N_0, N_1, N_2, \ldots, N_k, \ldots, N_K) \\
&= I_0 - L_0(1+i)^{-N_0} + \sum_{j=1}^{N_0} C_{0j}(1+i)^{-j} \\
&\quad + [I_1 - L_1(1+i)^{-N_1} + \sum_{j=1}^{N_1} C_{1j}(1+i)^{-j}](1+i)^{-N_0} \\
&\quad + [I_2 - L_2(1+i)^{-N_2} + \sum_{j=1}^{N_2} C_{2j}(1+i)^{-j}](1+i)^{-(N_0+N_1)} \\
&\quad \cdot \\
&\quad \cdot \\
&\quad \cdot \\
&\quad + [I_K - L_K(1+i)^{-N_K} + \sum_{j=1}^{N_K} C_{Kj}(1+i)^{-j}](1+i)^{-(N_0+N_1+\cdots+N_{K-1})} \\
&= \sum_{k=0}^{K} [I_k - L_k(1+i)^{-N_k} + \sum_{j=1}^{N_k} C_{kj}(1+i)^{-j}](1+i)^{-(N_0+N_1+\cdots+N_{k-1})} \qquad (8.1)
\end{aligned}
$$

where K is the total number of replacements to be considered over the planning horizon. In the event of an indeterminate planning horizon, K equals infinity. It will also be noted that values of I_k (except I_0) and L_k in the above expression depend upon the values selected for N_k.

There are no simple, direct methods for determining those values for N_k which will minimize the net discounted present worth of the system.[2] Indeed, most mathematical models currently available generally entail a number of important simplifying assumptions.

In the following section we examine one of the more interesting and widely used of these solution procedures.

THE MAPI MODEL. The research staff of the Machinery and Allied Products Institute (MAPI), under the direction of George Terborgh, has constructed a number of mathematical models to be used for replacement studies. The first of these models appeared in *Dynamic Equipment Policy* (*see Bibliography*) in 1949; the MAPI *Replacement Manual* was issued in 1950; *Business Investment Policy* (*see Bibliography*) appeared in 1958; and *Business Investment Management* (*see Bibliography*) was published in 1967. Our treatment of replacement problems would be incomplete without at least a brief discussion of the principal concepts and procedures presented in the earlier MAPI publications.

Consider a challenger which may be purchased immediately for $1,000, and assume that this challenger's salvage value is zero at all times. Further, assume that the operating costs during the first year for this challenger are $2,200 and that these disbursements increase at the rate of $100 per year thereafter. Assume that, due to technological progress, the initial cost of the challenger which will become available next year is expected to be only $2,000 and, finally, assume that these patterns repeat themselves, that is, the first costs of future challengers decrease at the same rate of $200 per year, annual disbursements of each challenger increase at the rate of $100 per year, and the salvage value of all challengers is always zero.

The annual disbursements of the current and next year's challengers, as well as their successors, are shown in Figure 8-3. (In the Figure it is assumed that all challengers will be replaced at the end of each four years. The analysis which follows indicates that this is indeed the economic life of all challengers with the given assumptions.) It will be noted that the current challenger will be "inferior" to next year's challenger by $300, of which $200 is due to the decrease in initial cost and the other $100 is due to the increase in annual disbursements. In *Dynamic Equipment Policy*, the rate of which the current challenger accumulates inferiority to future challengers ($300 in the example) is known as the *inferiority gradient*.

Determination of the economic life of the current challenger (as well as

[2] Although beyond the scope of this text, we note parenthetically that the generalized replacement model may be cast into a framework convenient for solution by the use of dynamic programming. An earlier article discussing this procedure, including a numerical example, is: Dreyfus, Stuart E., "A Generalized Equipment Replacement Study," *Journal of the Society for Industrial and Applied Mathematics*, Vol. 8, No. 3, Sept. 1960, pp. 425–35.

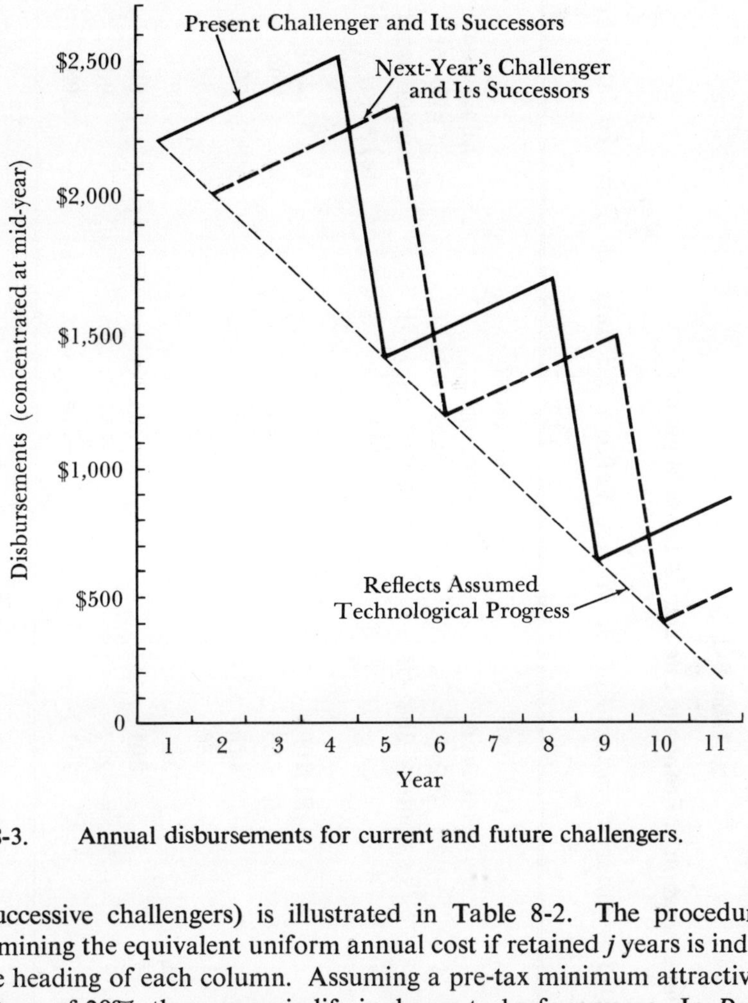

Fig. 8-3. Annual disbursements for current and future challengers.

all successive challengers) is illustrated in Table 8-2. The procedure for determining the equivalent uniform annual cost if retained j years is indicated at the heading of each column. Assuming a pre-tax minimum attractive rate of return of 20%, the economic life is shown to be four years. In *Dynamic Equipment Policy* the equivalent uniform annual cost at the economic life ($687 in the example) is known as the *challenger's adverse minimum.* The cumulative inferiority in Column (b) is the difference between the disbursements for the current challenger in the jth year and the disbursements which would occur if a new challenger is purchased at the start of the jth year. It will be noted that the economic life occurs at that point where the cumulative inferiority becomes larger than the equivalent uniform annual cost.

In *Dynamic Equipment Policy* an approximate formula is recommended for determining the challenger's adverse minimum (CAM):

$$CAM = \sqrt{2CG} + \frac{iC - G}{2}$$

Table 8-2

Determination of Economic Life and "Adverse Minimum"

Challenger: First Cost $1,000, Inferiority Gradient $3,000, Salvage Value at all times 0, Assumed Interest Rate 20%.

Year j (a)	Cumulative Inferiority (b)	Capital Recovery Cost $1,000(*CR*-20%-*j*) (c)	Cumulative Inferiority, Annualized $300(*GUS*-20%-*j*) (d)	Equivalent Uniform Annual Cost (e) = (c) + (d)
1	$ 0	$1,200	$ 0	$1,200
2	300	655	135	790
3	600	475	264	739
4	900	386	381	687
5	1,200	334	492	826
6	1,500	301	594	895
7	1,800	277	687	964
8	2,100	261	774	1,035

where C is the initial cost, G is the inferiority gradient, and i is the interest rate. As before, this formula assumes zero salvage value at all times. It is approximate in that it averages cash flows rather than determining equivalent values using compound interest factors.

The defender in our replacement problem must now be examined. Assume that the defender's next year's disbursements are $2,500 and that the disbursements of subsequent years will be even higher. If the defender has no salvage value now or at any time in the future, it is clear that no year will be as inexpensive as next year. Thus, since there are no capital costs, the next year's operating inferiority to the present challenger is simply $300(= $2,500 − $2,200), and this represents the *defender's adverse minimum.* Since the challengers adverse minimum, $687, is larger, the defender should be retained. In other words, it would be more costly to replace the defender today with the current challenger than it would be to forego replacement for one more year and then replace with next year's challenger.

The MAPI methods presented in the more recent *Business Investment Policy* differ considerably from those of the earlier publications. The previous methods compared next year dollar values, whereas the *MAPI urgency rating* is used in the 1958 publication. The urgency rating is the next year after-tax rate of return assuming a 50% tax rate and a 3:1 equity:debt ratio for capital funds. An interest rate of 3% is assumed for debt capital, and a rate of return of 10% is required from equity funds. As before, the rate of technological progress is assumed constant, but the 1958 techniques also allow the analyst to assume that operating disbursements increase at an (*a*) increasing or (*b*) decreasing rate as well as the (*c*) constant rate used in *Dynamic Equipment Policy*. The analyst may also choose between the straight line or sum of years digits depreciation methods.

This discussion of the MAPI techniques is necessarily abbreviated. It is recommended that students interested in extensive discussions of the MAPI methods consult the source publications directly. The Grant–Ireson text (*see Bibliography*) is also an excellent reference.

SUMMARY

Of those problems of interest in the capital allocation context, questions of retirement and replacement probably occur most frequently in the real world. Moreover, these problems present special conceptual and computational difficulties. It is for these reasons that a separate chapter has been devoted to discussion of retirement and replacement.

The simplest special case occurs when an existing asset is to be retired but not replaced. In this instance the net present value of all prospective consequences during the remaining life of the asset is evaluated. If the present value is positive the asset should be retained; otherwise it should be terminated. This procedure indicates the economic life of an asset.

An additional complexity is generated when the problem of replacement is added to that of simple retirement. If the existing asset (defender) is to be replaced by an *identical* new asset (challenger), and if the challenger which will become available in future years will also be identical to the defender, the appropriate replacement decision is indicated by determining whether the economic life of the defender has been equalled or exceeded. In this case the defender should be retained if its actual life is less than its economic life. (Replacement must occur, of course, if the physical life of the asset has been met.)

In the event that the challenger under consideration is *different* from the defender but *identical* or superior to all challengers which may become available in the future, the first step in resolving the replacement problem is determination of the economic life of the challenger. The equivalent uniform annual cost of the challenger at this life is then compared to the cost of keeping the defender in service one more year. If the *EUAC* of the defender is lower, then retention is in order; if it is higher than the *EUAC* of the challenger, then the *EUAC* of the defender if kept *two* more years must be determined. The questions are then repeated. If the *EUAC* of the defender with two-year life is less than the *EUAC* of the challenger, the defender should not be replaced; if it is greater, then the *EUAC* of the defender if kept *three* more years should be computed. This procedure is repeated until such time as retention is indicated or the physical life of the defender has been met. If there is no defender life resulting in an *EUAC* less than that of the best challenger, the defender should be replaced.

The most difficult problems arise from cases in which the current challenger is *different* from the defender and, further, succeeding challengers are still *different* from the existing challenger. It is possible to structure a mathematical model which describes the general situation, but optimal solutions for this model are extremely difficult to determine.[3] (For the generalized model given on p. 133, it may be shown that, if an improved challenger becomes available each year, there are 2^N possible solutions for a planning horizon of N years. For example, a planning horizon of only ten years will produce over 1,000 solutions.)

A number of simplified mathematical models have been structured, among the most interesting and widely used being those developed by George Terborgh and the research staff of the Machinery and Allied Products Institute (MAPI). In the earlier MAPI publications, it was proposed that the replacement decision be based upon comparison of the *challenger's adverse minimum* (the sum of the challenger's capital recovery cost and the present worth of the disadvantage resulting from having the current challenger and its

[3] See discussion, footnote 2.

successors rather than next year's challenger and its successors) and the *defender's adverse minimum* (the sum of the defender's next year operating inferiority and the next year capital costs). In *Business Investment Policy* the "adverse minimum" concept was abandoned in favor of an *urgency rating* (the next year rate of return). All MAPI models include a formalized allowance for the superiority of future challengers compared to the current challenger.

PROBLEMS

In the following problems it is assumed that future challengers will not differ significantly from the current challenger. Further, those assumptions apply which are given (pp. 120–121) for the problems of Chapter 7.

1. The Blue Company owns a machine which cost $26,000 ten years ago. It is being depreciated by the straight line method over 12 years to an estimated $2,000 salvage value. A new machine is available which will cost $11,000 and, if purchased, will save $2,000 annually. This new machine will be depreciated by the sum of years digits method over 4 years to an estimated $1,000 salvage value.

   If the new machine is purchased, the old machine will be sold for $8,000. If the old machine is continued in use, it will be scrapped in 5 years for zero salvage value. Assume that the estimated salvage value of the new machine will be $1,000 at the end of 5 years, that the minimum attractive rate of return after taxes is 12%, and that the incremental income tax rate is 50%. Should the existing machine be replaced with the challenger as described above? Why?

2. The manager of the western division of the Brown Manufacturing Company has received a request from the superintendent of the Los Angeles plant for a new heavy duty generator to replace existing equipment. The manager has forwarded the request to Corporate Headquarters for approval. The existing generator was purchased 5 years ago for $5,000. It was depreciated by the straight line method over 5 years to zero salvage value.

   Although its present book value is zero, it is believed that it may remain in operation for another 8 years before it must be scrapped. The existing generator is specialized equipment but, fortunately, there currently is a buyer who is willing to pay $600 for the equipment. This will probably be the last chance to sell it at any price, however.

   The proposed equipment will cost $6,000 and has an expected useful life of 10 years. If purchased, sum of years digits depreciation will be used with a 5-year life and zero salvage value. It is expected that the actual market value of the equipment at any time will be the same as its book value at that time. The estimated annual operating costs for the new equipment is \$600; operating costs for the existing equipment are expected to be \$1,800 per year.

The company plans to sell the plant and all its equipment in 5 years. The sale price will be independent of the present decision concerning the generator.

Assuming an after-tax minimum attractive rate of return of 10% and an incremental tax rate of 50%, should the new equipment be purchased? Why?

3. A high speed, special-purpose, automatic strip-feed punch press costing \$15,000 is proposed to replace three hand-fed presses now in use. The life of this automatic press has been estimated to be 5 years. Expenditures for labor, maintenance, etc., are estimated to be \$3,000 per year.

   The general-purpose, hand-fed punch presses cost \$2,000 each 10 years ago and were estimated to have a life of 20 years, with salvage value of \$200 each at the end of that time. Their present net realizable value is \$750 each. Operating expenditures for labor, etc., will be about \$2,850 per machine per year. The net salvage value is expected to decrease at the rate of about \$100 per press per year. It is expected that the required service will continue for only 5 years more and that the salvage value of the challenger will be \$5,000 at the end of that time.

   The company's after-tax minimum attractive rate of return is 12%. The incremental income tax rate is 50%.

   Although the expected service life if the challenger is only 5 years, it will be necessary to use 15-year life (with zero salvage value) in conjunction with the sum of years digits method for depreciation. Straight line depreciation has been used for the defenders.

   Make an after-tax annual cost analysis to determine if the defenders should be replaced.

4. The Core Corporation is considering replacing or remodeling a small commercial structure. A new building will cost \$60,000 and will have an estimated useful life of 20 years. It is expected that the present structure, if repaired, will have an additional useful life of 7 years. Remodeling costs are estimated to be \$18,000. The existing building may be sold for \$8,000 in its present condition but, if remodeled and retained for another 7 years, will have no value upon disposal at that time. The terminal salvage value of a replacement structure after 20 years is estimated to be \$100,000. All other costs will be unaffected by the replacement decision.

If the before-tax minimum attractive rate of return is 15%, determine the equivalent uniform annual costs of the two alternatives.

5. The General Hospital is considering purchase of certain new kitchen equipment to replace its present 3-year old equipment. The total physical life of the present equipment is 5 years. Cost history for the past three years — and estimates for the next two years — are as follows:

DISBURSEMENTS

Year	Operations	Maintenance	End-of-Year Salvage Value
1	$ 600	$100	—
2	800	300	—
3	1,000	500	$1,400
4	1,200	700	1,100
5	1,400	900	900

The kitchen superintendent has suggested that this equipment be replaced by a new model costing $6,000. The manufacturer claims that this new equipment will require no maintenance and, further, will reduce operating costs by $100 per year over the corresponding costs with the old equipment.

Assuming a 5-year physical life for the challenger with a $1,000 terminal salvage value, make a pre-tax comparison of equivalent annual costs using a minimum attractive rate of return of 10% before taxes.

6. Consider the problem of replacement with an identical asset. An alternative formulation of the decision rule for determining the economic life of the defender is: "The minimum equivalent uniform annual cost occurs when the cost of extending service one additional year is greater than the equivalent uniform annual cost up to date." Why is this true? Demonstrate this principle using the example presented in Table 8-1. Plot the results.

7. Assume that we are considering a finite planning horizon N and that this time period is such that not more than one replacement will be made between now and time N. This is to say that either no replacement will be made or, if the challenger is obtained at any time, it will be retained until time N. After time N the requirement will cease. Also assume that the operating costs (including maintenance) for both the challenger and defender are nondecreasing with time. Show, in general, that replacement should not occur as long as the cost of one additional year of ser-

vice for the defender is less than the savings resulting from postponing the acquisition of the challenger one year.

8. A new piece of equipment is being considered to replace a certain existing asset. If the defender is replaced, the net effect next year will be as follows: revenue will be increased by $1,000 due to improved quality of the product, direct labor costs of operation will be reduced by $4,500, maintenance costs will be reduced by $500, and insurance costs will increase by $200. The present market value of the defender is $900; the market value will drop to $600 if kept one more year. The defender is now 10 years old. The first cost of the proposed new equipment is $15,000, and the expected salvage value of the challenger is zero.

   Assuming a pre-tax minimum attractive rate of return of 20%, use the method advocated in *Dynamic Equipment Policy* to determine if the defender should be immediately replaced. (Hint: Recall, the defender's adverse minimum is the sum of next year's operating inferiority and next year's capital costs. The challenger's adverse minimum may be determined by using the approximate zero-salvage value formula shown in the text. Since the inferiority gradient is required in the formula, estimate this value by determining the past value and assuming that it will continue into the future. The past gradient is determined by dividing the defender's operating inferiority next year by its age.) What is the implied economic life of the challenger?

9. In the zero-salvage value case, the *MAPI Replacement Manual* gives the following formula for the challenger's adverse minimum:

$$CAM = \frac{CNi^2}{iN + (1 + i)^{-N} - 1}$$

   Where C is the initial cost of the challenger, N is the economic life, and i is the interest rate. Assuming an economic life of 12 years for the challenger described in Problem 8, use the formula to determine the implied gradient. (Recall the gradient is the adverse minimum divided by the life.)

10. Show that the formula given in Problem 9 may be derived directly from:

$$CAM = C(CR - i\% - N) + G(GUS - i\% - N)$$

   when the challenger's adverse *minimum* is equal to NG. Provide a verbal explanation of this equation.

9

THE UNCERTAIN FUTURE

Problems of capital allocation invariably concern the future. The past is of interest only insofar as it provides information about the expected amounts and timing of future cash flows. In view of this emphasis, it is necessary to address ourselves briefly to the problem of uncertainty which is always associated with estimates of future events. In the following discussion several techniques are presented which may be used to consider uncertainty explicitly in capital budgeting analyses.

SENSITIVITY ANALYSIS

Procedure

When a small change in the value of a particular estimate results in a change in the choice of alternative, the decision is said to be *sensitive* to that estimate. Conversely, the decision is insensitive to the estimate if relatively wide variations in the original estimate do not change the original solution. It is clearly of considerable interest to the analyst to determine those factors which are sensitive in any given study. As illustrated in the following example, either graphic or algebraic techniques (or a combination of the two) may be used for the sensitivity analysis.

An Example: A firm is considering the possibility of investing in a small subsidiary operation. This proposal will require an initial outlay of $90,000 for capital equipment and an additional \$10,000 for working capital. It is assumed that the investment will be terminated at the end of fifteen years, at which time the equipment will be sold for a net salvage value of \$10,000. The company expects to sell 7,000 units per year at a price of \$12 each. Variable costs per unit are assumed to be \$10. If the firm requires a return of at least 10% on its investment before taxes, does this proposal appear to be profitable?

The basic solution is rather straightforward. The negative cash flow at date zero is \$100,000 (= \$90,000 + \$10,000) and the total positive cash flow at the end of fifteen years is \$20,000 (= \$10,000 + \$10,000). Finally, since the variable profit per unit is \$2, the annual excess of receipts over disbursements is \$14,000 (= \$2 × 7000). Assuming a minimum attractive rate of return of 10% before taxes, the equivalent uniform annual benefit is:

$$
\begin{aligned}
&-(\$100{,}000 - \$20{,}000)(CR - 10\% - 15) - (\$20{,}000)(0.10) + \$2(7000) \\
&= -\ \$80{,}000(0.13147) - \$2{,}000 + \$14{,}000 \\
&= \$1{,}482
\end{aligned}
$$

Although the solution indicates that the proposal should be accepted (all other things being equal), it is prudent to conduct a sensitivity analysis to determine to which of the input parameters the solution may be sensitive. There are at least eight parameters which could be examined in this problem — first cost of equipment, salvage value of equipment, working capital required, variable costs per unit, revenue per unit, number of units sold each year, life of the project, and the interest rate used in the study — but examination of only one of these inputs will serve to illustrate the technique.

The equivalent uniform annual benefit is clearly a function of the number of units sold each year. Suppose that, although we assumed 7,000 units per year in the original calculation, management has reason to believe that it is "extremely unlikely" that annual sales will be less than 6,500 units. We test for sensitivity by recomputing the equivalent uniform annual benefits with this most pessimistic sales forecast. Thus:

$$-\ \$80{,}000(CR - 10\% - 15) - \$2{,}000 + \$2(6{,}500) = \$482$$

and we conclude that the solution is not sensitive to this particular parameter.

It is frequently helpful, particularly when presenting solutions to management for review, to conduct the sensitivity analysis in graphic form. The solution as a function of the number of units sold per year is readily apparent from Figure 9-1.

Break-Even Analysis

Rather than recompute the solution for estimates of the parameter other than the expected value, it may be more desirable to determine the value at which the solution will change. To determine this *break-even* or *equal cost* point, first equate the annual costs (or annual benefits, present worths, rates of return, etc.) for the pair(s) of alternatives, keeping as the uncertain factor the

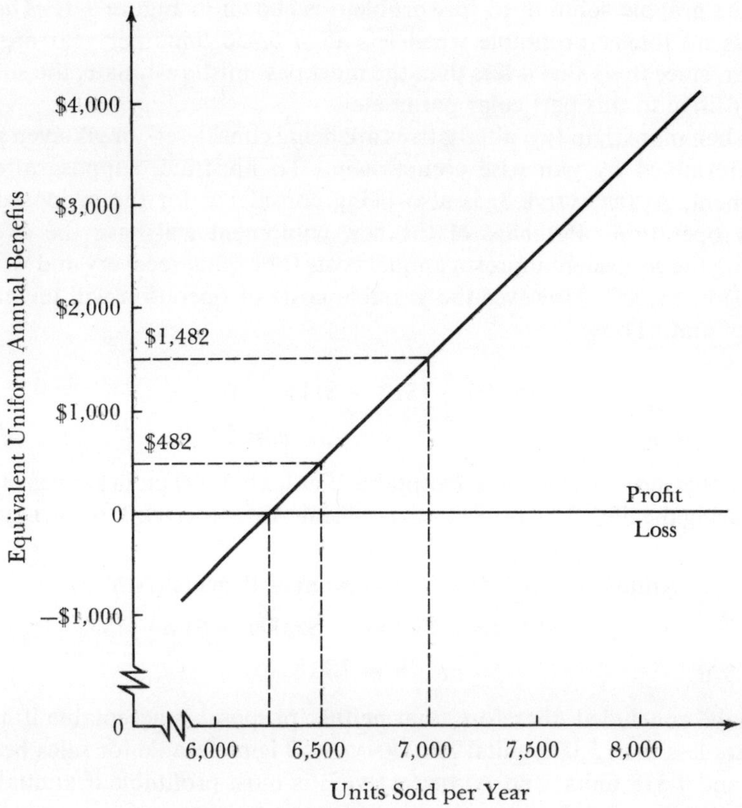

Fig. 9-1. Graphic sensitivity analysis.

unknown quantity on each side of the equation. Then solve for the unknown and compare the result to the range of expected values. If the break-even point lies within the range, then additional refinement of the estimate is required or, if this is infeasible, the uncertainty should be considered as an irreducible before the final decision is made. On the other hand, insensitivity is indicated if the break-even point lies outside the range of expected values.

The break-even point may be determined algebraically or graphically. Referring to the previous example, the two alternatives are: (1) not to invest in the proposal but, rather, invest elsewhere at the minimum attractive rate of return or (2) invest in the subsidiary operation. To determine the break-even point for the number of units sold per year, n, first equate the equivalent uniform annual benefits for ALTERNATIVES 1 and 2:

$$-\$80{,}000(CR - 10\% - 15) - \$2{,}000 + 2n = 0$$
$$-\$12{,}518 + \$2n = 0$$
$$n = 6{,}256$$

The graphic solution to this problem is shown in Figure 9-1. The proposal is no longer profitable when less than 6,256 units per year are sold. Further, since this value is less than the most pessimistic estimate, the solution is insensitive to this particular parameter.

When more than two alternatives are being considered, break-even points are determined by pair-wise comparison. To illustrate, suppose alternate equipment, ALTERNATIVE 3, is also being considered for the proposed subsidiary operation. Purchase of the new equipment will have the effect of reducing the equivalent uniform annual costs (or capital recovery and working capital) to \$5,000. However the variable costs of operation will increase to \$11 per unit. Thus:

$$- \$5{,}000 + (\$12 - \$11)n = 0$$
$$n = 5{,}000$$

That is, this new alternative is acceptable if at least 5,000 units per year will be sold during the life of the project. Comparing ALTERNATIVE 3 to ALTERNATIVE 2:

$$\text{Annual Benefits (ALT. 2)} = \text{Annual Benefits (ALT. 3)}$$
$$- \$12{,}518 + \$2n = - \$5{,}000 + \$1\,n$$
$$n = 7{,}518$$

It may be concluded, therefore, that neither proposal is acceptable if annual sales are less than 5,000 units; ALTERNATIVE 2 is preferable for sales between 5,000 and 7,518 units; and ALTERNATIVE 3 is most profitable if annual sales are greater than 7,518 units.

A graphic solution for this problem is given in Figure 9-2. Graphic solutions sacrifice some numerical accuracy, but they are generally easier to interpret than algebraic solutions, particularly when more than two alternatives are being considered.

UNKNOWN PROBABILITIES OF FUTURE OUTCOMES

Problem Statement

The International Investment Corporation is considering five mutually exclusive alternatives for constructing a new manufacturing plant in a certain Latin American country. The costs of each of the alternatives, stated in terms of equivalent uniform annual costs, are dependent upon the outcome of negotiations which are currently underway between the Corporation, lending agencies, and the government of the host country. The Corporation's ana-

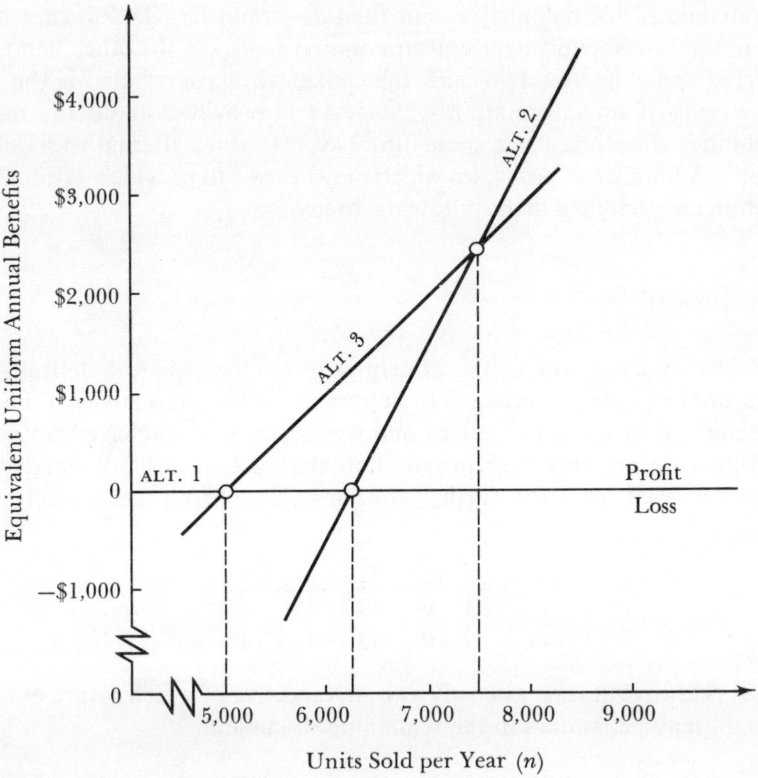

Fig. 9-2. Sensitivity analysis for three ALTERNATIVES.

lysts have concluded that four specific mutually exclusive outcomes are possible, and they have computed the equivalent uniform annual cost for each alternative-outcome combination. These are shown as cell values in the following *cost matrix;*

Possible Outcomes

		s_1	s_2	s_3	s_4
	a_1	18	11	11	10
	a_2	16	16	16	16
Alternatives	a_3	17	20	8	17
	a_4	9	12	17	16
	a_5	10	13	17	18

(cell entries are multiples of $10,000)

If the future is known with certainty, then the least costly alternative may be selected by any of the methods of Chapter 6. For example, if it is known that outcome s_3 will definitely occur, then a_3 should be selected since it will result in the lowest equivalent uniform annual cost. On the other hand, if a_3 is selected and s_2 perversely occurs, the choice will have resulted in the most costly event. If no information whatsoever is provided about the relative probabilities of occurrence of these future events, which alternative should be selected? A number of principles which may be used to provide a rationale for a solution are presented in the following discussion.

Dominance

Before applying any of the principles of choice, it is first desirable (although not absolutely necessary) to determine which alternatives, if any, are dominated. If of two alternatives one would never be preferred no matter what future occurs, this unpreferred alternative is said to be dominated and may be removed from any further consideration. From the example, consider a_4 and a_5:

	s_1	s_2	s_3	s_4
a_4	9	12	17	16
a_5	10	13	17	18

Since a_5 is always at least as costly as a_4 irrespective of which future outcome occurs, a_5 may be ignored in the remaining discussion.

Minimax (or Maximin)

The *minimax principle* is pessimistic in the extreme. It assumes that, if an alternative is selected, the worst possible outcome will occur. The maximum cost associated with each alternative is examined, and that alternative is selected which *minimizes* the *maximum* cost. From the example:

	Maximum Cost
a_1	\$180,000
(a_2)	160,000
a_3	200,000
a_4	170,000

Adopting this conservative position, a_2 should be selected since it minimizes costs assuming the worst possible conditions.

The mirror image, the *maximin principle*, may be applied when the matrix contains *profit* or *revenue* measures. In this case the most pessimistic view suggests that the alternative to be selected is that which *maximizes* the *minimum* profit or revenue associated with each alternative.

Minimin (or Maximax)

The *minimin principle* is based on the view that the best possible outcome occurs when a given alternative is selected. It is optimistic in the extreme. The minimum cost associated with each alternative is examined, and that alternative is selected which *minimizes* the *minimum* cost. From the example:

	Minimum Cost
a_1	\$100,000
a_2	160,000
(a_3)	80,000
a_4	90,000

As a corollary, the *maximax principle* is appropriate when the decision maker is optimistic in the extreme and the matrix contains measures of profit or revenue. The maximum profit (or revenue) associated with each alternative is examined, and that alternative is selected which *maximizes* the *maximum* profit (or revenue).

Hurwicz Principle[1]

It may be argued that decision makers need not be totally optimistic nor pessimistic in the extreme, in which case this principle permits selection of a position between the two limits. For each alternative a_1, the "Hurwicz Criterion" is computed as follows:

$$H(a_1) = \alpha\left[\min_j (v_{ij})\right] + (1 - \alpha)\left[\max_j (v_{ij})\right] \tag{9.1}$$

where α is the "index of optimism" such that $0 \leqslant \alpha \leqslant 1$, and v_{ij} is the cell value for the *i*th alternative and the *j*th possible outcome. Extreme pessimism is defined by $\alpha = 0$; extreme optimism is defined by $\alpha = 1$. The value of α used in any particular analysis will be selected by the decision maker based upon his subjective judgment. The alternative which *minimizes* the quantity $H(a_1)$ is the alternative to be selected.

From the example, the Hurwicz criteria are determined as follows:

$$H(a_1) = \alpha\,(\$100{,}000) + (1 - \alpha)(\$180{,}000)$$
$$H(a_2) = \alpha\,(\$160{,}000) + (1 - \alpha)(\$160{,}000)$$
$$H(a_3) = \alpha\,(\$\ 80{,}000) + (1 - \alpha)(\$200{,}000)$$
$$H(a_4) = \alpha\,(\$\ 90{,}000) + (1 - \alpha)(\$170{,}000)$$

[1] Named after the econometrician, Leonid Hurwicz.

The values of $H(a_1)$ are plotted in Figure 9-3. We may determine graphically (or algebraically) that a_2 will be chosen for $0 \leqslant \alpha \leqslant 0.125$, a_4 will be selected for $0.125 \leqslant \alpha \leqslant 0.75$, and a_3 is least costly for $0.75 \leqslant \alpha \leqslant 1.00$. Suppose that the personnel of the International Investment Corporation concerned with this decision agree that there is no particular reason for being either optimistic or pessimistic, and thus their value for α is approximately 0.5. Under this assumption the Hurwicz principle indicates that a_4 should be selected.

It should be noted that the above definition of the Hurwicz criterion is applicable only to minimization (cost) problems. If we are dealing with a maximization (revenues or profits) problem, the alternative which *maximizes*

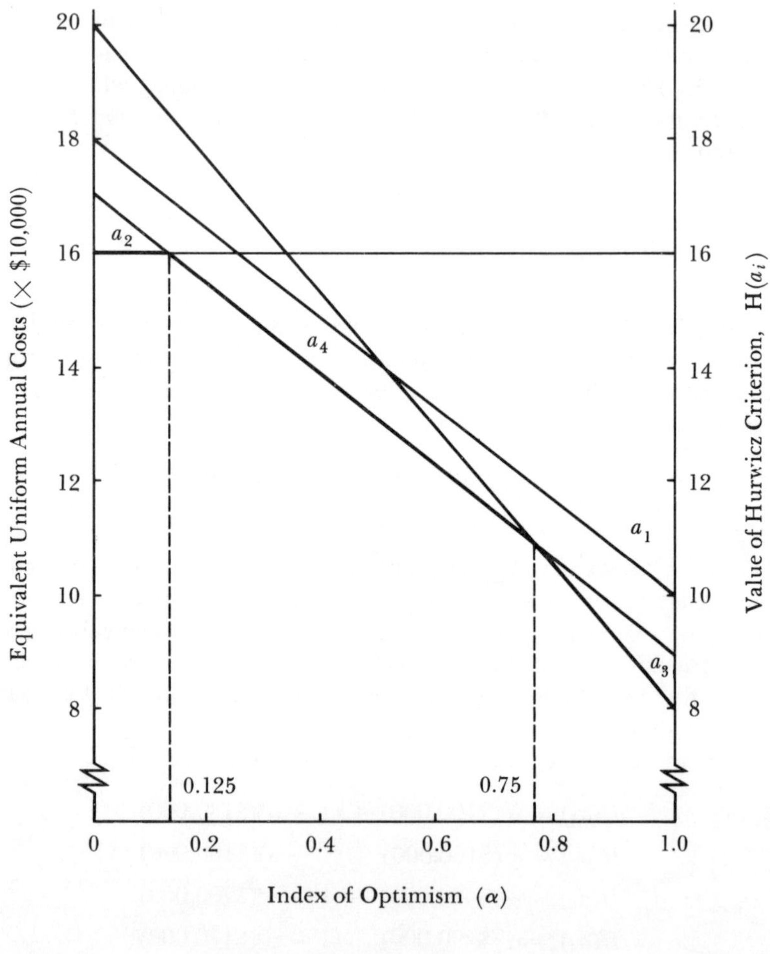

Fig. 9-3. Hurwicz criteria as function of α.

$$H(a_1) = \alpha \left[\max_{j} (v_{ij}) \right] + (1 - \alpha) \left[\min_{j} (v_{ij}) \right] \tag{9.2}$$

is the alternative which should be selected.

Laplace Principle[2]

The Laplace Principle, sometimes known as the "Principle of Insufficient Reason," assumes that the probabilities of occurrence of future events are equal. That is, in the absence of any information to the contrary, it is assumed that each future outcome is equally likely to occur. The expected cost (or profit/revenue) of each alternative is then computed, and that alternative is selected which yields the minimum expected cost (or maximum expected profit/revenue).

Before proceeding it will be necessary to establish two important results of probability theory.[3] First, *the sum of probabilities of exhaustive events is unity*. Using this relative frequency definition,

$$\sum_{x} Pr[x] = 1 \tag{9.3}$$

where $Pr[x]$ is the probability of occurrence of the random variable x. Second, the *expected value* of a random variable, $E[x]$, is defined as:

$$E[x] = \sum_{x} xPr[x] \tag{9.4}$$

To illustrate these concepts, consider a single roll of a pair of six-sided dice. Suppose a win occurs if the player rolls either a 7 or 11, a loss occurs if he rolls a 2, 3, or 12, and any other sum results in a draw. Then:

$$Pr[\text{win}] + Pr[\text{loss}] + Pr[\text{draw}] = 1$$

$$Pr[7,11] + Pr[2,3,12] + Pr[4,5,6,8,9,10] = 1$$

Independently computing the relative probability of rolling a 2, 3, 4, ..., 12 on a single roll of the dice, we can determine the probability of a win, loss, or draw. These are: $Pr[\text{win}] = 8/36$, $Pr[\text{loss}] = 4/36$, $Pr[\text{draw}] = 24/36$. Now suppose \$1 is wagered on the outcome of one roll of the dice. The amount which the player can expect to win is:

$$\begin{aligned} E[\text{winning}] &= \$1Pr[\text{win}] - \$1Pr[\text{loss}] + \$0Pr[\text{draw}] \\ &= \$1(8/36) - \$1(4/36) \\ &= \$1/9 \end{aligned}$$

[2] Named after an eighteenth century French mathematician.
[3] Our discussion of probability is necessarily limited here. The relevant theory is presented only with sufficient rigor to permit clear understanding of these few simple applications.

Returning now to the example, the assumption that the possible outcomes are equally likely indicates that $Pr(s_1] = Pr[s_2] = Pr[s_3] = Pr[s_4] = \frac{1}{4}$. We can now compute the expected cost of each of the alternatives, $E[C(a_1)]$, using these probabilities.

$$\text{In general: } E[v_{ij}] = \tfrac{1}{4}v_{i1} + \tfrac{1}{4}v_{i2} + \tfrac{1}{4}v_{i3} + \tfrac{1}{4}v_{i4}$$

$$\text{or } E[C(a_1)] = \tfrac{1}{4}\sum_{j=1}^{4} v_{ij}$$

Using data from the example:

$$E[C(a_1)] = \tfrac{1}{4}(18 + 11 + 11 + 10) = 12.5$$
$$E[C(a_2)] = \tfrac{1}{4}(16 + 16 + 16 + 16) = 16.0$$
$$E[C(a_3)] = \tfrac{1}{4}(17 + 20 + 8 + 17) = 15.5$$
$$E[C(a_4)] = \tfrac{1}{4}(9 + 12 + 17 + 16) = 13.5$$

Alternative a_1 should therefore be selected since it results in the minimum expected equivalent uniform annual cost.

Savage Principle[4] (Minimax Regret)

The Savage Principle is based on the assumption that the decision maker's primary interest is the *difference* between the actual outcome and that which would have occurred had he been able to accurately predict the future. Given these differences, or *regrets*, he then adopts a conservative position and selects that alternative which will minimize his maximum potential regret for each alternative.

A *regret matrix* is computed, having for its cell values:

$$R_{ij} = v_{ij} - \underset{i}{Min}\,(v_{ij}) \tag{9.5}$$

for all j, where R_{ij} is the regret for the ith row (alternative) and jth column (possible future). The regret matrix for the example is as follows:

Possible Outcomes

		s_1	s_2	s_3	s_4
Alternatives	a_1	$18 - 9 = 9$	$11 - 11 = 0$	$11 - 8 = 3$	$10 - 10 = 0$
	a_2	$16 - 9 = 7$	$16 - 11 = 5$	$16 - 8 = 8$	$16 - 10 = 6$
	a_3	$17 - 9 = 8$	$20 - 11 = 9$	$8 - 8 = 0$	$17 - 10 = 7$
	a_4	$9 - 9 = 0$	$12 - 11 = 1$	$17 - 8 = 9$	$16 - 10 = 6$

[4] Named after L. J. Savage, the contemporary statistician.

Having completed the regret matrix, the alternative is selected which *minimizes* the *maximum* regret. From the example:

Alternative	*Maximum Regret*
a_1	9
(a_2)	8
a_3	9
a_4	9

Thus, according to the Savage Principle of Minimax Regret, alternative a_2 will be selected.

A major inconsistency using this principle is that the solution can be altered by adding still another alternative which itself is not selected as the most desirable. To illustrate, suppose that we are considering still another alternative, a_6, with the following equivalent uniform annual costs:

	S_1	S_2	S_3	S_4
a_6	19	18	6	18

Inclusion of this new alternative will result in a revised regret matrix:

	S_1	S_2	S_3	S_4
a_1	9	0	5	0
a_2	7	5	10	6
a_3	8	9	2	7
a_4	0	1	11	6
a_6	10	7	0	8

Now, minimizing the maximum regret:

(a_1)	9
a_2	10
(a_3)	9
a_4	11
a_6	10

In this instance addition of the alternative a_6 has shifted the solution from a_2 to a_1 or a_3. Does this appear to be reasonable?

Some Additional Comments

There is no special reason why each of the principles discussed above yields the same solution. In fact, in our example all alternatives were selected at least once:

Principle of Choice	*Alternative Recommended*
Minimax	a_2
Minimin	a_3
Hurwicz ($\alpha = 0.5$)	a_4
Laplace (Insufficient Reason)	a_1
Savage (Minimax Regret)	a_2

Is one of these principles more "correct" than any other? There is no simple answer to this question since the choice of principle is largely dependent upon the predisposition of the decision maker. Each principle has certain obvious advantages, and each is deficient in one or more desirable characteristics.[5] Nevertheless, the principles in this section are useful if for no other reason than they shed some light on the subjective decision process.

KNOWN PROBABILITIES OF FUTURE OUTCOMES

Problem Statement

We continue with the problem being considered by the International Investment Corporation, but now let us assume that sufficient information exists to warrant statements about the relative probabilities of the possible future outcomes. Specifically, these probabilities (expected relative frequencies) are:

$$Pr[s_1] = 0.3 \qquad Pr[s_3] = 0.2$$
$$Pr[s_2] = 0.4 \qquad Pr[s_4] = 0.1$$

Given this additional information, which alternative should be selected? A number of principles which may be applied in this situation are discussed in the following sub-sections.[6]

Most Probable Future

Let us view the future somewhat myopically; in particular, let us assume that the future event to be expected is precisely that which is most likely. Thus, observing that s_2 has the highest probability of occurrence, we assume that s_2 will in fact occur. In this case we note that a_1 (with a cost of $110,000) is the least costly of the four available alternatives.

[5] Our discussion has primarily focused upon simple structures and areas of application; little has been said of the major deficiencies of the principles of choice. For more extensive discussion, see the Morris text or the collection of papers edited by Thrall, Coombs, and Davis cited in Bibliography.

[6] In the literature of decision theory, a semantic distinction is frequently made between cases where nothing at all is known about the relative probabilities of expected future events and those cases where probability statements can be made. The former situation is known as "decisions under *uncertainty*" and the latter as "decisions under *risk*."

It would appear that this principle is particularly appealing in those cases where one future is significantly more probable than all other possibilities. To illustrate, we may admit to the finite probability that we may not survive the trip on the freeway to the office in the morning but, since safe transit is significantly more likely than death or injury in an automobile accident, we do drive!

Principle of Expectation

Determination of the expected value of a random variable was discussed in the preceding section. Recall:

$$E[x] = \sum_{x} xPr[x]$$

The Principle of Expectation states that the alternative to be selected is that which has the minimum expected cost (or maximum expected profit or revenue). From the example:

$$\begin{aligned}
E[C(a_1)] &= 0.3(18) + 0.4(11) + 0.2(11) + 0.1(10) = 13.0 \\
E[C(a_2)] &= 0.3(16) + 0.4(16) + 0.2(16) + 0.1(16) = 16.0 \\
E[C(a_3)] &= 0.3(17) + 0.4(20) + 0.2(\ 8) + 0.1(17) = 16.4 \\
E[C(a_4)] &= 0.3(\ 9) + 0.4(12) + 0.2(17) + 0.1(16) = 12.5
\end{aligned}$$

where $E[C(a_1)]$ is the expected cost of alternative a_1. Here a_4 should be selected since it yields the minimum expected cost. (The entries in the cost matrix are multiples of \$10,000; hence the minimum expected cost is \$125,000.)

It will be noted that the Laplace Principle (Insufficient Reason) discussed previously is a special case of the Expectation Principle in that the former simply assumes equal probabilities for each of the possible outcomes.

Principles which depend upon determination of expected values by the mathematics of probability theory are frequently criticized on the grounds that the theory holds only when "trials" are repeated large numbers of times. That is, the relative frequency of a tail resulting from the flip of a fair coin approaches 0.5 as the number of flips (trials) gets larger and larger. If the number of flips is extremely large, one is reasonably confident that the relative frequency of tails will indeed be 0.5. On the other hand, this confidence is unwarranted if the number of flips is small. It is argued that, for certain types of decisions — for example, to finance a major expansion — expectation is meaningless since this type of decision is not made very often. According to the counter-argument, even if it is not faced with a large number of repetitive decisions, the firm should apply the principle to many different decisions and thus realize the long-run effects. Moreover, even if the decision is unique, the only way to approach these types of decisions (where probabilities are known) is to behave as if the decision were a repetitive one, and thus minimize expected cost or maximize expected revenue or profit.

Expectation–Variance

This principle focuses attention on the variability of the possible results for each of the alternatives. It formally allows for the view that variability is of great interest to the decision maker and, if feasible, it is desirable to minimize this measure of uncertainty. Thus the Expectation-Variance Principle states that, if two or more alternatives have the same expected cost or return, choose the one with the smallest variance of cost or return; if two or more alternatives have the same variance, choose the one with the smallest expected cost or largest expected return.

Before proceeding, it will be necessary to discuss variance as a statistical measure of dispersion. The variance of a random variable, Var[x], is defined as:

$$\text{Var}[x] = E[x^2] - \{E[x]\}^2 \tag{9.6}$$

where

$$E[x^2] = \sum_x x^2 Pr[x] \tag{9.7}$$

and

$$\{E[x]\}^2 = \{\sum_x xPr[x]\}^2 \tag{9.8}$$

Returning to the example, the variances of the random variable (cost) for each of the alternatives are as follows:

$$\begin{aligned}
\text{Var}[C(a_1)] &= [0.3(18)^2 + 0.4(11)^2 + 0.2(11)^2 + 0.1(10)^2] - (13)^2 \\
&= 179.8 - 169 \\
&= 10.8, \text{ or } \$108{,}000 \\
\text{Var}[C(a_2)] &= [0.3(16)^2 + 0.4(16)^2 + 0.2(16)^2 + 0.1(16)^2] - (16)^2 \\
&= 256 - 256 \\
&= 0 \\
\text{Var}[C(a_3)] &= [0.3(17)^2 + 0.4(20)^2 + 0.2(8)^2 + 0.1(17)^2] - (16.4)^2 \\
&= 288.4 - 269.0 \\
&= 19.4, \text{ or } \$194{,}000 \\
\text{Var}[C(a_4)] &= 0.3(9)^2 + 0.4(12)^2 + 0.2(17)^2 + 0.1(16)^2] - (12.5)^2 \\
&= 165.3 - 156.3 \\
&= 9.0, \text{ or } \$90{,}000
\end{aligned}$$

From these results it is clear that variability is minimized if a_2 is selected; there is zero dispersion of possible results. But the expected cost for a_2 ($160,000) is considerably greater than that for either a_1 ($130,000) or a_4

($125,000), and thus a_2 would not be chosen unless a large implicit cost were to be associated with variability of possible future events.

Since expected values and variances are rarely exactly equal for two or more alternatives, the Expectation-Variance Principle in effect calls for the maximization of some function of the expectation and the variance. To illustrate, consider alternatives a_2 and a_4.

$$E[C(a_2)] = \$160,000 \qquad \text{Var}[C(a_2)] = 0$$
$$E[C(a_4)] = \$125,000 \qquad \text{Var}[C(a_4)] = \$90,000$$

To determine which alternative is preferable, it is first necessary to decide upon the relative value, or utility, of a dollar of expected cost as compared to a dollar of variance. Suppose, for example, that an increase of \$1.00 in expected cost is equivalent to an increase of \$0.50 in variance. Then the difference in expected costs between a_2 and a_4, \$35,000, is more than offset by the corresponding value of the adjusted difference in variances, \$45,000. Computing the total implicit cost for each of the four alternatives:

$$\text{Implicit cost } (a_1) = \$130,000 + 0.5(\$108,000) = \$184,000$$
$$\text{Implicit cost } (a_2) = \$160,000 + 0.5(0) = \$160,000$$
$$\text{Implicit cost } (a_3) = \$164,000 + 0.5(\$194,000) = \$261,000$$
$$\text{Implicit cost } (a_4) = \$125,000 + 0.5(\$90,000) = \$170,000$$

Consequently, if we assume the 2:1 relationship between equivalent uniform annual cost and variance, the total cost is minimized if a_2 is selected.

Parenthetically, it should be noted that the *range* of values is frequently used as an *estimate* of the variance, where

$$\text{Range}(x) = x_{\text{max}} - x_{\text{min}} \tag{9.9}$$

To illustrate, consider the data from the example:

Alt.	Maximum	Minimum	Range	Variance
a_1	\$180,000	\$100,000	\$ 80,000	\$108,000
a_2	160,000	160,000	0	0
a_3	200,000	80,000	120,000	194,000
a_4	170,000	90,000	80,000	90,000

Although the range is only an approximate measure of dispersion, it may be especially useful when the analyst is unfamiliar with the mathematics required to calculate variance. The ability of the range to estimate the variance is improved as the number of values (possible outcomes) is increased.

Aspiration Level

This principle requires the establishment of a goal or level of aspiration. Then that alternative should be selected which maximizes the probability that the goal will be met or exceeded. To illustrate, suppose that management of the International Investment Corporation specifies that it wishes to minimize the probability that equivalent uniform annual costs will exceed $150,000. (Note that this is identical to the requirement that we maximize the probability that costs will *not* exceed $150,000.) The probabilities are:

$$Pr[C(a_1) > \$150{,}000] = 0.3$$

$$Pr[C(a_2) > \$150{,}000] = 0.3 + 0.4 + 0.2 + 0.1 = 1.0$$

$$Pr[C(a_3) > \$150{,}000] = 0.3 + 0.4 \qquad + 0.1 = 0.8$$

$$Pr[C(a_4) > \$150{,}000] = \qquad + 0.2 + 0.1 = 0.3$$

Thus the aspiration level will be met if either a_1 or a_4 is selected.

Summary of Results

Clearly, the selection from among mutually exclusive alternatives is a matter of which principle is used to guide the decision. From the example:

Principle of Choice	Alternative Recommended
Most Probable Future	a_1
Expectation	a_4
Expectation–Variance	a_2
Aspiration Level	a_1 or a_4

SOME ADDITIONAL APPROACHES

Statistical Techniques

In recent years a number of procedures have been advocated wherein mathematical statistics and probability theory are applied to problems of risk and uncertainty. Many of these procedures provide management with incomplete information upon which to base decisions; others assume availability of input data which is extremely difficult to obtain. Nevertheless, some of these techniques appear to be quite useful, and it is likely that they will be applied with increasing frequency in the future. Neither space nor time allow for complete exposition at this time, however, and, moreover, the knowledge of statistics and probability theory required for reasonable comprehension of these techniques is probably beyond that of most readers. For those students who wish to search the literature independently, the articles by F. S. Hillier, Joel Cord and David Hertz, provide interesting samples (*see Bibliography*).

Increase Minimum Attractive Rate of Return

Some analysts advocate that the minimum attractive rate of return be adjusted to compensate for risky investments. This is to suggest that, since the future is uncertain, stipulation of a minimum attractive rate of return of, say, $i + \Delta i$ will insure that i will be earned in the long run. Since some investments will not turn out as well as expected, these failures will have been compensated for by the incremental "safety margin," Δi. It is our view, however, that this approach fails to come to grips with the risk or uncertainty associated with estimates for specific alternatives, and thus an element Δi in the minimum attractive rate of return penalizes all alternatives equally.

Rates of Return Differentiated by Risk Class

Rather than build the "safety margin" into a single minimum attractive rate of return, some firms establish several risk classes with separate standards for each class. For example, the firm may require low-risk investments to yield at least 10%, medium-risk investments to yield at least 12%, and the minimum attractive rate of return is defined as 15% for high-risk proposals. The analyst makes a judgment as to which class the specific proposal belongs, and the relevant minimum attractive rate of return is then used in the analysis. Although this approach is a step in the direction away from treating all alternatives equally, it is less than satisfactory in that it fails to focus attention on the uncertainty associated with the individual proposals. No two proposals have precisely the same degree of risk, and grouping alternatives by class obscures this point. Moreover, the attention of the decision maker should be directed to the causes of uncertainty, that is, to the individual estimates.

Decrease Expected Project Life

Still another procedure frequently employed to compensate for uncertainty is to decrease the expected project life. It is argued that estimates become less and less reliable as they occur further and further into the future, and thus shortening project life is equivalent to ignoring those distant, unreliable estimates. Further, distant consequences are more likely to be favorable than unfavorable, that is, distant estimated cash flows are generally positive (resulting from net revenues) and estimated cash flows near date zero are more likely to be negative (resulting from start-up costs). Reducing expected project life has the effect of penalizing the proposal by precluding possible future benefits, thereby allowing for risk in much the same way as increasing the minimum attractive rate of return penalizes marginally attractive proposals. Again, this procedure is to be criticized on the basis that it obscures uncertain estimates from the decision maker.

SUMMARY

Limited capital is allocated to competing investment proposals on the basis of estimates of future consequences. Since the future can never be known with absolute certainty, it follows that procedures must be developed which the analyst may use when dealing with risk and uncertainty in capital budgeting problems. Several of those procedures are discussed in this chapter.

Sensitivity (or break-even) analysis is widely used because of its simplicity and ability to focus on particular estimates. It generally treats only one estimate at a time, however, and is difficult to apply when determining possible effects of combinations of errors in the estimates.

Decision theory provides a number of principles which may be used to select from among mutually exclusive alternatives when various future outcomes are possible. They may be grouped into two classes: (*a*) those which are applicable when nothing at all is known about the relative probabilities of future events, and (*b*) those which are applicable when these probabilities can be defined with reasonable precision. There are significant differences between these principles and, in some instances, they are mutually contradictory. In any event, they are helpful in formalizing the decision process and thereby exposing the relative strengths and weaknesses of the various viewpoints.

Some firms adjust for risk and uncertainty by requiring prospective investments to promise somewhat higher returns than would normally be expected if future consequences were known with perfect certainty. In some cases the minimum attractive rate of return is increased above the risk-free rate; in others expected project life is truncated. These approaches are criticized primarily on the grounds that they penalize all alternatives equally and, further, they tend to obscure the degree of uncertainty associated with specific estimates.

There are no simple, widely accepted techniques for effectively dealing with risk and uncertainty in capital budgeting. Although some promising advances have been made in recent years with the application of probability theory and decision theory, practical application remains as much an art as a science.

PROBLEMS

1. Review the various principles of choice discussed in this chapter and then develop still another principle which you feel may be useful. Give

the rationale for your principle and illustrate its use with a numerical example. Distinguish between cases where expected probabilities of future events are both known (or estimated) and unknown.

2. A phased program of plant expansion is to be compared with a program wherein full expansion is to be undertaken immediately with a total initial investment of $1,400,000. The phased program requires $800,000 now, $600,000 in 5 years, and another $600,000 in 10 years. If the full program is selected, estimated annual disbursement will be $40,000 more during the first 5 years and $20,000 more during the second 5 years. There are no other differences between alternatives.
   (a) If the pre-tax minimum attractive rate of return is 10%, which alternative should be selected?
   (b) At what range of values for the minimum attractive rate of return will the phased program be economically superior?

3. Management is attempting to determine which cleaning equipment it will purchase for its California plant. The decision is dependent upon wage rates used in the analysis, but these rates are uncertain as they are the subject of current negotiations with the union. Unfortunately, the investment decision must be made immediately. The following table represents, in thousands of dollars, the annual bencfits (reduction in labor and other operating costs) which may result from four different alternatives coupled with the four possible outcomes of the current wage negotiations.

		Possible Outcome			
		s_1	s_2	s_3	s_4
Mutually Exclusive Alternatives	a_1	1	2	3	4
	a_2	3	2	1	0
	a_3	2	3	4	2
	a_4	3	4	2	1

   (a) If the relative probabilities of occurrence of each of the outcomes are unknown, determine which alternative is indicated by each of the following decision rules: Maximin, Maximax, Hurwicz Criterion with $\alpha = 0.5$, Savage (Minimax Regret), and Laplace (Insufficient Reason).
   (b) Suppose there is reason to believe that $Pr[s_1] = \frac{1}{8}$, $Pr[s_2] = \frac{1}{8}$, $Pr[s_3] = \frac{1}{4}$, and $Pr[s_4] = \frac{1}{2}$. Determine which alternative is indicated by the following decision rules: expectation, most probable future, and expectation-variance.

4. The plant manager is considering two mutually exclusive alternatives: (a_1) expand the existing warehouse, or (a_2) build an additional warehouse.

Three possible future events are likely: (s_1) there will be no change in output other than normal growth, (s_3) new product A will be manufactured at the plant, or (s_3) new product B will be manufactured at the plant.

(a) The matrix of equivalent uniform annual costs which is to be considered by the plant manager is as follows:

	s_1	s_2	s_3
a_1	$140,000	$300,000	$300,000
a_2	$200,000	$250,000	$250,000

Using the Laplace Principle of Insufficient Reason, which alternative should be selected?

(b) Suppose the decision is reviewed by the comptroller at corporate headquarters. Noting that costs are dependent only upon whether or not a new product line is to be manufactured at the plant, he simplifies the cost matrix as follows:

	s_1	s_2
a_1	$140,000	$300,000
a_2	$200,000	$250,000

In the revised matrix s_2 represents the outcome "A new product line is to be manufactured at the plant." Which alternative should be selected if the Laplace Principle is applied?

(c) Comment on the results for (a) and (b) above.

5. The following questions refer to the maximin principle.

(a) Consider the following profit matrix:

	s_1	s_2
a_1	$1	$100
a_2	$2	$2

Alternative a_2 is chosen under the maximin principle of choice. What in general may be inferred from this problem?

(b) Consider the following profit matrix:

CASE I

	s_1	s_2
a_1	$1	$4
a_2	$3	$2

Now suppose that additional information has been developed which indicates that, if s_1 occurs, profits will be increased by $3 over the original values. Moreover, this will be the case regardless of the alternative selected. The revised profit matrix is:

CASE II

	s_1	s_2
a_1	$4	$4
a_2	$6	$2

Comment on the maximin solutions for these two cases.

6. The following table gives the costs that would result from alternative testing sequences required in connection with a certain research program. All costs are in thousands of dollars:

Possible Outcomes

		s_1	s_2	s_3	s_4	s_5
Mutually Exclusive Alternatives	a_1	18	16	10	14	15
	a_2	14	15	15	14	15
	a_3	5	16	12	10	15
	a_4	14	22	10	12	15
	a_5	10	12	15	10	15

(a) Apply the principles of choice discussed in the chapter under the assumption that relative probabilities of future events are unknown. Comment on the results.

(b) In (a), if any alternative remains unchosen under any principle, eliminate it, and then determine if your original solutions would still apply.

(c) Suppose that information is available which suggests that failure patterns will occur with probabilities as follows:

$Pr[s_1] = 0.20$ $Pr[s_2] = 0.15$ $Pr[s_3] = 0.40$ $Pr[s_4] = 0.10$ and $Pr[s_5] = 0.05$.

Apply criteria for decision making when probabilities are known or estimated and comment on the results.

7. The Research Director and the Controller of the Truline Trucking Company are discussing the merits of a proposed labor saving device designed to eliminate a certain freight handling operation. The proposal has a first cost of $8,000, estimated life of 10 years, and zero net salvage value. The manual operation which it will replace currently requires 100 hours per year at a cost of $2.50 per hour. There are no other differ-

ences between alternatives. The minimum attractive rate of return is 12% before taxes.

(a) The Controller believes the investment should not be made? Is he correct? Why?

(b) The Research Director claims that labor costs may be expected to increase by about 5% per year (over the first year). That is, cost per man-hour will be \$2.50 the first year, \$2.63 the second, \$2.75 the third, etc. Under these conditions, he says, the new device should be purchased. Is he correct? Why?

8. A manufacturing firm is planning to construct a large industrial smoke stack which, because of certain design characteristics, may be either 80 feet or 150 feet high. The tall stack can be accommodated by a large footing only, whereas the short stack can be built with either a large or small footing. The initial costs are:

Big footing:	\$40,000	Tall stack:	\$140,000
Little footing:	\$20,000	Short stack:	\$ 40,000

At first glance it appears as though the company should build the short stack with the little footing with a total first cost of \$60,000. But, unfortunately, life is not quite so simple. If a short stack is built, the company risks being cited by the local "air pollution control board" and forced to build a tall stack.

The tall stack and the footings are permanent, but the short stack will be replaced by a tall one in 10 years in any case. If the minimum attractive rate of return is 10% before taxes, analyze this problem in a way that you believe will give management a reasonable basis for decision. Assume that cash expenses during any year will be concentrated at the end of that year.

9. An industrial sales firm is considering purchase of a desk computer for \$10,000. If this computer is purchased, clerical costs will be reduced by \$1,000 per year. The computer will be used for 10 years, at the end of which time the net salvage value will be zero. The firm requires a minimum attractive rate of return of 15% before taxes.

(a) Assuming no other relevant differences between alternatives, should the computer be purchased?

(b) Test the sensitivity of the solution in (a) to the assumption concerning annual labor costs by assuming that these costs will increase by \$50 per year, that is, \$1,000 the first year, \$1,050 the second, \$1,100 the third, etc.

(c) By how much, in terms of dollars per year, must the cost of labor increase if the proposed investment is to be economically sound?

10. A firm is planning to keep a certain old machine for another two years. The maintenance department advises that the machine will probably break down and require repair sometime during these two years unless an immediate overhaul is made. They estimate that, without an overhaul, the probability is 0.5 that the machine will break down the first year and 0.3 that the machine will survive the first year but break down during the second year.

Repairing the machine *after* a breakdown would (a) cost an estimated \$1,000, (b) guarantee against further breakdowns in the next two years, and (c) add \$500 to the salvage value. Overhauling the machine *now* would (a) cost \$800, (b) guarantee against further breakdown in the next two years, and (c) add \$500 to the salvage value. The minimum attractive rate of return is 10% before taxes.

Use "expected cost" calculations and the end-of-year convention to determine whether the machine should be repaired now. Assume that cash expenses during any year will be concentrated at the end of that year.

10

COST OF CAPITAL

All of the principal methods of capital budgeting require an explicit or implicit determination of the minimum attractive rate of return. This value is used directly as the interest rate i in the present worth and annual cost methods; in the rate of return method, project rates of return on incremental investments must exceed this "hurdle" rate. Some other descriptive titles given to this value are: financial standard, target rate of return, and cut off rate.

Although the minimum attractive rate of return is necessarily an integral part of the capital budgeting process, there currently exists considerable controversy as to the manner in which this value should be determined. The discussion which follows closely parallels the so-called "traditional view" although some important alternative formulations are also discussed.[1]

Sources of Capital

Each dollar invested within the firm may be classified as *debt* or *equity* according to the nature of its source. *Equity capital* may be defined as those funds which are provided by the owners of the firm in the form of profits realized from prior operations and retained for reinvestment or from infusion of new capital raised from new owners through the sale of additional shares of common stock. *Debt capital*, on the other hand, consists of funds provided by individuals and institutions in the form of loans which must be repaid according to some contractual arrangements. Bonds are the most common type

[1] The texts of Robichek and Meyers, and Quirin present interesting attempts to reconcile prevailing cost of capital theories. The reader is also referred to the Solomon text for an extensive discussion (*see Bibliography*).

of debt capital. Both bonds and preferred stock are frequently referred to as "senior securities" in that holders of these securities have claim to the assets of the firm ahead of owners of common stock.[2] The principal sources of investment funds are illustrated in Figure 10-1.

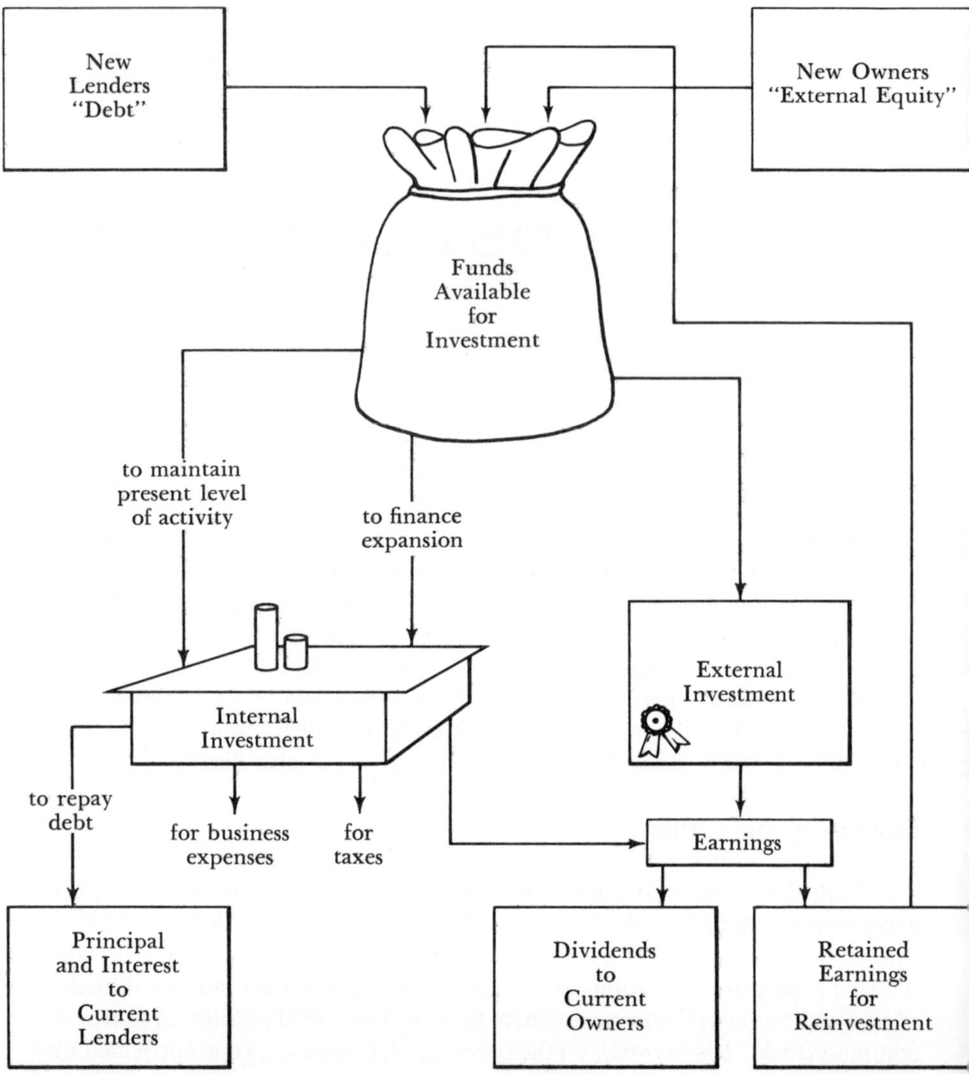

Fig. 10-1. Flow of investment capital.

[2] For our purposes here, preferred stock will be classified as a form of debt financing.

Usefulness of the Cost of Capital Concept

In the real world of limited resources, both debt and equity capital are costly in the sense that, if these funds were *not* employed within the firm, certain costs associated with borrowing could be avoided and "freed" capital could be profitably invested elsewhere. Clearly, in order to avoid uneconomic operation, each increment of internal investment must provide a return at least as great as the incremental cost of the associated funds. The cost of capital establishes a lower bound, or minimum level, against which all prospective investments may be measured.

A secondary and closely related function of the cost of capital formulation is determination of optimal capital structure for a given firm. That is, if cost of capital is a function of the relative amounts of debt and equity capital employed, then, for any total amount of capital required, there is a certain balance of debt to equity which will minimize overall cost of capital. This issue is examined at some length in our subsequent discussion of "leverage."[3]

Uncertainty

The previous statement relating cost of capital to the minimum attractive rate of return must be suitably modified in view of the uncertainty associated with real world estimates. Future receipts and disbursements are never known with absolute certainty, and thus measures such as present worth and project rate of return are at best only expected values. Moreover, there is an unmeasurable uncertainty associated with the cost of capital, particularly with respect to equity funds. In spite of these difficulties, however, it is our view that use of (the best estimate of) the cost of capital as a minimum attractive rate of return is an acceptable policy. The point is that selection of *some* value simply cannot be avoided, and the cost of capital approach seems to offer the most reasonable rationale.

Parenthetically, it is to be noted that, while most firms do not reveal the explicit basis upon which their figures for minimum attractive rate of return are based, it appears as though the cost of capital approach is not extensively used. The precise reasons for this are still open to question, although it may be surmised that the concept is not widely understood and, further, there are certain procedural difficulties inherent in measuring capital costs. These difficulties become apparent during the course of the following discussion.

SOURCES AND COSTS OF INVESTMENT FUNDS

Retained Earnings

In stating basic principles to guide investment decisions, it is first necessary to establish from whose point of view the relative merits of the decisions

[3] Some authors draw a formal distinction between *investment decisions* and *financing decisions*. Although our emphasis is upon the former, both are discussed in this chapter.

are to be judged. Here it would seem reasonable to assume that the viewpoint to be adopted is that of the current owners of the firm. Moreover, we will assume that owners are profit maximizers and investment decisions are rational, and thus the principal investment criterion is maximization, over the long run, of the interests of the existing group of owners. This statement of the fundamental investment principal is not intended to preclude such management objectives as level employment, product safety, community service, and so on. Indeed, management decisions are affected in a variety of ways. It may be argued, however, that in order to continue as a viable enterprise in a competitive economy, there are at least *some* decisions which have as their basis an economic justification. Our discussion of the rationale of capital allocation belongs in this frame of reference.

Rather than retaining earnings for reinvestment, it is possible to return these earnings to the stockholder so that he may invest in other opportunities. Thus it is necessary that all funds employed within the firm provide a return at least as great as that which could be earned by stockholders if these same funds were to be invested elsewhere. (As before, *return* may be defined as the equivalent net discounted present value of all expected future cash flows.)

What is the "value" of earnings to the individual stockholder? Ignoring the question of taxes for the moment, this figure may be inferred by examining an alternative which is always available: sale of the ownership share in the stock market. Suppose, for example that the market value, $\mathcal{M}$, of a share of common stock is $30, and suppose further that the earnings per share, $\mathcal{E}$, are expected to be $3 over the indeterminate future. The *capitalization rate for earnings*, k_e, is the same as the rate of return for an initial investment and an infinite series of uniform cash flows:

$$k_e = \mathcal{E}/\mathcal{M} \tag{10.1}$$

In this example the capitalization rate is $3/$30 = 0.10. Since the stockholder has the option of foregoing a 10% return by selling his ownership for $30 per share, we may infer that all retained earnings must return at least 10%. Because of this possibility of *disinvestment*, internal investments must yield at least $k_e = \mathcal{E}/\mathcal{M}$.

The numerator in Equation 10.1 represents the expected earnings per share *after* corporate taxes but *before* individual income taxes. Given the two alternatives (a) retention and reinvestment within the firm or (b) distribution as dividends and reinvestment elsewhere, individual income taxes must be paid in the latter case. When taxes are considered, the stream of earnings, available to the stockholders is reduced by t_p, where t_p is the personal income tax rate, and the capitalization rate becomes:

$$k_{ep} = (1 - t_p)\,\mathcal{E}/\mathcal{M} \tag{10.2}$$

To illustrate, suppose that the $3 earnings per share are distributed as dividends, and assume that the shareowners' incremental personal income rate is (and is expected to continue to be) 0.30. With a current market value of \$30 per share, the implied capitalization rate is:

$$k_{ep} = (1 - 0.30)(\$3)/\$30$$
$$= 0.07$$

It is extremely difficult to determine a representative incremental personal income tax rate for all stockholders in large, publicly held corporations, and the formulation given by Equation 10.2 is generally not feasible as a practical matter. We may avoid this complication, of course, by simply ignoring personal taxes altogether or assuming that retained earnings, if not reinvested within the firm, are used for outside investment opportunities. For example, retained earnings may be used to purchase 5,000 shares in Company Y or 60% of Company Z. When the outside ownership interest is sufficient to permit a consolidated corporate income tax return — that is, when the outside investment represents majority control — there is no *immediate* tax effect and the equity capitalization rate is consequently that given by Equation 10.1.

In the remaining discussion of cost of capital, personal income taxes are ignored on the additional grounds that the value of the stock as established in the marketplace reflects the tax consequences for individual shareholders. That is, faced with the prospect of an indefinite series of earnings, $\mathcal{E}$, continued ownership of the stock having a certain market value per share, $\mathfrak{M}$, suggests a capitalization rate, k_e, for each and every shareholder, as given by Equation 10.1. Both Mr. Smith and Mr. Jones, for example, with incremental personal income tax rates of 30% and 60%, respectively, will presumably continue to own their shares having market value $\mathfrak{M}$ per share if the earnings are reinvested in projects yielding returns of at least k_e.

Before leaving this section, we should point out that retained earnings may not, to some readers, represent all equity funds which are generated within the firm. In an accounting sense, internally generated investment funds are obtained through depreciation and other capital-consumption allowances as well as from retained earnings. In the context in which it is used here, however, "earnings" refers to the net cash flows available for additional investment or disinvestment, after a provision has been made for reinvestment sufficient for the maintenance of earnings at the projected level. That is, net earnings E are equal to total cash earnings (net positive cash flow) less the capital consumption allowances necessary to maintain the flow of cash earnings.

New (External) Equity

In addition to equity funds owned by current shareholders in the form of retained earnings (internal equity), additional investment funds may be generated by selling new ownership shares to willing investors (external equity). We now attempt to formulate an expression for the cost of external equity funds.

Consider an all-equity firm with the following characteristics:

Number of shares outstanding (Q)	\$100,000.00
Total book value of the firm (B)	\$2,800,000.00
Current market price per share ($\mathcal{M}$)	\$30.00
Current earnings per share ($\mathcal{E}_c$)	\$3.60
Expected earnings per share ($\mathcal{E}$)	\$4.20

The interests of existing owners may be determined by examining *current market value* with reference to expected *future earnings*. Book value is merely an accounting estimate of the current net worth of the firm; the actual worth of the firm is determined in the market place by buyers and sellers of ownership shares. Moreover, market price of ownership shares is based upon the expectations of buyers and sellers over the foreseeable future, and thus current earnings are relevant only insofar as they may suggest the nature of future earnings. In the example, then, current shareholders own stock valued at \$30 per share in the expectation that future earnings will approximate \$4.20 per share. (These comments, of course, also apply to the determination of k_e in the preceding section.)

Let us now suppose that a new proposal is under consideration requiring an initial incremental investment of \$290,000 and promising a rate of return of 13% over an indefinite period. We will further suppose that this new project may be financed by selling additional shares of stock at market value (\$30) but, due to the costs associated with the issue (for example, underwriting fees), the net proceeds to the firm $\mathcal{P}$ are only \$29 per share. In order to raise \$290,000 in external equity capital, 10,000 additional shares must be sold, thereby increasing the number of shares outstanding to 110,000. The earnings per share upon adoption of the new proposal will be:

$$\frac{\$420{,}000 + 0.13(\$290{,}000)}{110{,}000} = \$4.16$$

Since the expected earnings per share *without* the new project were \$4.20, it is clear that there has been a slight diminution in value to the initial owner caused by acceptance of an "unprofitable" proposal.

What rate of return on the new project is necessary to support the decision to raise external equity funds? In order that the current earnings per share not be decreased, it is necessary that total earnings be equal to (or greater than) \$4.20 $\times$ 110,000 shares = \$462,000. Of this amount \$420,000 is expected to be earned with internal equity only; the remaining \$42,000 per year must be generated from the initial investment of \$290,000. Thus the rate of return required for the new project is \$42,000/\$290,000 = 14.48%. In equation form:

$$\frac{\$4.20(100{,}000) + \Delta k_e(10{,}000)(\$29)}{100{,}000 + 10{,}000} = \$4.20$$

$$\Delta k_e = 14.48\%$$

where Δk_e is the capitalization rate, or cost, of the external equity. Restating this more generally:

$$\frac{\mathcal{E}(Q) + \Delta k_e(\Delta Q)(\mathcal{P})}{Q + \Delta Q} = \mathcal{E} \qquad (10.3)$$

$$\Delta k_e = \frac{\mathcal{E}}{\mathcal{P}} \qquad (10.4)$$

In the event that the distribution costs for the new stock are either negligible or ignored, $\Delta k_e = \mathcal{E}/\mathcal{M}$, which is the same as the expression given for k_e in Equation 10.1. As a practical matter, it is probably sufficient to adopt this simplification, thereby defining the cost of all equity capital, both internal and external, as $\mathcal{E}/\mathcal{M}$.

It should be noted that new equity capital may be raised in a variety of ways other than the simple distribution of new issues on the open market. For example, existing owners may exercise preemptive rights to purchase additional shares, or other classes of securities may be converted to common stock. The conclusions of the preceding paragraphs are equally applicable in these instances however, since it is only the *identity* of new owners which is affected. In all cases, the market price per share of existing (current) shares must be protected by insuring that investment will not be undertaken which will diminish future earnings per share.

Debt Capital

The total cost of an increment of debt capital may be defined as the direct "price" paid for borrowed funds *in addition* to the effect of the new borrowing on costs of other capital. The secondary, or induced, effects will be discussed in a subsequent section. Our comments here are limited to the direct costs of borrowed funds.

Unlike equity capital, the cost of debt capital need not be inferred by reference to market valuation. On the contrary, the direct price paid for debt capital is explicitly stated at the time of the loan in the form of contractual conditions regarding the amount and timing of repayment of principal and interest. The pre-tax direct cost of debt capital is:

$$k'_d = \frac{I'}{D} \qquad (10.5)$$

where I' represents the total annual interest charges before taxes on borrowed funds and D represents the total market value of long-term debt.

Interest charges are deductible as interest expense when computing taxable income, and thus the *after-tax* direct cost of debt capital is:

$$k_d = (1 - t)\frac{I'}{D}$$

$$= \frac{I}{D} \tag{10.6}$$

where t is the relevant income tax rate for the firm.

To illustrate these concepts, consider a firm with annual interest payments of \$200,000 based upon total debt of \$4,000,000. The pre-tax direct cost of debt capital is determined from Equation 10.5 to be 0.05. Assuming an incremental income tax rate of 0.40, the after-tax cost of debt is (1 − 0.40) (0.05), or only 0.03.

Combined Cost of Debt and Equity

Given a specific capital structure defined by proportion w_1 of equity and w_2 of debt, the overall cost of capital k_o may be determined by averaging the costs of both debt and equity funds. Ignoring the transfer costs associated with the sale of ownership shares, the cost of equity capital is given by Equation 10.1 as $k_e = \mathcal{E}/\mathfrak{M}$ where $\mathcal{E}$ represents expected future earnings per share after corporate income taxes. An alternative formulation is:

$$k_e = \frac{E}{M} \tag{10.7}$$

where E represents total after-tax earnings and M represents total market value of the firm's outstanding common stock. Note that $E = \mathcal{E}Q$ and $M = \mathfrak{M}Q$. The after-tax cost of debt capital is given by Equation 10.6 as $k_d = (1 - t)I/D$. The average cost of capital, after consideration of corporate income taxes, is the average of the costs of debt and equity weighted by the amount of each in the capital structure. Thus:

$$k_o = \frac{k_e M + k_d D}{M + D} \tag{10.8}$$

or:

$$k_o = w_1 k_e + w_2 k_d \tag{10.9}$$

It is frequently desirable to determine the weighted average cost of capital *before* corporate income taxes, k'_o, for use in those instances in which tax effects of investment proposals are temporarily ignored. This may easily be shown to be:

$$k'_o = w_1 k'_e + w_2 k'_d \tag{10.10}$$

where k'_e and k'_d are the pre-tax costs of equity and debt, respectively.

To illustrate the procedure for determining the weighted average cost of capital, both before and after taxes, consider the following data for a fictitious firm:

Total market value of equity (M)	\$6,000,000
Total market value of debt (D)	\$4,000,000
Total expected cash earnings for the year	\$5,000,000
Capital required to maintain flow of cash earnings at expected levels (tax deductible)	\$3,600,000
Total interest charges on borrowed funds (I')	\$200,000
Incremental corporate income tax rate (t)	0.40

We first determine the *before-tax* weighted average cost of capital. Of the total expected cash earnings per year, \$3,600,000 is required to maintain the earnings level and an additional \$200,000 is required to pay interest on debt. Thus the expected taxable income, E', is \$1,200,000, and k'_e = \$1,200,000/\$6,000,000 = 0.20. The cost of debt capital is k'_d = \$200,000/ \$4,000,000 = 0.05. Thus, from equation 10.10:

$$\begin{aligned} k'_o &= w_1 k'_e + w_2 k'_d \\ &= \frac{\$6{,}000{,}000}{\$10{,}000{,}000}(0.20) + \frac{\$4{,}000{,}000}{\$10{,}000{,}000}(0.05) \\ &= 0.14 \end{aligned}$$

The after-tax weighted average cost of capital may be determined in a similar manner.

Total cash earnings	\$5,000,000
Costs to maintain earnings level	3,600,000
Net operating earnings	\$1,400,000
Interest on debt (I')	200,000
Net earnings before taxes (E')	\$1,200,000
Income taxes @ 0.40	480,000
Net earnings after taxes (E)	\$720,000

With these results:

$$k_e = \frac{E}{M} = \frac{\$720{,}000}{\$6{,}000{,}000} = 0.12$$

$$k_d = \frac{(1-t)I'}{D} = \frac{(1-0.40)(\$200{,}000)}{\$4{,}000{,}000} = 0.03$$

$$k_o = w_1 k_e + w_2 k_d = 0.6(0.12) + 0.4(0.03) = 0.084$$

COST OF CAPITAL AS INVESTMENT CRITERION

Given an existing mixture of debt and equity, and given conditions in the capital market which affect costs of these funds, a weighted average cost of capital may be determined as outlined above. The resulting values, k_o or k'_o, specify a minimum return which must be obtained by new investment proposals in order that the ownership value of existing owners of the firm will not be reduced. On a before-tax basis, for example, the criterion for acceptance of a new proposal is:

$$\frac{\Delta E}{C} > k_o \qquad (10.11)$$

where C represents the initial cost of the project and ΔE represents the uniform annual net benefits resulting from the project.[4]

In the absence of specific information to the contrary, the initial investment is assumed to consist of debt and equity funds in equal proportion to the total mix in the firm. If, in fact, the investment funds for a particular proposal can be clearly identified as to source and associated cost, and if the use of these funds will result in no change to the the cost of other funds, then the minimum attractive rate of return for the proposal should reflect these conditions. In such cases a revised value of k_o or k'_o should be evaluated using the relevant value for k_d.

LEVERAGE AND OPTIMAL CAPITAL STRUCTURE

The preceding sections focused upon the problem of determining the cost of capital for a certain mix of debt and equity and with given conditions in the capital market. We now turn briefly to an associated issue which has generated a good deal of discussion in recent years: with given conditions in the capital market, how is the optimum capital structure determined? That is, what mix of debt and equity will result in minimum overall cost of capital?

If leverage λ is defined as the ratio of debt D to total value of the firm at market prices $D + M$, determination of optimal capital structure clearly depends upon the behavior of weighted average cost of capital as λ varies. Optimal leverage is that mix of equity and debt which maximizes the total market value of the firm.

The Traditional View

Figure 10-2 graphically illustrates the traditional view of the response of the market value of a firm to changes in leverage. Essentially there are three

[4] The project rate of return is given by $\Delta E/C$ only in the case of uniform infinite cash flows. The formulation shown here is by way of illustration only. It is our intent to indicate that the left side of the inequality represents the project rate of return.

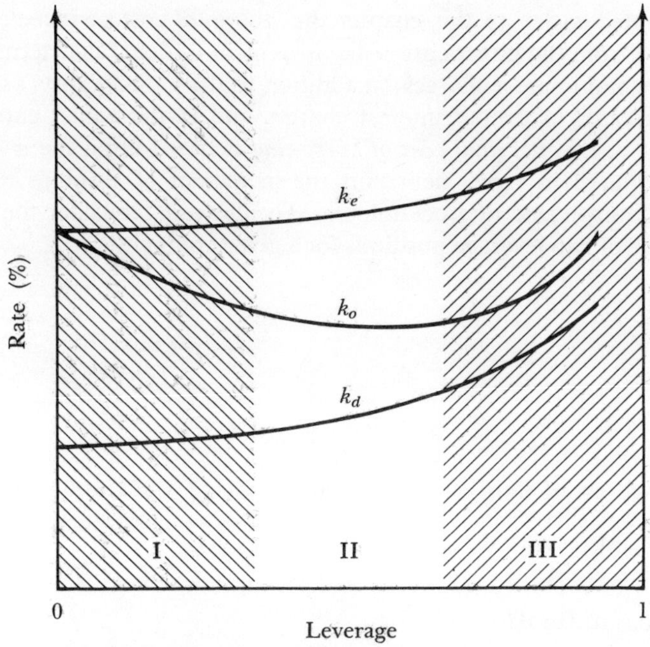

Fig. 10-2. The effect of leverage on cost of capital.

general phases. During the *first* phase, market value is increased as leverage increases since the cost of debt (k_d) rises rather slowly and the cost of equity capital (k_e) remains virtually constant. Recall from equation 10.9 that:

$$k_o = w_1 k_e + w_2 k_d$$

As the proportion of equity (w_1) decreases and the proportion of debt (w_2) increases, it is clear the weighted average cost of capital k_o will decrease as long as k_d is less than k_e and k_e remains constant. In the *third* phase, it is postulated that k_o increases due to the reaction of the market to the large proportion of debt incurred by the firm. This is to say that both stockholders and lenders become more apprehensive as the relative proportion of debt increases, and each of these groups requires a higher price for their capital as the result of added risk. The market price of stock will decrease as debt is increased beyond the point considered by investors to be acceptable. Lenders will react in a similar manner, charging even higher interest rates for their loans. During the *second* phase, total market value remains virtually constant as the opposite effects of the first and third phases tend to cancel each other. Thus the traditional view holds that cost of capital as a function of leverage is U-shaped, and an optimum (minimum) point does indeed exist.[5]

[5] Over the range where k_e remains constant and $k_d < k_e$, it may be shown that k_o will continue to decrease to the point where the marginal rate of interest on debt equals the average cost of equity capital. The proof is left as an exercise for the reader.

We noted earlier in this chapter that the *total* cost of increased debt is determined from the direct cost of the increment of debt (as determined from the incremental interest charges) in addition to the indirect costs as measured by the increases in overall interest charges and in the equity capitalization rate. That is, the *marginal cost of borrowing* is based upon the increment of interest required to repay debt plus the increment of earnings required to maintain equity value of stockholders. To illustrate, consider the following comparison of two leverage positions for a given company.

		λ_1 Smaller Leverage	λ_2 Larger Leverage
Given:			
Market value of debt	(D)	\$5,000	\$6,000
Average interest rate paid on all debt	(k_d)	0.04	0.05
Equity capitalization rate	(k_e)	0.12	0.13
Expected annual net operating earnings[a]	$(\hat{E})$	\$1,400	\$1,400
Analysis:			
Interest	$(I = Dk_d)$	\$200	\$300
Expected annual net earnings	$(E = \hat{E} - I)$	\$1,200	\$1,100
Market value of equity	$(M = E/k_e)$	\$10,000	\$8,460
Total market value of firm	$(V = D + M)$	\$15,000	\$14,460
Average cost of capital	$(k_o = \hat{E}/V)$	0.093	0.097
Leverage	$(\lambda = D/V)$	0.333	0.415

[a] Expected annual net operating earnings $(\hat{E})$ includes profits after taxes but before interest payments. That is, $\hat{E} = E + I$.

The addition of \$1,000 of debt capital (replacing \$1,000 of equity) results in an increase of \$100 in interest payments as well as a slight increase in the equity capitalization rate. To preserve the equity value of existing stockholders, market value of equity should not fall below \$9,000 since \$1,000 of equity has been replaced by a like amount of debt. With new capitalization rate $k_e = 0.13$, expected annual net earnings should be \$1,170, or \$70 more than estimated. Thus the additional \$1,000 of debt results in a total marginal cost of \$170.

As long as the *marginal* cost of capital remains below the *average* cost of capital, the average cost will continue to decline; the average cost will increase as long as the marginal cost is higher. Therefore, the minimum average cost of capital will occur at the point at which the average cost is equal to the marginal cost. From the example above, the marginal cost, stated as a percentage, is 17% when leverage is increased from 0.333 to 0.415. Since the average cost of capital is only 9.3% with the smaller leverage, the average cost increases with the increase in leverage.

The Modigliani–Miller Thesis

An important alternative to the traditional view has been articulately presented by Professors Franco Modigliani and Merton H. Miller (*see Bibliography*). It is their position that average cost of capital is *independent* of the capital structure of the firm and, as a corollary, the total market value of the firm is unaffected by the relative proportions of debt and equity. Thus there is no "optimal" capital structure defined by the minimum average cost of capital.

Although space does not permit a complete discussion of the Modigliani-Miller thesis, a simple example serves to illustrate an essential feature of their position:[6]

	Company A	Company B
Annual net operating earnings $(\hat{E})$	\$ 10,000	\$ 10,000
Market value of debt (D)	—	\$ 30,000
Interest @ 4% (I)	—	\$ 1,200
Annual net earnings (after interest payments) $(E = \hat{E} - I)$	\$ 10,000	\$ 8,800
Equity capitalization rate (k_e)	0.10	0.11
Market value of equity $(M = E/k_e)$	\$100,000	\$ 80,000
Total market value of firm $(V = D + M)$	\$100,000	\$110,000
Leverage $(\lambda = D/V)$	—	0.2727

Modigliani–Miller assert that the increase in market value for Company B is not possible given rational investors and perfect capital markets. A stockholder owning \$10,000 of common stock in Company B, for example,

[6] This example is based upon data provided by Barges (p. 80) for two hypothetical firms.

will find that his investment yields only \$1,100. However, he may sell his stock in Company B, borrow an additional \$3,750 at 4% (the same rate as is available to Company B), and then invest the entire \$13,750 in the stock of Company A. With this strategy the investor will receive \$1,225 for his investment, determined as follows:

Total yield from Company A	0.10(\$13,750) =	\$1,375
Interest on debt	0.04(\$3,750) =	150
Net yield from \$10,000 investment	=	\$1,225

This *arbitrage process* is available to all stockholders, of course, and thus equality in the total market values of the two companies will result from continued exchanges.

The views of Modigliani and Miller have been seriously questioned by a number of authors. Solomon, for example, summarizes the principal objections to this simple arbitrage model as follows: "It ignores the tax-deductibility of interest payments . . . . It ignores the difference between corporate debt and personal debt . . . (and it) ignores the attitude of lenders and its effect on lending rates." (pp.102–04) In addition to providing an interesting theoretical discussion of the Modigliani–Miller position, Professor Alexander Barges has attempted to verify the thesis using statistical analysis of real world data relating equity capitalization rates and yields for various industries. Barges concludes that there *is* some dependence between average cost and capital structure, although the k_o curve appears to be reasonably flat over a wide range.

Although the controversy continues at this writing, it appears that the preponderance of theoretical discussion as well as empirical data support the view that there *is* some leverage position which will maximize the value of the firm, although a reasonable degree of precision may be lacking. Much additional research clearly remains to be done in this important area.

A Contrary Note

As a practical matter — that is, when considering its implementation within a realistic context — the method which has been advocated for determining cost of capital presents a number of troublesome problems. Before leaving this chapter, we briefly discuss several of them.

First, note that the current market price per share of common stock ($\mathfrak{M}$) must be specified. But what is that value? We know, of course, that day-to-day variations are quite normal, and, in some instances, these swings are relatively large. Price variations on the order of 20% during the year are not unusual, for example. Thus it would appear that the value chosen for $\mathfrak{M}$ should represent an average over a sufficient time interval to account for short term fluctuations.

Second, expected future earnings must also be specified, and this, too, presents a difficult problem in estimation. Suppose a stock is currently selling for $100 per share, for example, and the firm is currently earning at the rate of $2 per share. Clearly the high price-earnings ratio is due to the stockholders' expectations of markedly higher earnings in the future. But what value should be used? Shall a representative sample of stockholders be polled in order to arrive at a group guess? Shall we poll a group of knowledgeable market analysts or, perhaps, the management of the firm? Unfortunately, there is no simple answer to this very difficult question.

Third, most business firms are not static institutions, and thus we should not expect future earnings, even if known, to remain *constant* from year to year. Moreover, we should not expect them to grow at a uniform *rate*. Since earnings generally assume a nonuniform pattern, what values should be used when predicting future earnings so as to compute the cost of equity? And how should the model for cost of capital (k_o) be adjusted to reflect these irregularities?

A number of other troublesome issues could be raised at this point but, as noted earlier, an extensive discussion of the cost of capital concept is beyond the scope of this text. It should be clear to the reader, however, that this is an area which presents formidable difficulties in practical implementation as well as in theoretical understanding.

SUMMARY

The minimum attractive rate of return required of all new investment proposals is determined by the over-all cost of funds to be employed. Since these investment funds are provided by both equity and debt sources, the over-all cost of capital is the average cost of equity and debt weighted by the relative amount of each in the capital structure.

Equity capital consists of the funds of the existing stockholders (retained earnings) and of new equity raised through the sale of additional shares of common stock. The cost of equity capital (k_e) is given as the ratio of expected future net earnings after interest and corporate taxes (E) to the market value of the ownership shares (M). The direct cost of debt capital (k_d) is given as the ratio of annual interest charges (I) to market value of debt (D). The weighted average cost of capital after taxes is:

$$k_o = \frac{k_e M + k_d D}{M + D}$$

Using the above formulation, it is possible to compute average cost of capital for various degrees of leverage. In this manner the optimal capital structure is determined by that leverage which yields minimum over-all average cost of capital. Optimal leverage is also defined as the point at which average cost of capital is equal to marginal cost of capital, where marginal cost is the total of (a) the increase in interest charges brought about by the increased debt and (b) the increase in earnings required to maintain the equity value of shareholders.

The traditional view holds that average cost of capital is a U-shaped function of leverage since there are initial advantages in increasing the proportion of relatively low-cost debt capital but, beyond a certain critical point, this advantage is more than offset by increases in interest rates for debt and increases in the equity capitalization rate. An alternative view presented by Professor Modigliani and Professor Miller asserts that, due to the use of arbitrage in a perfect capital market, over-all cost of capital for a given firm must be independent of leverage. The issue is by no means clearly decided.

PROBLEMS

1. Consider the following prospective (assumed) capitalization rates for various leverage positions:

Market Value of Debt D	Effective Interest Rate Paid on Debt k_d	Expected Annual Net Operating Earnings $\hat{E}$	Equity Capitalization Rate k_e
$ —	—	$1,000	0.120
1,000	0.045	1,000	.120
2,000	.045	1,000	.122
3,000	.047	1,000	.125
4,000	.050	1,000	.130
5,000	.054	1,000	.140
6,000	.069	1,000	.150
7,000	.075	1,000	.170
8,000	.082	1,000	.200
9,000	uncertain	1,000	uncertain

Using these data, determine the (a) annual interest charge, (b) expected annual net earnings, (c) market value of the stock, and (d) total market value of the firm for each of the ten leverage positions as shown above. Show these results in tabular form.

2. Using the data from Problem 1, determine the overall cost of capital k_o and leverage λ for each of the indicated situations. Prepare a graph of k_o

as a function of λ and discuss the results. (In this problem define λ as the ratio of debt to total market value of the firm, that is, $\lambda = D/V$.)

3. Using the data from Problem 1, determine the over-all average cost of capital k_o and the "marginal cost of borrowing" for each of the indicated leverage positions. Plot these marginal costs and average costs as a function of leverage λ and discuss the results.

4. Construct a numerical example (similar to the text discussion, pp. 179–180) indicating the effect of arbitrage. Discuss the arbitrage process within the context of your example.

5. Professor Barges has tested the Modigliani–Miller thesis with respect to empirical data for certain selected industries: Class I railroads, department store companies, and the cement industry (Chapters 5.1, 5.2, and 5.3). It is suggested that students replicate the Barges investigations using data from other industries.

11

CAPITAL BUDGETING PROCEDURES

Decisions affecting capital allocation are made at many levels throughout a business organization. Capital budgeting is commonly understood to be the function which takes place at the highest levels of management — Office of the Controller, Corporate Planning Committee, and Executive Review Committee are illustrations — but it is noteworthy that decisions made at lower levels in the management hierarchy directly affect those proposals which are ultimately considered as contenders in the capital budget. For example, before the alternatives for plant relocation can be completely defined prior to final analysis and decision, it may be necessary to select from among *sub-alternatives* such items as design of loading docks for truck and rail traffic, and number, type, and method of financing new office equipment; or perhaps alternative locations within a given community will be examined in order to select the "most feasible" site for each community. Our distinction between the *capital budgeting* and *design* levels in the following discussion is not merely semantic. As will be shown, capital allocation procedures are appropriately different between these two levels.

THE DESIGN LEVEL

Two types of economically-based decisions occur at the design level. First, decisions must be made regarding the characteristics of those proposals which are to be presented to the capital budgeting level for consideration. Since it is the responsibility of the design level to specify materials, dimensions, and construction scheduling, for example, it is necessary that "designers" be guided in their decisions by procedures which are consistent with corporate economic objectives. Second, many final decisions concerning capital allocation are made by personnel below the capital budgeting level of the firm. That is, rather than burden senior executives unnecessarily, it is generally corporate policy to allow line managers to make limited expenditures without additional review. As in the case of design decisions, appropriate procedures should be available and uniformly applied to insure that economic consequences are properly evaluated.

Parenthetically, it should be noted that formal economic evaluation is not required for *all* design decisions and nonreview expenditures. There are many instances, of course, where the amount of money involved is clearly not sufficient to warrant the time (and associated expense) required to complete formal analysis, and in these cases the combined intuition and experience of the decision maker is probably reliable. Although this critical level is not easily delineated, the appropriate strategy usually will be apparent.

Selection of the Interest Rate

The minimum attractive rate of return must be precisely stated in order to proceed with any of the equivalent evaluation techniques to which we referred in earlier chapters. For example, if the present worth method is used, the index of value (PW) for a specific proposal is the solution of the following equation:

$$PW = \sum_{j=0}^{N} C_j(1 + i)^{-j} \qquad (11.1)$$

where N is the number of compounding periods, C_j is the cash flow in period j, and i is the minimum attractive rate of return. If the rate of return method is used, on the other hand, the project rate of return (i) is the solution of the following equation:

$$0 = \sum_{j=0}^{N} C_j(1 + i)^{-j} \qquad (11.2)$$

The value of i which is the solution of Equation 11.2 is then compared to the minimum attractive rate of return in order to determine whether or not the investment is justified. Since all other proper techniques are but variations of the present worth and rate of return methods, it follows that a clear expression of the minimum attractive rate of return must be provided to the decision maker at the design level.

As outlined in the preceding Chapter, the average cost of capital (k_o) is based upon a weighted average of the costs of funds obtained from both equity and debt sources. The cost of equity capital (k_e) is a function of prospective internal investment opportunities as well as external alternatives available to current owners; the cost of debt capital (k_d) is determined by the interest payments required for debt in a given capital structure. Therefore, since the weighted average cost of capital represents a "price" paid for each dollar available for investments, it is equivalent to the *minimum* return which must be achieved if the value of the firm to current owners is not to be decreased. That is, the desired rate of return must be at least as great as the weighted average cost of capital.

Precise determination of the average cost of capital is rather difficult at any point in time, especially because of the short term variation in market price of common stocks. (Leverage also undergoes short-term fluctuations, but these are generally relatively minor and can usually be ignored.) There is no simple solution to this vexing problem of measurements, although some sort of time averaging should prove satisfactory in most cases. In any event, this lack of precision must be viewed simply as any other real world uncertainty to be dealt with in a reasonably consistent manner. Difficulties in measurement do not in themselves justify abandonment of precedures which are otherwise conceptually sound.

Estimates of Expected Consequences

Procedures relating to capital allocation decisions at the design level generally require three types of input data: estimates of amounts and timing of cash flows, expected project life, and a statement, either mathematical or verbal, of the risk or uncertainty associated with these estimates. In addition, those consequences which cannot or will not be reduced to monetary terms should also be noted.

It is useful to distinguish four separate categories of cash flow consequences for management decisions:

- Capital investment
- Working capital
- Operating results
- Disposal (salvage) values

Although each of these categories is simply descriptive of the movement of cash at points in time, their delineation is illuminating in the sense that investment strategy may well depend on the *source* of expected cash flows. For example, a negative cash flow of $100,000 at time zero may be due to either initial purchase of capital equipment or provision of working capital; a positive cash flow of $25,000 at the end of year ten may be due to either net salvage value realized upon the disposal of assets or recovery of working capital. Recognition of the sources of expected cash flows provides some insight into the relative uncertainty associated with the cash flows and, further, it presents data in a form which may be used when preparing *pro forma* balance sheets and profit and loss statements.

A suggested format for input data is presented in Table 11-1. "Date zero" is arbitrarily selected as the time at which the allocation decision is to be made, rather than the time at which the proposal is expected to be fully operable. Conceptually, the question of which point in time will be selected as "date zero" is unimportant; it is only necessary that a common date be used when comparing two or more alternatives.

The simplified work sheet shown as Table 11-1 illustrates one possibility for presenting estimates of expected consequences. Depending upon the needs of any given firm, additional detail may be included as desired. For example, analysts may wish to distinguish between cash flows which take place *during* the period and those which take place at the *end* of the interest period; months, rather than years, may be used as the interest period; a provision may be made for detailing future capital investments (for example, plant expansion) which will be required at some future date; investment in inventories may be described in additional detail (for example, raw materials, work in process, finished goods); equipment may be described more completely (such as plant production machinery, vehicles); and period-by-period estimates of production output may also be included. Although the format of the work sheet is specified by the requirements of the individual firm, it is necessary that the amounts and timing of *all* expected cash flows arising from the decision to accept the proposal be included.

Depreciation and Taxes

After all expected consequences have been defined and the estimated timing and amounts of cash flows associated with these consequences have been determined, it is necessary to evaluate the cash flows due to income taxes. (This step will not be required of course in those cases where only a pre-tax analysis is expected. These instances are likely to arise at the design level, especially with regard to those proposals whose capitalized component is relatively small.)

As a first step, the appropriate depreciation schedule should be determined for each asset to be capitalized. Corporate policy, guided by relevant governmental regulations, will normally establish the depreciation method to be used in any given instance. First costs, net salvage values, and depreciable lives are provided by the analyst. As indicated in Table 11-2, the expected annual depreciation expenses are determined for each of the capital assets in the proposal and then summed to yield the total year-by-year charges.

Given the annual depreciation charges and the relevant *incremental* tax rate, total after-tax cash flows may be determined as outlined in Table 11-3. Referring to the table, *internal cash flows* are those which have no effect on taxable income, such as initial expenditures for capitalized items and investment in working capital. The accountant will not record a business expense in either of these instances, although a cash commitment to the project has

Table 11-1

Simplified Work Sheet for Summarizing Economic Consequences of Investment Proposal

	19____	19____	19____	Total
Initial Investment				
Capitalized:				
Land				
Building				
Equipment				
____				
Expensed:				
Site Preparation				
____				
Working Capital				
Accounts Receivable				
Inventories				
____				

Year	Receipts	Expen-ditures	Net

Year	Receipts	Expen-ditures	Net
*			

*Salvage value

Comments: ____

____

Table 11-2

Sample Depreciation Schedule for Proposed Investment

	Grinder	Shaper		
First Cost	$20,000	$15,000		
Net Salvage Value	5,000	4,200		
Depreciable Amount	$15,000	$10,000		
Depreciable Life	10 Yrs	8 Yrs		
Depreciation Method	SL	SOYD		

Year: Relative	Year: Calendar	Depreciation Expense: Grinder	Depreciation Expense: Shaper			Total
1	1969	$1,500	$2,400			$3,900
2	1970	1,500	2,100			3,600
3	1971	1,500	1,800			3,300
4	1972	1,500	1,500			3,000
5	1973	1,500	1,200			2,700
6	1974	1,500	900			2,400
7	1975	1,500	600			2,100
8	1976	1,500	300			1,800
9	1977	1,500				1,500
10	1978	1,500				1,500
11						
12						

Table 11-3

Sample Cash Flow Table for Proposed Investment

Year	"Internal" Cash Flows	Profit Before Depreciation	Depreciation and Depletion Expense	Taxable Income	Cash Flow for Taxes @ 40%	Cash Flow After Taxes
1969	– $40,000	– $5,000	– $3,900	– $8,900	$3,560	– $41,400
1970	– 10,000	– 5,000	– 3,600	– 8,600	3,440	– 11,560
1971		-0-	– 3,300	– 3,300	1,320	1,320
1972		5,000	– 3,000	2,000	– 800	4,200
1973		10,000	– 2,700	7,300	– 2,920	7,080
1974		12,000	– 2,400	9,600	– 3,840	8,160
1975		12,000	– 2,100	9,900	– 3,960	8,040
1976		12,000	– 1,800	10,200	– 4,080	7,920
1977	5,000	8,000	– 1,500	6,500	– 2,600	10,400
1978	19,200	4,000	– 1,500	2,500	– 1,000	22,200

Comments: $5,000 of working capital committed in 1969, another $10,000 committed in 1970. $5,000 of working capital recovered in 1977; another $10,000 recovered in 1978. Assume all equipment sold in 1978 at book value.

clearly been made. *Profit before depreciation* represents the total of those cash flows which take place during the period and which affect taxable income for the period.[1] Since *depreciation and depletion* are not cash items, they are listed separately. *Taxable income* is the algebraic sum of the profit before depreciation and the depreciation expense, and *cash flow for taxes* is determined by multiplying taxable income by the appropriate incremental tax rate. Finally, *cash flow after taxes* is computed for each period by adding the internal cash flows, profit before depreciation, and cash flow for taxes. In summary form:

$$\begin{aligned}\text{Cash flow after taxes} &= [\text{cash flow before taxes}] + [\text{cash flow for taxes}]\\ &= [\text{internal cash flows}] +\\ &\quad\ [\text{cash income} - \text{cash expenses}] +\\ &\quad\ [\text{tax rate}]\cdot[(\text{profit before depreciation}) -\\ &\quad\ (\text{depreciation and depletion expenses})]\end{aligned}$$

In the example of Table 11-3, it is assumed that profit before depreciation is equal to cash income less cash expenses.

Present Worth or Rate of Return

After the cash flows have been completely specified with respect to amount and timing, the appropriate measure of attractiveness may be determined. In most cases, this measure will take the form of either net present worth or project rate of return. (Other correct measures, such as equivalent uniform annual cost, are but variants of present worth or rate of return, and thus the following discussion is suitable in these instances with only minor modification.)

Continuing the example, Table 11-4 illustrates a suggested format for determining the net present worth with an assumed interest rate of 10%. By preprinting the single payment present worth factors, subsequent calculations need not be made by someone intimately familiar with compound interest mathematics; rather, a clerk or secretary may complete the calculations by multiplying across each row and adding the figures in the last column.

In the example, the net present worth is a negative value, – $13,573, thereby indicating that the proposal is economically unacceptable with the given assumptions. The rate of return method also yields the same result since the negative present worth at 10% clearly indicates a project rate of

[1] In addition to depreciation and depletion, some items shown as income and expenses on the profit and loss statement for a given accounting period do not represent actual cash flows during the period. For example, a liability or obligation may be incurred in one period but the actual payment may not be made until some later time, in which event the accountant may note the "expense" in the earlier period. The analyst must exercise special care to insure that the appropriate distinction is made between the timing of cash flows for operations and the subsequent effect upon taxable income.

Table 11-4

Determination of Project Net Present Worth

Year	Cash Flow After Taxes and *PW* @ 0%	Present Worth Factor for $i = 10\%$	Present Worth at 10%
1	−$41,440	0.9091	−$37,673
2	− 11,560	0.8264	− 9,553
3	1,320	0.7513	992
4	4 200	0.6830	2,869
5	7,080	0.6209	4,396
6	8,160	0.5645	4,606
7	8,040	0.5132	4,126
8	7,920	0.4665	3,695
9	10,400	0.4241	4,411
10	22,200	0.3855	8,558
11		0.3505	
12		0.3186	
Total	$16,320		−$13,573

return somewhat less than 10%. The precise rate of return of the project may be determined by successive trial-and-error solutions of the equation

$$0 = \sum_{j=1}^{10} C_j(1 + i)^{-j}$$

for various values of *i*. An effective method of carrying out these rather burdensome calculations is suggested in Table 11-5 and Figure 11-1.

As in Table 11-4, the appropriate single payment present worth factors are preprinted for those interest rates most likely to be encountered, and net present worths are then computed in the usual way. The resulting present values are then plotted on a preprinted graph, the points are connected, and the project rate of return is determined by dropping a perpendicular from the zero intercept. Since the actual present worth function is convex as shown in

Table 11-5

Determination of Net Present Worths at Various Interest Rates

	0%	5%		10%		15%		20%	
0	—	1.000	—	1.0000	—	1.0000	—	1.0000	—
1	-$41,440	0.9524	-$39,467	0.9091	-$37,673	0.8696	-$36,036	0.8333	-$35,532
2	-11,560	0.9070	-10,485	0.8264	9,553	0.7561	-8,741	0.6944	-8,027
3	1,320	0.8638	1,140	0.7513	992	0.6575	868	0.5787	764
4	4,200	0.8227	3,455	0.6830	2,869	0.5718	2,402	0.4823	2,026
5	7,080	0.7835	5,547	0.6209	4,396	0.4972	3,520	0.4019	2,845
6	8,160	0.7462	6,089	0.5645	4,606	0.4323	4,428	0.3349	2,733
7	8,040	0.7107	5,714	0.5132	4,126	0.3759	3,022	0.2791	2,244
8	7,920	0.6768	5,360	0.4665	3,695	0.3269	2,589	0.2326	1,842
9	10,400	0.6446	6,704	0.4241	4,411	0.2843	2,957	0.1938	2,016
10	22,200	0.6139	13,629	0.3855	8,558	0.2472	5,488	0.1615	3,585
11		0.5847		0.3505		0.2149		0.1346	
12		0.5568		0.3186		0.1869		0.1122	
Total:	$16,320		-$2,314		-$13,573		-$19,503		-$25,504

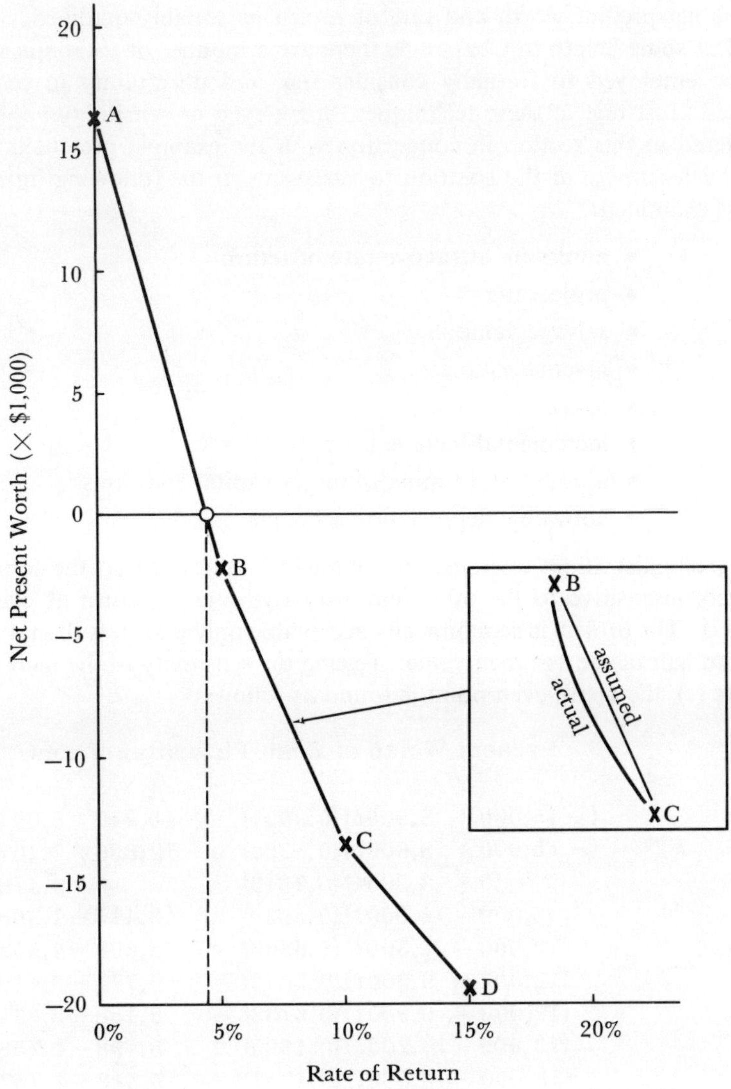

Fig. 11-1. Graphic solution of project rate of return.

Figure 11-1, the solution resulting from this graphic form of linear interpolation is only approximate. The inaccuracy is generally tolerable, however, especially in view of the advantage gained by clerical simplicity.

Risk and Uncertainty

Because of the unavoidable uncertainty associated with estimates of future events, it is desirable, if not essential, that measures of attractiveness such as net present worth and rate of return be suitably qualified. As discussed at some length in Chapter 9, there are a number of techniques which may be employed to formally consider risk and uncertainty in economic analyses. Just one of these techniques, break-even or sensitivity analysis, is considered in this section in connection with the example presented above.

The *sensitivity* of the solution to variations in the following input data may be examined:

- minimum attractive rate of return
- project life
- salvage value
- revenue estimates
- operating costs
- incremental income tax rate
- account and timing of major capital additions
- allowable depreciation schedule

By way of illustration, reference to Figure 11-1 indicates that the solution is relatively insensitive to the minimum attractive rate of return as originally specified. The project is economically acceptable only if i is less than 4.5%, or less than half of the assumed value. Testing the sensitivity to the incremental tax rate (t), the break-even point is found as follows:

Year	Present Worth of Cash Flow after Taxes	
1	$(-45{,}000 + 8{,}900t)(0.9091)$ =	$-40{,}910 + 8{,}091t$
2	$(-15{,}000 + 8{,}600t)(0.8264)$ =	$-12{,}396 + 7{,}107t$
3	$(0 + 3{,}300t)(0.7513)$ =	$0 + 2{,}479t$
4	$(5{,}000 - 2{,}000t)(0.6830)$ =	$3{,}415 - 1{,}366t$
5	$(10{,}000 - 7{,}300t)(0.6209)$ =	$6{,}209 - 4{,}532t$
6	$(12{,}000 - 9{,}600t)(0.5645)$ =	$6{,}774 - 5{,}419t$
7	$(12{,}000 - 9{,}900t)(0.5132)$ =	$6{,}158 - 5{,}081t$
8	$(12{,}000 - 10{,}200t)(0.4665)$ =	$5{,}598 - 4{,}758t$
9	$[(13{,}000 - 6{,}500t)(0.4241)]$ =	$5{,}513 - 2{,}757t$
10	$(23{,}200 - 2{,}500t)(0.3855)$ =	$8{,}944 - 964t$
	Total:	$-10{,}695 - 17{,}895t = 0$

$$\text{Thus: } t = \frac{10{,}695}{-17{,}895} = -0.6$$

Since t is a negative value, we conclude that there is no incremental income tax rate which would cause the project to be economically acceptable. The minimum possible tax rate, zero percent, will result in a negative net present worth of $10,695.

With the exception of those parameters which obviously have no effect upon the original solution, sensitivity tests should be conducted to provide decision makers with all reasonable data upon which to base decisions. The appropriate techniques should be made part of capital budgeting procedures.

Irreducibles

No analysis is complete without careful description and consideration of the irreducibles, that is, those prospective consequences of the proposal investment which cannot readily be reduced to monetary terms. In many cases a proposal will appear unattractive on the basis of its economic consequences, but it will be approved because of the favorable aspects of the irreducibles. It is frequently advisable to list by category most relevant irreducibles when prescribing capital budgeting procedures. This check list has the effect of insuring that certain important consequences will be considered in the final decision.

THE CAPITAL BUDGETING LEVEL

In general, decisions at the capital budgeting level are concerned with allocation of limited capital among an array of investment proposals, each of which has been evaluated at the design level and found to be economically justifiable. All prospective consequences have been described and evaluated, the amount and timing of pre-tax and post-tax cash flows have been determined, and net present worths (or project rates of return) are available for contending projects. The problem is now one of determining the optimum capital budget.

Under Conditions of Fixed Capital Available

If a specified capital structure is available — that is, the available amounts of debt and equity capital are fixed — the capital allocation problem is one of determining which investment strategy will maximize the net present value of the firm. This is to say that a combination of alternative investment proposals should be selected which, within the constraint of the capital available, will affect the equivalent present worth of the firm more positively than any other combination of investments. The appropriate discounting rate will directly reflect the given capital structure.

To illustrate this view, refer to Figure 11-2a. Here we indicate the functional relationship between increase in present worth and total funds expended, as shown by the curves $O-A$ and $O-B$. Point C represents the total amount of funds available; D represents the total amount of funds which

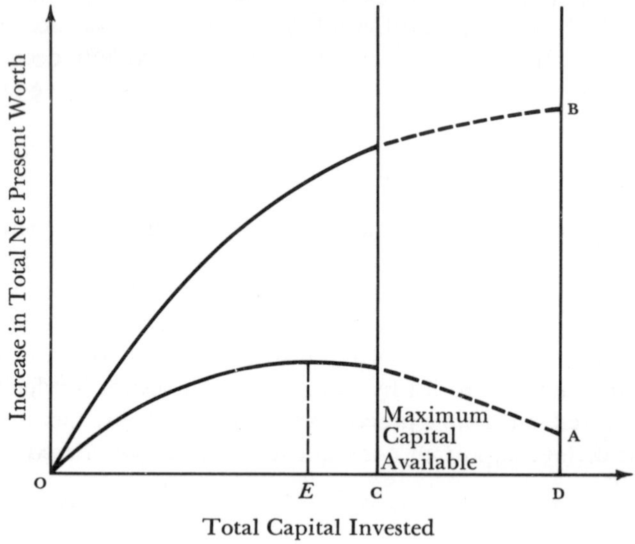

Fig. 11-2a. Investment strategy with fixed funds available.

would be required in order to accept *all* the alternatives under consideration. Presumably, but not necessarily, the available budget (supply) will be something less than the total funds required (demand). The curve $O-A$ illustrates the case in which the increase in total net present worth may be obtained at a level of expenditure (E) somewhat less than the total capital available. The more usual case, however, is represented by the curve $O - B$, that is, the value of contending investments is such that the optimal strategy requires expenditure of all available funds. This would be especially true in those instances where preselection based upon economic analysis takes place at the design level.

As one approach to the choice of the optimal combination of projects, we may consider the problem to be one of selection from among multiple alternatives, where each alternative is represented by a "package," or combination, of projects. To illustrate, consider the three alternatives, *A*, *B*, and *C*, discussed in Chapter 5:

Alternative	Initial Cost	Net Present Worth
A	$10,000	$1,982
B	20,000	2,934
C	50,000	4,832

As before, let us assume that the projects are not technically mutually exclusive and that only $75,000 is available for investment. Thus there are eight "packages," or investment strategies, which may be considered:

Package	Alternatives	Initial Cost	Net Present Worth
I	do nothing	0	0
II	A	$10,000	$1,982
III	B	20,000	2,934
IV	C	50,000	4,832
V	AB	30,000	4,916
VI	AC	60,000	6,814
VII	BC	70,000	7,766
VIII	ABC	80,000	9,748

As shown graphically in Figure 11-2b, the optimal strategy is represented by package VII, the selection of ALTERNATIVES B and C.

When using the rate of return method in conjunction with this "package" formulation of the problem, care should be taken to insure that alternative strategies are not ranked in descending order of rates of return. Rather, alternative budget packages should be established, the cost of each being equal to or less than the total capital available. Then the optimal package is selected by successive examination of incremental rates of return.

A second error, discussed in Chapter 5, may arise due to preliminary selection from among technically mutually exclusive alternatives at the design

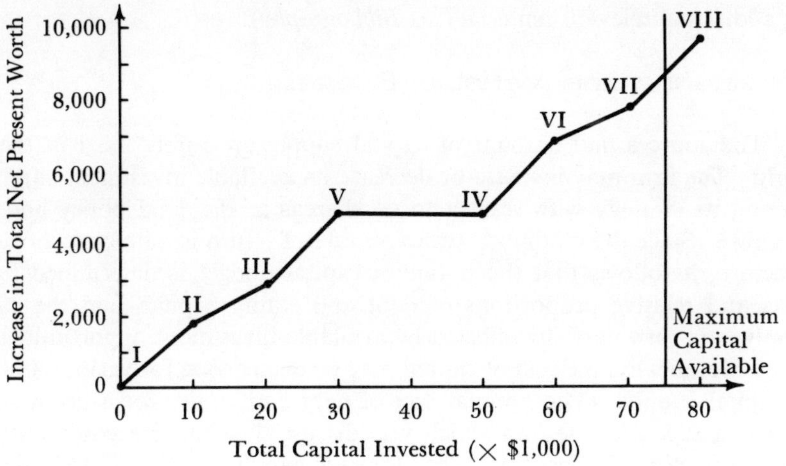

Fig. 11-2b. Investment strategy using example from text.

level. For example, Machine M1 may not be as economically attractive as a more expensive but technically equivalent Machine M2, so M2 is recommended to the capital budgeting level for inclusion in the final budget. However, it is possible that acceptance of M2 may preclude another alternative, Facility F, and acceptance of the less expensive Machine M1 will allow Facility F also to be included in the budget. If M1 and F together are more desirable than M2 alone, this fact will be obscured unless data regarding the temporarily rejected alternatives are also forwarded to the capital budgeting level. Care should be taken to avoid the "preselection error" whenever possible, although this is a problem which is extremely difficult to avoid in practice. Obviously, *all* technically equivalent alternatives cannot be considered at *all* review levels. Since some preselection must take place, it is suggested that particular attention be paid to those alternatives which are relatively expensive or otherwise affect the capital budget significantly.

It should be noted that the "package" formulation as discussed here and in Chapter 5 is especially useful when the rate of return method is employed in the solution of the capital budgeting problem, but it is relatively inefficient when the net present worth is used as the criterion measure.[2] In the latter event, the "package" formulation requires evaluation of 2^n packages when considering n projects. For example, if only ten projects are being considered in the capital budget, then as many as 1,024 separate packages must be evaluated. Fortunately, however, there are certain of the mathematical methods of operations research, such as linear and integer programming, and dynamic programming, that may be used to select the optimal combination of projects in an efficient manner; that is, all possible combinations need not be evaluated. A further discussion of these techniques is beyond the scope of this text. The interested reader is referred to the excellent article by Weingartner for additional relevant material (*see Bibliography*).

Considering the Variable Budget

The sources and amount of capital supply are rarely fixed in the real world. The firm may increase or decrease its available investment capital by altering its strategy with respect to such areas as dividend policy and debt structure. Since the minimum attractive rate of return is a function of capital structure, it follows that the optimum capital budget is determined by the costs and relative proportions of debt and equity capital, and the capital supply is in turn partially affected by available investment opportunities.

Theoretically, the cost of capital may be determined for various amounts of capital supply. (The optimal mix of debt and equity for a given supply level is a separate question which was discussed in the preceding chapter.) Then the optimal budget "package" for each supply level is selected using the appropriate minimum attractive rate of return for that level and, finally, that

[2] The essential difference here is the hierarchical character of the criterion measure, that is, the appropriateness of using the criterion measure as an index to *rank* alternatives.

combination of capital supply and demand resulting in the maximum net present worth is established in the final capital budget.

Figure 11-3 is a graphic illustration of this concept. The amount of available investment funds may be increased by withholding dividends and/or

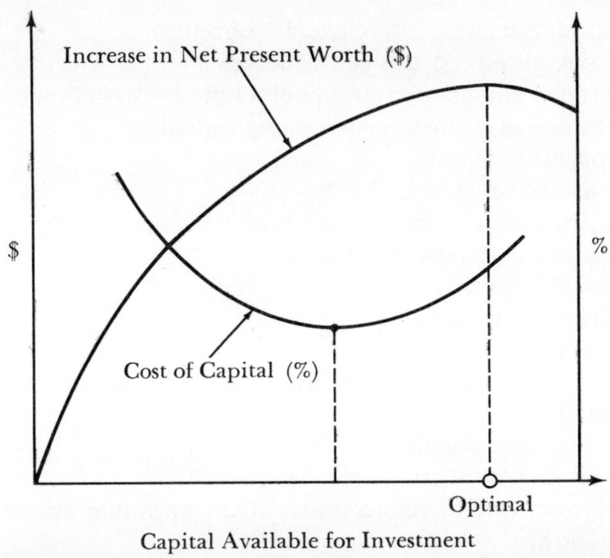

Fig. 11-3. Optimal level of capital investment.

adding relatively inexpensive debt capital, thereby lowering the over-all (weighted average) cost of capital up to a certain point, but the over-all cost begins to rise as lenders recognize the weakened capital structure of the firm and attractive investment opportunities become more scarce. Associated with each cost of capital is a potential increase in the firm's net present worth which is expected to occur at that level of investment. Available capital, a direct function of leverage, should be increased up to the point where the marginal increment no longer adds to the equivalent present value of the firm.

As a practical matter, variations in capital supply are generally quite small over the short term, and it may be reasonable to assume a fixed capital structure when planning the capital budget. Budgeting procedures are considerably simplified, of course, if the assumption of fixed capital supply appears reasonable.

SUMMARY

Because of the difference in emphasis and variations in procedures, it is fruitful to distinguish between capital allocation decisions at the design level and the capital budgeting level. In general, design level decisions are concerned with selection from among technically mutually exclusive alternatives; decisions at the capital budgeting level are concerned with selection from among technically independent alternatives competing for limited investment funds. The procedures are summarized as follows:

A. Design level
   1. Establish minimum attractive rate of return
   2. Describe all prospective consequences
   3. Determine amount and timing of all pre-tax cash flows
      a. capital investment and working capital
      b. operating results
      c. salvage value
   4. Describe depreciation (or depletion) schedule
   5. Determine cash flows after taxes
      a. taxable income
      b. incremental tax rate
      c. cash flows for taxes
   6. Determine measure of effectiveness (present worth, rate of return, etc.)
   7. Compare with criteria
      a. net present worth greater than zero?
      b. project rate of return greater than minimum attractive rate of return?
   8. Formally consider risk and uncertainty
   9. Consider irreducibles prior to decision

B. Capital budgeting level
   1. For fixed capital supply:
      a. determine cost of capital for given capital structure
      b. either select from among multiple alternatives by:
         1) defining mutually exclusive budget "packages"
         2) and selecting optimal package, or
      c. select optimal combination of projects by applying
         1) linear programming, integer programming algorithm, or
         2) dynamic programming
   2. For variable capital supply:
      a. determine cost of capital for each budget level
      b. using this cost of capital, determine optimal combination of projects and total contribution of this strategy to net present value of the firm
      c. select that combination of investment level and projects resulting in maximum net present value.

GLOSSARY

A	uniform, period-by-period, end of period series
$\bar{A}$	cash flows taking place continuously during each and every period from the first through the Nth period
a_j	depreciation *rate* in year j (no subscript if constant for all j)
B	total book value of the firm
b_j	book value of the individual asset at the end of the jth year
C	first cost of proposal (initial investment)
D	market value of long-term debt
d_j	depreciation *charge* in jth year
$\hat{E}$	total after-tax earnings available for owners and lenders
E	annual net earnings (after taxes and interest payments)
E'	annual taxable income (before taxes but after interest payments)
$\mathcal{E}$	expected after-tax earnings per share (but before personal income taxes)
$\mathcal{E}_c$	current after-tax earnings per share
e	exponential $\simeq 2.8$
F	future sum at the end of N periods
$\bar{F}$	cash flow taking place continuously during the Nth period
f	federal income tax rate
G	gradient (uniform increase or decrease in cash flow)
I'	interest charges on borrowed funds (before taxes)
I	interest charges on borrowed funds (after taxes)
i	effective interest rate per interest period (also the minimum attractive rate of return and the project rate of return)
i'	effective interest rate per year
j	index for number of interest periods
K	number of sequential replacements
k_d	average interest rate paid on long-term debt (after corporate income taxes)

k'_d	average interest rate paid on long-term debt (before corporate income taxes)
k_e	equity capitalization rate (after corporate income taxes)
k_{ep}	equity capitalization rate (after corporate and personal income taxes)
k_o	over-all cost of capital (after corporate income taxes)
k'_o	over-all cost of capital (before corporate income taxes)
L	net salvage value
L_a	*expected* (or actual) salvage value
L_d	salvage value used for *depreciation* purposes
M	number of compounding periods per year (also total market value of firm's equity)
$\mathfrak{M}$	market value per share of common stock
N	number of interest periods
N_a	*expected* (or actual) life of project
N_d	life of project used for *depreciation* purposes
P or PW	equivalent present worth of current and/or future sums
$\bar{P}$	cash flow taking place continuously during the first of N periods
$\mathcal{P}$	net proceeds per share resulting from the sale of new equity
Q	number of shares outstanding
r	nominal interest rate per year
s	state income tax rate
t	corporate income tax rate
t_p	personal income tax rate
V	total value of the firm
w_1	relative proportion of equity in capital structure
w_2	relative proportion of debt in capital structure
λ	leverage = ratio of debt to total market value
α	Hurwicz "index of optimism"

APPENDIX: COMPOUND INTEREST TABLES

The following interest rates are included in these tables:

.005	.055	.11	.25
.01	.06	.12	.30
.015	.065	.13	.35
.02	.07	.14	.40
.025	.075	.15	.45
.03	.08	.16	.50
.035	.085	.17	
.04	.09	.18	
.045	.095	.19	
.05	.10	.20	

N	SINGLE PAYMENT			UNIFORM	
	COMPOUND AMOUNT	PRESENT WORTH		COMPOUND	AMOUNT
	CA	PW	CPW	SCA	CSCA
1	1.005	.9950	.9975	1.000	1.002
2	1.010	.9901	.9925	2.005	2.010
3	1.015	.9851	.9876	3.015	3.023
4	1.020	.9802	.9827	4.030	4.040
5	1.025	.9754	.9778	5.050	5.063
6	1.030	.9705	.9729	6.076	6.091
7	1.036	.9657	.9681	7.106	7.124
8	1.041	.9609	.9633	8.141	8.162
9	1.046	.9561	.9585	9.182	9.205
10	1.051	.9513	.9537	10.228	10.254
11	1.056	.9466	.9490	11.279	11.307
12	1.062	.9419	.9443	12.336	12.366
13	1.067	.9372	.9396	13.397	13.431
14	1.072	.9326	.9349	14.464	14.500
15	1.078	.9279	.9302	15.537	15.575
16	1.083	.9233	.9256	16.614	16.656
17	1.088	.9187	.9210	17.697	17.742
18	1.094	.9141	.9164	18.786	18.833
19	1.099	.9096	.9119	19.880	19.929
20	1.105	.9051	.9073	20.979	21.032
21	1.110	.9006	.9028	22.084	22.139
22	1.116	.8961	.8983	23.194	23.252
23	1.122	.8916	.8938	24.310	24.371
24	1.127	.8872	.8894	25.432	25.495
25	1.133	.8828	.8850	26.559	26.625
26	1.138	.8784	.8806	27.692	27.761
27	1.144	.8740	.8762	28.830	28.902
28	1.150	.8697	.8718	29.975	30.049
29	1.156	.8653	.8675	31.124	31.202
30	1.161	.8610	.8632	32.280	32.361
31	1.167	.8567	.8589	33.441	33.525
32	1.173	.8525	.8546	34.609	34.695
33	1.179	.8482	.8504	35.782	35.87
34	1.185	.8440	.8461	36.961	37.05
35	1.191	.8398	.8419	38.145	38.24
40	1.221	.8191	.8212	44.159	44.269
45	1.252	.7990	.8010	50.324	50.450
50	1.283	.7793	.7812	56.645	56.787
55	1.316	.7601	.7620	63.126	63.283
60	1.349	.7414	.7432	69.770	69.944
65	1.383	.7231	.7249	76.582	76.773
70	1.418	.7053	.7071	83.566	83.775
80	1.490	.6710	.6727	98.068	98.313
90	1.567	.6383	.6399	113.311	113.594
100	1.647	.6073	.6088	129.334	129.657

I= .00500

ANNUAL SERIES				GRADIENT SERIES		
PRESENT WORTH		SINKING FUND	CAPITAL RECOVERY	UNIFORM SERIES	PRESENT WORTH	N
PW	CSPW	SF	CR	GUS	GPW	
.995	.998	1.00000	1.00500	.000	.000	1
1.985	1.990	.49875	.50375	.499	.990	2
2.970	2.978	.33167	.33667	.997	2.960	3
3.950	3.960	.24813	.25313	1.494	5.901	4
4.926	4.938	.19801	.20301	1.990	9.803	5
5.896	5.911	.16460	.16960	2.485	14.655	6
6.862	6.879	.14073	.14573	2.980	20.449	7
7.823	7.843	.12283	.12783	3.474	27.176	8
8.779	8.801	.10891	.11391	3.967	34.824	9
9.730	9.755	.09777	.10277	4.459	43.386	10
10.677	10.704	.08866	.09366	4.950	52.853	11
11.619	11.648	.08107	.08607	5.441	63.214	12
12.556	12.588	.07464	.07964	5.930	74.460	13
13.489	13.522	.06914	.07414	6.419	86.583	14
14.417	14.453	.06436	.06936	6.907	99.574	15
15.340	15.378	.06019	.06519	7.394	113.424	16
16.259	16.299	.05651	.06151	7.880	128.123	17
17.173	17.216	.05323	.05823	8.366	143.663	18
18.082	18.128	.05030	.05530	8.850	160.036	19
18.987	19.035	.04767	.05267	9.334	177.232	20
19.888	19.938	.04528	.05028	9.817	195.243	21
20.784	20.836	.04311	.04811	10.299	214.061	22
21.676	21.730	.04113	.04613	10.781	233.677	23
22.563	22.619	.03932	.04432	11.261	254.082	24
23.446	23.504	.03765	.04265	11.741	275.269	25
24.324	24.385	.03611	.04111	12.220	297.228	26
25.198	25.261	.03469	.03969	12.698	319.952	27
26.068	26.133	.03336	.03836	13.175	343.433	28
26.933	27.000	.03213	.03713	13.651	367.663	29
27.794	27.863	.03098	.03598	14.126	392.632	30
28.651	28.722	.02990	.03490	14.601	418.335	31
29.503	29.577	.02889	.03389	15.075	444.762	32
30.352	30.427	.02795	.03295	15.548	471.906	33
31.196	31.273	.02706	.03206	16.020	499.758	34
32.035	32.115	.02622	.03122	16.492	528.312	35
36.172	36.263	.02265	.02765	18.836	681.335	40
40.207	40.308	.01987	.02487	21.159	850.763	45
44.143	44.253	.01765	.02265	23.462	1035.697	50
47.981	48.101	.01584	.02084	25.745	1235.269	55
51.726	51.855	.01433	.01933	28.006	1448.646	60
55.377	55.516	.01306	.01806	30.247	1675.027	65
58.939	59.087	.01197	.01697	32.468	1913.643	70
65.802	65.967	.01020	.01520	36.847	2424.645	80
72.331	72.512	.00883	.01383	41.145	2976.077	90
78.543	78.739	.00773	.01273	45.361	3562.793	100

N	SINGLE PAYMENT			UNIFORM	
	COMPOUND AMOUNT	PRESENT WORTH		COMPOUND AMOUNT	
	CA	PW	CPW	SCA	CSCA
1	1.010	.9901	.9950	1.000	1.005
2	1.020	.9803	.9852	2.010	2.020
3	1.030	.9706	.9754	3.030	3.045
4	1.041	.9610	.9658	4.060	4.081
5	1.051	.9515	.9562	5.101	5.126
6	1.062	.9420	.9467	6.152	6.183
7	1.072	.9327	.9374	7.214	7.250
8	1.083	.9235	.9281	8.286	8.327
9	1.094	.9143	.9189	9.369	9.415
10	1.105	.9053	.9098	10.462	10.514
11	1.116	.8963	.9008	11.567	11.625
12	1.127	.8874	.8919	12.683	12.746
13	1.138	.8787	.8830	13.809	13.878
14	1.149	.8700	.8743	14.947	15.022
15	1.161	.8613	.8656	16.097	16.177
16	1.173	.8528	.8571	17.258	17.344
17	1.184	.8444	.8486	18.430	18.522
18	1.196	.8360	.8402	19.615	19.713
19	1.208	.8277	.8319	20.811	20.915
20	1.220	.8195	.8236	22.019	22.129
21	1.232	.8114	.8155	23.239	23.355
22	1.245	.8034	.8074	24.472	24.594
23	1.257	.7954	.7994	25.716	25.845
24	1.270	.7876	.7915	26.973	27.108
25	1.282	.7798	.7837	28.243	28.384
26	1.295	.7720	.7759	29.526	29.673
27	1.308	.7644	.7682	30.821	30.975
28	1.321	.7568	.7606	32.129	32.289
29	1.335	.7493	.7531	33.450	33.617
30	1.348	.7419	.7456	34.785	34.959
31	1.361	.7346	.7382	36.133	36.313
32	1.375	.7273	.7309	37.494	37.681
33	1.389	.7201	.7237	38.869	39.063
34	1.403	.7130	.7165	40.258	40.459
35	1.417	.7059	.7094	41.660	41.868
40	1.489	.6717	.6750	48.886	49.130
45	1.565	.6391	.6422	56.481	56.763
50	1.645	.6080	.6111	64.463	64.785
55	1.729	.5785	.5814	72.852	73.216
60	1.817	.5504	.5532	81.670	82.077
65	1.909	.5237	.5263	90.937	91.391
70	2.007	.4983	.5008	100.676	101.179
80	2.217	.4511	.4534	121.672	122.279
90	2.449	.4084	.4104	144.863	145.586
100	2.705	.3697	.3716	170.481	171.332

I= .01000

ANNUAL SERIES				GRADIENT SERIES		
PRESENT WORTH		SINKING FUND	CAPITAL RECOVERY	UNIFORM SERIES	PRESENT WORTH	N
PW	CSPW	SF	CR	GUS	GPW	
.990	.995	1.00000	1.01000	.000	.000	1
1.970	1.980	.49751	.50751	.498	.980	2
2.941	2.956	.33002	.34002	.993	2.921	3
3.902	3.921	.24628	.25628	1.488	5.804	4
4.853	4.878	.19604	.20604	1.980	9.610	5
5.795	5.824	.16255	.17255	2.471	14.321	6
6.728	6.762	.13863	.14863	2.960	19.917	7
7.652	7.690	.12069	.13069	3.448	26.381	8
8.566	8.609	.10674	.11674	3.934	33.696	9
9.471	9.519	.09558	.10558	4.418	41.843	10
10.368	10.419	.08645	.09645	4.901	50.807	11
11.255	11.311	.07885	.08885	5.381	60.569	12
12.134	12.194	.07241	.08241	5.861	71.113	13
13.004	13.069	.06690	.07690	6.338	82.422	14
13.865	13.934	.06212	.07212	6.814	94.481	15
14.718	14.791	.05794	.06794	7.289	107.273	16
15.562	15.640	.05426	.06426	7.761	120.783	17
16.398	16.480	.05098	.06098	8.232	134.996	18
17.226	17.312	.04805	.05805	8.702	149.895	19
18.046	18.136	.04542	.05542	9.169	165.466	20
18.857	18.951	.04303	.05303	9.635	181.695	21
19.660	19.759	.04086	.05086	10.100	198.566	22
20.456	20.558	.03889	.04889	10.563	216.066	23
21.243	21.349	.03707	.04707	11.024	234.180	24
22.023	22.133	.03541	.04541	11.483	252.894	25
22.795	22.909	.03387	.04387	11.941	272.196	26
23.560	23.677	.03245	.04245	12.397	292.070	27
24.316	24.438	.03112	.04112	12.852	312.505	28
25.066	25.191	.02990	.03990	13.304	333.486	29
25.808	25.937	.02875	.03875	13.756	355.002	30
26.542	26.675	.02768	.03768	14.205	377.039	31
27.270	27.406	.02667	.03667	14.653	399.586	32
27.990	28.129	.02573	.03573	15.099	422.629	33
28.703	28.846	.02484	.03484	15.544	446.157	34
29.409	29.555	.02400	.03400	15.987	470.158	35
32.835	32.999	.02046	.03046	18.178	596.856	40
36.095	36.275	.01771	.02771	20.327	733.704	45
39.196	39.392	.01551	.02551	22.436	879.418	50
42.147	42.358	.01373	.02373	24.505	1032.815	55
44.955	45.179	.01224	.02224	26.533	1192.806	60
47.627	47.864	.01100	.02100	28.522	1358.390	65
50.169	50.419	.00993	.01993	30.470	1528.647	70
54.888	55.162	.00822	.01822	34.249	1879.877	80
59.161	59.456	.00690	.01690	37.872	2240.567	90
63.029	63.344	.00587	.01587	41.343	2605.776	100

N	SINGLE PAYMENT			UNIFORM	
	COMPOUND AMOUNT	PRESENT WORTH		COMPOUND	AMOUNT
	CA	PW	CPW	SCA	CSCA
1	1.015	.9852	.9926	1.000	1.007
2	1.030	.9707	.9779	2.015	2.030
3	1.046	.9563	.9635	3.045	3.068
4	1.061	.9422	.9492	4.091	4.122
5	1.077	.9283	.9352	5.152	5.191
6	1.093	.9145	.9214	6.230	6.276
7	1.110	.9010	.9078	7.323	7.378
8	1.126	.8877	.8944	8.433	8.496
9	1.143	.8746	.8811	9.559	9.631
10	1.161	.8617	.8681	10.703	10.783
11	1.178	.8489	.8553	11.863	11.952
12	1.196	.8364	.8426	13.041	13.139
13	1.214	.8240	.8302	14.237	14.343
14	1.232	.8118	.8179	15.450	15.566
15	1.250	.7999	.8058	16.682	16.807
16	1.269	.7880	.7939	17.932	18.067
17	1.288	.7764	.7822	19.201	19.345
18	1.307	.7649	.7706	20.489	20.643
19	1.327	.7536	.7592	21.797	21.960
20	1.347	.7425	.7480	23.124	23.297
21	1.367	.7315	.7370	24.471	24.654
22	1.388	.7207	.7261	25.838	26.031
23	1.408	.7100	.7153	27.225	27.429
24	1.430	.6995	.7048	28.634	28.848
25	1.451	.6892	.6944	30.063	30.288
26	1.473	.6790	.6841	31.514	31.750
27	1.495	.6690	.6740	32.987	33.233
28	1.517	.6591	.6640	34.481	34.739
29	1.540	.6494	.6542	35.999	36.268
30	1.563	.6398	.6445	37.539	37.820
31	1.587	.6303	.6350	39.102	39.394
32	1.610	.6210	.6256	40.688	40.993
33	1.634	.6118	.6164	42.299	42.615
34	1.659	.6028	.6073	43.933	44.262
35	1.684	.5939	.5983	45.592	45.933
40	1.814	.5513	.5554	54.268	54.674
45	1.954	.5117	.5155	63.614	64.090
50	2.105	.4750	.4786	73.683	74.234
55	2.268	.4409	.4442	84.530	85.162
60	2.443	.4093	.4124	96.215	96.934
65	2.632	.3799	.3828	108.803	109.617
70	2.835	.3527	.3553	122.364	123.279
80	3.291	.3039	.3062	152.711	153.853
90	3.819	.2619	.2638	187.930	189.336
100	4.432	.2256	.2273	228.803	230.515

I= .01500

ANNUAL SERIES				GRADIENT SERIES		
PRESENT WORTH		SINKING FUND	CAPITAL RECOVERY	UNIFORM SERIES	PRESENT WORTH	N
PW	CSPW	SF	CR	GUS	GPW	
.985	.993	1.00000	1.01500	.000	.000	1
1.956	1.971	.49628	.51128	.496	.971	2
2.912	2.934	.32838	.34338	.990	2.883	3
3.854	3.883	.24444	.25944	1.481	5.710	4
4.783	4.818	.19409	.20909	1.970	9.423	5
5.697	5.740	.16053	.17553	2.457	13.996	6
6.598	6.648	.13656	.15156	2.940	19.402	7
7.486	7.542	.11858	.13358	3.422	25.616	8
8.361	8.423	.10461	.11961	3.901	32.612	9
9.222	9.291	.09343	.10843	4.377	40.367	10
10.071	10.146	.08429	.09929	4.851	48.857	11
10.908	10.989	.07668	.09168	5.323	58.057	12
11.732	11.819	.07024	.08524	5.792	67.945	13
12.543	12.637	.06472	.07972	6.258	78.499	14
13.343	13.443	.05994	.07494	6.722	89.697	15
14.131	14.237	.05577	.07077	7.184	101.518	16
14.908	15.019	.05208	.06708	7.643	113.940	17
15.673	15.790	.04881	.06381	8.100	126.943	18
16.426	16.549	.04588	.06088	8.554	140.508	19
17.169	17.297	.04325	.05825	9.006	154.615	20
17.900	18.034	.04087	.05587	9.455	169.245	21
18.621	18.760	.03870	.05370	9.902	184.380	22
19.331	19.475	.03673	.05173	10.346	200.001	23
20.030	20.180	.03492	.04992	10.788	216.090	24
20.720	20.875	.03326	.04826	11.228	232.631	25
21.399	21.559	.03173	.04673	11.665	249.607	26
22.068	22.233	.03032	.04532	12.099	267.000	27
22.727	22.897	.02900	.04400	12.531	284.796	28
23.376	23.551	.02778	.04278	12.961	302.978	29
24.016	24.196	.02664	.04164	13.388	321.531	30
24.646	24.831	.02557	.04057	13.813	340.440	31
25.267	25.456	.02458	.03958	14.236	359.691	32
25.879	26.073	.02364	.03864	14.656	379.269	33
26.482	26.680	.02276	.03776	15.073	399.161	34
27.076	27.278	.02193	.03693	15.488	419.352	35
29.916	30.140	.01843	.03343	17.528	524.357	40
32.552	32.796	.01572	.03072	19.507	635.011	45
35.000	35.262	.01357	.02857	21.428	749.964	50
37.271	37.550	.01183	.02683	23.289	868.028	55
39.380	39.675	.01039	.02539	25.093	988.167	60
41.338	41.647	.00919	.02419	26.839	1109.475	65
43.155	43.478	.00817	.02317	28.529	1231.166	70
46.407	46.755	.00655	.02155	31.742	1473.074	80
49.210	49.578	.00532	.02032	34.740	1709.544	90
51.625	52.011	.00437	.01937	37.530	1937.451	100

N	SINGLE PAYMENT			U N I F O R M	
	COMPOUND AMOUNT	PRESENT WORTH		COMPOUND	AMOUNT
	CA	PW	CPW	SCA	CSCA
1	1.020	.9804	.9902	1.000	1.010
2	1.040	.9612	.9707	2.020	2.040
3	1.061	.9423	.9517	3.060	3.091
4	1.082	.9238	.9331	4.122	4.163
5	1.104	.9057	.9148	5.204	5.256
6	1.126	.8880	.8968	6.308	6.371
7	1.149	.8706	.8792	7.434	7.508
8	1.172	.8535	.8620	8.583	8.669
9	1.195	.8368	.8451	9.755	9.852
10	1.219	.8203	.8285	10.950	11.059
11	1.243	.8043	.8123	12.169	12.290
12	1.268	.7885	.7964	13.412	13.546
13	1.294	.7730	.7807	14.680	14.827
14	1.319	.7579	.7654	15.974	16.133
15	1.346	.7430	.7504	17.293	17.466
16	1.373	.7284	.7357	18.639	18.825
17	1.400	.7142	.7213	20.012	20.212
18	1.428	.7002	.7071	21.412	21.626
19	1.457	.6864	.6933	22.841	23.068
20	1.486	.6730	.6797	24.297	24.540
21	1.516	.6598	.6664	25.783	26.040
22	1.546	.6468	.6533	27.299	27.571
23	1.577	.6342	.6405	28.845	29.132
24	1.608	.6217	.6279	30.422	30.725
25	1.641	.6095	.6156	32.030	32.350
26	1.673	.5976	.6035	33.671	34.007
27	1.707	.5859	.5917	35.344	35.697
28	1.741	.5744	.5801	37.051	37.420
29	1.776	.5631	.5687	38.792	39.179
30	1.811	.5521	.5576	40.568	40.972
31	1.848	.5412	.5466	42.379	42.802
32	1.885	.5306	.5359	44.227	44.668
33	1.922	.5202	.5254	46.112	46.571
34	1.961	.5100	.5151	48.034	48.513
35	2.000	.5000	.5050	49.994	50.493
40	2.208	.4529	.4574	60.402	61.004
45	2.438	.4102	.4143	71.893	72.609
50	2.692	.3715	.3752	84.579	85.422
55	2.972	.3365	.3399	98.587	99.569
60	3.281	.3048	.3078	114.052	115.188
65	3.623	.2761	.2788	131.126	132.433
70	4.000	.2500	.2525	149.978	151.473
80	4.875	.2051	.2072	193.772	195.703
90	5.943	.1683	.1699	247.157	249.620
100	7.245	.1380	.1394	312.232	315.344

I = .02000

ANNUAL SERIES				GRADIENT SERIES		
PRESENT WORTH		SINKING FUND	CAPITAL RECOVERY	UNIFORM SERIES	PRESENT WORTH	N
PW	CSPW	SF	CR	GUS	GPW	
.980	.990	1.00000	1.02000	.000	.000	1
1.942	1.961	.49505	.51505	.495	.961	2
2.884	2.913	.32675	.34675	.987	2.846	3
3.808	3.846	.24262	.26262	1.475	5.617	4
4.713	4.760	.19216	.21216	1.960	9.240	5
5.601	5.657	.15853	.17853	2.442	13.680	6
6.472	6.536	.13451	.15451	2.921	18.903	7
7.325	7.398	.11651	.13651	3.396	24.878	8
8.162	8.244	.10252	.12252	3.868	31.572	9
8.983	9.072	.09133	.11133	4.337	38.955	10
9.787	9.884	.08218	.10218	4.802	46.998	11
10.575	10.681	.07456	.09456	5.264	55.671	12
11.348	11.461	.06812	.08812	5.723	64.948	13
12.106	12.227	.06260	.08260	6.179	74.800	14
12.849	12.977	.05783	.07783	6.631	85.202	15
13.578	13.713	.05365	.07365	7.080	96.129	16
14.292	14.434	.04997	.06997	7.526	107.555	17
14.992	15.141	.04670	.06670	7.968	119.458	18
15.678	15.835	.04378	.06378	8.407	131.814	19
16.351	16.514	.04116	.06116	8.843	144.600	20
17.011	17.181	.03878	.05878	9.276	157.796	21
17.658	17.834	.03663	.05663	9.705	171.379	22
18.292	18.475	.03467	.05467	10.132	185.331	23
18.914	19.102	.03287	.05287	10.555	199.630	24
19.523	19.718	.03122	.05122	10.974	214.259	25
20.121	20.322	.02970	.04970	11.391	229.199	26
20.707	20.913	.02829	.04829	11.804	244.431	27
21.281	21.493	.02699	.04699	12.214	259.939	28
21.844	22.062	.02578	.04578	12.621	275.706	29
22.396	22.620	.02465	.04465	13.025	291.716	30
22.938	23.166	.02360	.04360	13.426	307.954	31
23.468	23.702	.02261	.04261	13.823	324.403	32
23.989	24.228	.02169	.04169	14.217	341.051	33
24.499	24.743	.02082	.04082	14.608	357.882	34
24.999	25.248	.02000	.04000	14.996	374.883	35
27.355	27.628	.01656	.03656	16.889	461.993	40
29.490	29.784	.01391	.03391	18.703	551.565	45
31.424	31.737	.01182	.03182	20.442	642.361	50
33.175	33.505	.01014	.03014	22.106	733.353	55
34.761	35.107	.00877	.02877	23.696	823.698	60
36.197	36.558	.00763	.02763	25.215	912.709	65
37.499	37.872	.00667	.02667	26.663	999.834	70
39.745	40.141	.00516	.02516	29.357	1166.787	80
41.587	42.001	.00405	.02405	31.793	1322.170	90
43.098	43.528	.00320	.02320	33.986	1464.753	100

N	SINGLE PAYMENT			UNIFORM	
	COMPOUND AMOUNT	PRESENT WORTH		COMPOUND	AMOUNT
	CA	PW	CPW	SCA	CSCA
1	1.025	.9756	.9878	1.000	1.012
2	1.051	.9518	.9637	2.025	2.050
3	1.077	.9286	.9402	3.076	3.114
4	1.104	.9060	.9172	4.153	4.204
5	1.131	.8839	.8949	5.256	5.322
6	1.160	.8623	.8730	6.388	6.467
7	1.189	.8413	.8517	7.547	7.641
8	1.218	.8207	.8310	8.736	8.845
9	1.249	.8007	.8107	9.955	10.078
10	1.280	.7812	.7909	11.203	11.343
11	1.312	.7621	.7716	12.483	12.639
12	1.345	.7436	.7528	13.796	13.967
13	1.379	.7254	.7345	15.140	15.329
14	1.413	.7077	.7165	16.519	16.725
15	1.448	.6908	.6991	17.932	18.155
16	1.485	.6736	.6820	19.380	19.621
17	1.522	.6572	.6654	20.865	21.124
18	1.560	.6412	.6491	22.386	22.665
19	1.599	.6255	.6333	23.946	24.244
20	1.639	.6103	.6179	25.545	25.863
21	1.680	.5954	.6028	27.183	27.522
22	1.722	.5809	.5881	28.863	29.222
23	1.765	.5667	.5738	30.584	30.965
24	1.809	.5529	.5598	32.349	32.752
25	1.854	.5394	.5461	34.158	34.583
26	1.900	.5262	.5328	36.012	36.460
27	1.948	.5134	.5198	37.912	38.384
28	1.996	.5009	.5071	39.860	40.356
29	2.046	.4887	.4947	41.856	42.377
30	2.098	.4767	.4827	43.903	44.449
31	2.150	.4651	.4709	46.000	46.573
32	2.204	.4538	.4594	48.150	48.750
33	2.259	.4427	.4482	50.354	50.981
34	2.315	.4319	.4373	52.613	53.268
35	2.373	.4214	.4266	54.928	55.612
40	2.685	.3724	.3771	67.403	68.242
45	3.038	.3292	.3333	81.516	82.531
50	3.437	.2909	.2946	97.484	98.698
55	3.889	.2572	.2604	115.551	116.989
60	4.400	.2273	.2301	135.992	137.684
65	4.978	.2009	.2034	159.118	161.099
70	5.632	.1776	.1798	185.284	187.591
80	7.210	.1387	.1404	248.383	251.475
90	9.229	.1084	.1097	329.154	333.252
100	11.814	.0846	.0857	432.549	437.933

I= .02500

ANNUAL SERIES				GRADIENT SERIES		
PRESENT WORTH		SINKING FUND	CAPITAL RECOVERY	UNIFORM SERIES	PRESENT WORTH	N
PW	CSPW	SF	CR	GUS	GPW	
.976	.988	1.00000	1.02500	.000	.000	1
1.927	1.951	.49383	.51883	.494	.952	2
2.856	2.892	.32514	.35014	.984	2.809	3
3.762	3.809	.24082	.26582	1.469	5.527	4
4.646	4.704	.19025	.21525	1.951	9.062	5
5.508	5.577	.15655	.18155	2.428	13.374	6
6.349	6.428	.13250	.15750	2.901	18.421	7
7.170	7.259	.11447	.13947	3.370	24.167	8
7.971	8.070	.10046	.12546	3.836	30.572	9
8.752	8.861	.08926	.11426	4.296	37.603	10
9.514	9.633	.08011	.10511	4.753	45.225	11
10.258	10.385	.07249	.09749	5.206	53.404	12
10.983	11.120	.06605	.09105	5.655	62.109	13
11.691	11.836	.06054	.08554	6.100	71.309	14
12.381	12.536	.05577	.08077	6.540	80.976	15
13.055	13.218	.05160	.07660	6.977	91.080	16
13.712	13.883	.04793	.07293	7.409	101.595	17
14.353	14.532	.04467	.06967	7.838	112.495	18
14.979	15.165	.04176	.06676	8.262	123.755	19
15.589	15.783	.03915	.06415	8.682	135.350	20
16.185	16.386	.03679	.06179	9.099	147.257	21
16.765	16.974	.03465	.05965	9.511	159.456	22
17.332	17.548	.03270	.05770	9.919	171.923	23
17.885	18.108	.03091	.05591	10.324	184.639	24
18.424	18.654	.02928	.05428	10.724	197.584	25
18.951	19.187	.02777	.05277	11.121	210.740	26
19.464	19.706	.02638	.05138	11.513	224.089	27
19.965	20.213	.02509	.05009	11.902	237.612	28
20.454	20.708	.02389	.04889	12.286	251.295	29
20.930	21.191	.02278	.04778	12.667	265.120	30
21.395	21.662	.02174	.04674	13.044	279.074	31
21.849	22.121	.02077	.04577	13.417	293.141	32
22.292	22.569	.01986	.04486	13.786	307.307	33
22.724	23.007	.01901	.04401	14.151	321.560	34
23.145	23.433	.01821	.04321	14.512	335.887	35
25.103	25.415	.01484	.03984	16.262	408.222	40
26.833	27.167	.01227	.03727	17.918	480.807	45
28.362	28.715	.01026	.03526	19.484	552.608	50
29.714	30.084	.00865	.03365	20.961	622.828	55
30.909	31.293	.00735	.03235	22.352	690.866	60
31.965	32.362	.00628	.03128	23.660	756.281	65
32.898	33.307	.00540	.03040	24.888	818.764	70
34.452	34.881	.00403	.02903	27.117	934.218	80
35.666	36.110	.00304	.02804	29.063	1036.550	90
36.614	37.070	.00231	.02731	30.752	1125.975	100

N	SINGLE PAYMENT			UNIFORM	
	COMPOUND AMOUNT	PRESENT WORTH		COMPOUND	AMOUNT
	CA	PW	CPW	SCA	CSCA
1	1.030	.9709	.9854	1.000	1.015
2	1.061	.9426	.9567	2.030	2.060
3	1.093	.9151	.9288	3.091	3.137
4	1.126	.8885	.9017	4.184	4.246
5	1.159	.8626	.8755	5.309	5.388
6	1.194	.8375	.8500	6.468	6.565
7	1.230	.8131	.8252	7.662	7.777
8	1.267	.7894	.8012	8.892	9.025
9	1.305	.7664	.7779	10.159	10.311
10	1.344	.7441	.7552	11.464	11.635
11	1.384	.7224	.7332	12.808	12.999
12	1.426	.7014	.7118	14.192	14.404
13	1.469	.6810	.6911	15.618	15.851
14	1.513	.6611	.6710	17.086	17.341
15	1.558	.6419	.6514	18.599	18.877
16	1.605	.6232	.6325	20.157	20.458
17	1.653	.6050	.6140	21.762	22.086
18	1.702	.5874	.5962	23.414	23.764
19	1.754	.5703	.5788	25.117	25.492
20	1.806	.5537	.5619	26.870	27.271
21	1.860	.5375	.5456	28.676	29.105
22	1.916	.5219	.5297	30.537	30.993
23	1.974	.5067	.5143	32.453	32.937
24	2.033	.4919	.4993	34.426	34.940
25	2.094	.4776	.4847	36.459	37.003
26	2.157	.4637	.4706	38.553	39.128
27	2.221	.4502	.4569	40.710	41.317
28	2.288	.4371	.4436	42.931	43.572
29	2.357	.4243	.4307	45.219	45.894
30	2.427	.4120	.4181	47.575	48.286
31	2.500	.4000	.4060	50.003	50.749
32	2.575	.3883	.3941	52.503	53.286
33	2.652	.3770	.3827	55.078	55.900
34	2.732	.3660	.3715	57.730	58.592
35	2.814	.3554	.3607	60.462	61.365
40	3.262	.3066	.3111	75.401	76.527
45	3.782	.2644	.2684	92.720	94.104
50	4.384	.2281	.2315	112.797	114.480
55	5.082	.1968	.1997	136.072	138.103
60	5.892	.1697	.1723	163.053	165.487
65	6.830	.1464	.1486	194.333	197.233
70	7.918	.1263	.1282	230.594	234.036
80	10.641	.0940	.0954	321.363	326.160
90	14.300	.0699	.0710	443.349	449.966
100	19.219	.0520	.0528	607.288	616.352

I= .03000

ANNUAL SERIES				GRADIENT SERIES		
PRESENT WORTH		SINKING FUND	CAPITAL RECOVERY	UNIFORM SERIES	PRESENT WORTH	N
PW	CSPW	SF	CR	GUS	GPW	
.971	.985	1.00000	1.03000	.000	.000	1
1.913	1.942	.49261	.52261	.493	.943	2
2.829	2.871	.32353	.35353	.980	2.773	3
3.717	3.773	.23903	.26903	1.463	5.438	4
4.580	4.648	.18835	.21835	1.941	8.889	5
5.417	5.498	.15460	.18460	2.414	13.076	6
6.230	6.323	.13051	.16051	2.882	17.955	7
7.020	7.124	.11246	.14246	3.345	23.481	8
7.786	7.902	.09843	.12843	3.803	29.612	9
8.530	8.658	.08723	.11723	4.256	36.309	10
9.253	9.391	.07808	.10808	4.705	43.533	11
9.954	10.103	.07046	.10046	5.148	51.248	12
10.635	10.794	.06403	.09403	5.587	59.420	13
11.296	11.465	.05853	.08853	6.021	68.014	14
11.938	12.116	.05377	.08377	6.450	77.000	15
12.561	12.749	.04961	.07961	6.874	86.348	16
13.166	13.363	.04595	.07595	7.294	96.028	17
13.754	13.959	.04271	.07271	7.708	106.014	18
14.324	14.538	.03981	.06981	8.118	116.279	19
14.877	15.100	.03722	.06722	8.523	126.799	20
15.415	15.645	.03487	.06487	8.923	137.550	21
15.937	16.175	.03275	.06275	9.319	148.509	22
16.444	16.689	.03081	.06081	9.709	159.657	23
16.936	17.188	.02905	.05905	10.095	170.971	24
17.413	17.673	.02743	.05743	10.477	182.434	25
17.877	18.144	.02594	.05594	10.853	194.026	26
18.327	18.601	.02456	.05456	11.226	205.731	27
18.764	19.044	.02329	.05329	11.593	217.532	28
19.188	19.475	.02211	.05211	11.956	229.414	29
19.600	19.893	.02102	.05102	12.314	241.361	30
20.000	20.299	.02000	.05000	12.668	253.361	31
20.389	20.693	.01905	.04905	13.017	265.399	32
20.766	21.076	.01816	.04816	13.362	277.464	33
21.132	21.447	.01732	.04732	13.702	289.544	34
21.487	21.808	.01654	.04654	14.037	301.627	35
23.115	23.460	.01326	.04326	15.650	361.750	40
24.519	24.885	.01079	.04079	17.156	420.632	45
25.730	26.114	.00887	.03887	18.558	477.480	50
26.774	27.174	.00735	.03735	19.860	531.741	55
27.676	28.089	.00613	.03613	21.067	583.053	60
28.453	28.878	.00515	.03515	22.184	631.201	65
29.123	29.558	.00434	.03434	23.215	676.087	70
30.201	30.652	.00311	.03311	25.035	756.087	80
31.002	31.465	.00226	.03226	26.567	823.630	90
31.599	32.071	.00165	.03165	27.844	879.854	100

N	SINGLE PAYMENT			UNIFORM	
	COMPOUND AMOUNT	PRESENT WORTH		COMPOUND	AMOUNT
	CA	PW	CPW	SCA	CSCA
1	1.035	.9662	.9830	1.000	1.017
2	1.071	.9335	.9498	2.035	2.070
3	1.109	.9019	.9176	3.106	3.160
4	1.148	.8714	.8866	4.215	4.288
5	1.188	.8420	.8566	5.362	5.456
6	1.229	.8135	.8277	6.550	6.664
7	1.272	.7860	.7997	7.779	7.915
8	1.317	.7594	.7726	9.052	9.209
9	1.363	.7337	.7465	10.368	10.549
10	1.411	.7089	.7213	11.731	11.936
11	1.460	.6849	.6969	13.142	13.371
12	1.511	.6618	.6733	14.602	14.856
13	1.564	.6394	.6505	16.113	16.393
14	1.619	.6178	.6285	17.677	17.985
15	1.675	.5969	.6073	19.296	19.631
16	1.734	.5767	.5867	20.971	21.336
17	1.795	.5572	.5669	22.705	23.100
18	1.857	.5384	.5477	24.500	24.926
19	1.923	.5202	.5292	26.357	26.816
20	1.990	.5026	.5113	28.280	28.772
21	2.059	.4856	.4940	30.269	30.796
22	2.132	.4692	.4773	32.329	32.891
23	2.206	.4533	.4612	34.460	35.060
24	2.283	.4380	.4456	36.667	37.305
25	2.363	.4231	.4305	38.950	39.628
26	2.446	.4088	.4160	41.313	42.032
27	2.532	.3950	.4019	43.759	44.520
28	2.620	.3817	.3883	46.291	47.096
29	2.712	.3687	.3752	48.911	49.762
30	2.807	.3563	.3625	51.623	52.521
31	2.905	.3442	.3502	54.429	55.377
32	3.007	.3326	.3384	57.335	58.332
33	3.112	.3213	.3269	60.341	61.391
34	3.221	.3105	.3159	63.453	64.557
35	3.334	.3000	.3052	66.674	67.834
40	3.959	.2526	.2570	84.550	86.021
45	4.702	.2127	.2164	105.782	107.622
50	5.585	.1791	.1822	130.998	133.277
55	6.633	.1508	.1534	160.947	163.747
60	7.878	.1269	.1291	196.517	199.936
65	9.357	.1069	.1087	238.763	242.917
70	11.113	.0900	.0916	288.938	293.965
80	15.676	.0638	.0649	419.307	426.603
90	22.112	.0452	.0460	603.205	613.701
100	31.191	.0321	.0326	862.612	877.621

I= .03500

ANNUAL SERIES				GRADIENT SERIES		
PRESENT WORTH		SINKING FUND	CAPITAL RECOVERY	UNIFORM SERIES	PRESENT WORTH	N
PW	CSPW	SF	CR	GUS	GPW	
.966	.983	1.00000	1.03500	.000	.000	1
1.900	1.933	.49140	.52640	.491	.934	2
2.802	2.850	.32193	.35693	.977	2.737	3
3.673	3.737	.23725	.27225	1.457	5.352	4
4.515	4.594	.18648	.22148	1.931	8.720	5
5.329	5.421	.15267	.18767	2.400	12.787	6
6.115	6.221	.12854	.16354	2.863	17.503	7
6.874	6.994	.11048	.14548	3.320	22.819	8
7.608	7.740	.09645	.13145	3.771	28.689	9
8.317	8.461	.08524	.12024	4.217	35.069	10
9.002	9.158	.07609	.11109	4.657	41.919	11
9.663	9.831	.06848	.10348	5.091	49.198	12
10.303	10.482	.06206	.09706	5.520	56.871	13
10.921	11.111	.05657	.09157	5.943	64.902	14
11.517	11.718	.05183	.08683	6.361	73.259	15
12.094	12.305	.04768	.08268	6.773	81.909	16
12.651	12.871	.04404	.07904	7.179	90.824	17
13.190	13.419	.04082	.07582	7.580	99.977	18
13.710	13.948	.03794	.07294	7.975	109.339	19
14.212	14.460	.03536	.07036	8.365	118.888	20
14.698	14.954	.03304	.06804	8.749	128.600	21
15.167	15.431	.03093	.06593	9.128	138.452	22
15.620	15.892	.02902	.06402	9.502	148.424	23
16.058	16.338	.02727	.06227	9.870	158.497	24
16.482	16.768	.02567	.06067	10.233	168.653	25
16.890	17.184	.02421	.05921	10.590	178.874	26
17.285	17.586	.02285	.05785	10.942	189.144	27
17.667	17.974	.02160	.05660	11.289	199.448	28
18.036	18.350	.02045	.05545	11.631	209.773	29
18.392	18.712	.01937	.05437	11.967	220.106	30
18.736	19.062	.01837	.05337	12.299	230.432	31
19.069	19.401	.01744	.05244	12.625	240.743	32
19.390	19.728	.01657	.05157	12.946	251.026	33
19.701	20.043	.01576	.05076	13.262	261.271	34
20.001	20.349	.01500	.05000	13.573	271.471	35
21.355	21.727	.01183	.04683	15.055	321.491	40
22.495	22.887	.00945	.04445	16.417	369.308	45
23.456	23.864	.00763	.04263	17.666	414.370	50
24.264	24.686	.00621	.04121	18.808	456.353	55
24.945	25.379	.00509	.04009	19.848	495.105	60
25.518	25.962	.00419	.03919	20.793	530.599	65
26.000	26.453	.00346	.03846	21.650	562.896	70
26.749	27.214	.00238	.03738	23.120	618.439	80
27.279	27.754	.00166	.03666	24.308	663.119	90
27.655	28.137	.00116	.03616	25.259	698.555	100

N	SINGLE PAYMENT			UNIFORM	
	COMPOUND AMOUNT	PRESENT WORTH		COMPOUND AMOUNT	
	CA	PW	CPW	SCA	CSCA
1	1.040	.9615	.9806	1.000	1.020
2	1.082	.9246	.9429	2.040	2.081
3	1.125	.8890	.9067	3.122	3.184
4	1.170	.8548	.8718	4.246	4.331
5	1.217	.8219	.8383	5.416	5.524
6	1.265	.7903	.8060	6.633	6.765
7	1.316	.7599	.7750	7.898	8.055
8	1.369	.7307	.7452	9.214	9.397
9	1.423	.7026	.7165	10.583	10.793
10	1.480	.6756	.6890	12.006	12.245
11	1.539	.6496	.6625	13.486	13.754
12	1.601	.6246	.6370	15.026	15.324
13	1.665	.6006	.6125	16.627	16.957
14	1.732	.5775	.5889	18.292	18.655
15	1.801	.5553	.5663	20.024	20.421
16	1.873	.5339	.5445	21.825	22.258
17	1.948	.5134	.5236	23.698	24.168
18	2.026	.4936	.5034	25.645	26.155
19	2.107	.4746	.4841	27.671	28.221
20	2.191	.4564	.4655	29.778	30.370
21	2.279	.4388	.4476	31.969	32.604
22	2.370	.4220	.4303	34.248	34.928
23	2.465	.4057	.4138	36.618	37.345
24	2.563	.3901	.3979	39.083	39.859
25	2.666	.3751	.3826	41.646	42.473
26	2.772	.3607	.3679	44.312	45.192
27	2.883	.3468	.3537	47.084	48.020
28	2.999	.3335	.3401	49.968	50.960
29	3.119	.3207	.3270	52.966	54.019
30	3.243	.3083	.3144	56.085	57.199
31	3.373	.2965	.3024	59.328	60.507
32	3.508	.2851	.2907	62.701	63.947
33	3.648	.2741	.2795	66.210	67.525
34	3.794	.2636	.2688	69.858	71.246
35	3.946	.2534	.2585	73.652	75.116
40	4.801	.2083	.2124	95.026	96.914
45	5.841	.1712	.1746	121.029	123.434
50	7.107	.1407	.1435	152.667	155.700
55	8.646	.1157	.1180	191.159	194.957
60	10.520	.0951	.0969	237.991	242.719
65	12.799	.0781	.0797	294.968	300.829
70	15.572	.0642	.0655	364.290	371.529
80	23.050	.0434	.0442	551.245	562.198
90	34.119	.0293	.0299	827.983	844.435
100	50.505	.0198	.0202	1237.624	1262.214

I= .04000

ANNUAL SERIES				GRADIENT SERIES		
PRESENT WORTH		SINKING FUND	CAPITAL RECOVERY	UNIFORM SERIES	PRESENT WORTH	N
PW	CSPW	SF	CR	GUS	GPW	
.962	.981	1.00000	1.04000	.000	.000	1
1.886	1.924	.49020	.53020	.490	.925	2
2.775	2.830	.32035	.36035	.974	2.703	3
3.630	3.702	.23549	.27549	1.451	5.267	4
4.452	4.540	.18463	.22463	1.922	8.555	5
5.242	5.346	.15076	.19076	2.386	12.506	6
6.002	6.121	.12661	.16661	2.843	17.066	7
6.733	6.867	.10853	.14853	3.294	22.181	8
7.435	7.583	.09449	.13449	3.739	27.801	9
8.111	8.272	.08329	.12329	4.177	33.881	10
8.760	8.935	.07415	.11415	4.609	40.377	11
9.385	9.572	.06655	.10655	5.034	47.248	12
9.986	10.184	.06014	.10014	5.453	54.455	13
10.563	10.773	.05467	.09467	5.866	61.962	14
11.118	11.339	.04994	.08994	6.272	69.735	15
11.652	11.884	.04582	.08582	6.672	77.744	16
12.166	12.407	.04220	.08220	7.066	85.958	17
12.659	12.911	.03899	.07899	7.453	94.350	18
13.134	13.395	.03614	.07614	7.834	102.893	19
13.590	13.860	.03358	.07358	8.209	111.565	20
14.029	14.308	.03128	.07128	8.578	120.341	21
14.451	14.738	.02920	.06920	8.941	129.202	22
14.857	15.152	.02731	.06731	9.297	138.128	23
15.247	15.550	.02559	.06559	9.648	147.101	24
15.622	15.932	.02401	.06401	9.993	156.104	25
15.983	16.300	.02257	.06257	10.331	165.121	26
16.330	16.654	.02124	.06124	10.664	174.138	27
16.663	16.994	.02001	.06001	10.991	183.142	28
16.984	17.321	.01888	.05888	11.312	192.121	29
17.292	17.636	.01783	.05783	11.627	201.062	30
17.588	17.938	.01686	.05686	11.937	209.956	31
17.874	18.229	.01595	.05595	12.241	218.792	32
18.148	18.508	.01510	.05510	12.540	227.563	33
18.411	18.777	.01431	.05431	12.832	236.261	34
18.665	19.035	.01358	.05358	13.120	244.877	35
19.793	20.186	.01052	.05052	14.477	286.530	40
20.720	21.132	.00826	.04826	15.705	325.403	45
21.482	21.909	.00655	.04655	16.812	361.164	50
22.109	22.548	.00523	.04523	17.807	393.689	55
22.623	23.073	.00420	.04420	18.697	422.997	60
23.047	23.505	.00339	.04339	19.491	449.201	65
23.395	23.859	.00275	.04275	20.196	472.479	70
23.915	24.391	.00181	.04181	21.372	511.116	80
24.267	24.749	.00121	.04121	22.283	540.737	90
24.505	24.992	.00081	.04081	22.980	563.125	100

N	SINGLE PAYMENT			UNIFORM	
	COMPOUND AMOUNT	PRESENT WORTH		COMPOUND	AMOUNT
	CA	PW	CPW	SCA	CSCA
1	1.045	.9569	.9783	1.000	1.022
2	1.092	.9157	.9362	2.045	2.091
3	1.141	.8763	.8959	3.137	3.207
4	1.193	.8386	.8573	4.278	4.374
5	1.246	.8025	.8204	5.471	5.593
6	1.302	.7679	.7850	6.717	6.867
7	1.361	.7348	.7512	8.019	8.198
8	1.422	.7032	.7189	9.388	9.590
9	1.486	.6729	.6879	10.802	11.043
10	1.553	.6439	.6583	12.288	12.563
11	1.623	.6162	.6300	13.841	14.150
12	1.696	.5897	.6028	15.464	15.809
13	1.772	.5643	.5769	17.160	17.543
14	1.852	.5400	.5520	18.932	19.355
15	1.935	.5167	.5283	20.784	21.248
16	2.022	.4945	.5055	22.719	23.227
17	2.113	.4732	.4637	24.742	25.294
18	2.208	.4528	.4629	26.855	27.455
19	2.308	.4333	.4430	29.064	29.713
20	2.412	.4146	.4239	31.371	32.072
21	2.520	.3968	.4056	33.783	34.538
22	2.634	.3797	.3882	36.303	37.114
23	2.752	.3634	.3715	38.937	39.807
24	2.876	.3477	.3555	41.689	42.620
25	3.005	.3327	.3402	44.565	45.561
26	3.141	.3184	.3255	47.571	48.633
27	3.282	.3047	.3115	50.711	51.844
28	3.430	.2916	.2981	53.993	55.199
29	3.584	.2790	.2852	57.423	58.706
30	3.745	.2670	.2730	61.007	62.370
31	3.914	.2555	.2612	64.752	66.199
32	4.090	.2445	.2500	68.666	70.200
33	4.274	.2340	.2392	72.756	74.381
34	4.466	.2239	.2289	77.030	78.751
35	4.667	.2143	.2190	81.497	83.317
40	5.816	.1719	.1758	107.030	109.421
45	7.248	.1380	.1410	138.850	141.951
50	9.033	.1107	.1132	178.503	182.490
55	11.256	.0888	.0908	227.918	233.008
60	14.027	.0713	.0729	289.498	295.964
65	17.481	.0572	.0585	366.238	374.418
70	21.784	.0459	.0469	461.870	472.186
80	33.830	.0296	.0302	729.558	745.852
90	52.537	.0190	.0195	1145.269	1170.849
100	81.589	.0123	.0125	1790.856	1830.855

I= .04500

ANNUAL SERIES				GRADIENT SERIES		
PRESENT WORTH		SINKING FUND	CAPITAL RECOVERY	UNIFORM SERIES	PRESENT WORTH	N
PW	CSPW	SF	CR	GUS	GPW	
.957	.978	1.00000	1.04500	.000	.000	1
1.873	1.914	.48900	.53400	.489	.916	2
2.749	2.810	.31877	.36377	.971	2.668	3
3.588	3.668	.23374	.27874	1.445	5.184	4
4.390	4.488	.18279	.22779	1.912	8.394	5
5.158	5.273	.14888	.19388	2.372	12.233	6
5.893	6.024	.12470	.16970	2.824	16.642	7
6.596	6.743	.10661	.15161	3.269	21.565	8
7.269	7.431	.09257	.13757	3.707	26.948	9
7.913	8.089	.08138	.12638	4.138	32.743	10
8.529	8.719	.07225	.11725	4.562	38.905	11
9.119	9.322	.06467	.10967	4.978	45.391	12
9.683	9.899	.05828	.10328	5.387	52.163	13
10.223	10.451	.05282	.09782	5.789	59.182	14
10.740	10.979	.04811	.09311	6.184	66.416	15
11.234	11.485	.04402	.08902	6.572	73.833	16
11.707	11.969	.04042	.08542	6.953	81.404	17
12.160	12.432	.03724	.08224	7.327	89.102	18
12.593	12.875	.03441	.07941	7.695	96.901	19
13.008	13.298	.03188	.07688	8.055	104.780	20
13.405	13.704	.02960	.07460	8.409	112.715	21
13.784	14.092	.02755	.07255	8.755	120.689	22
14.148	14.464	.02568	.07068	9.096	128.683	23
14.495	14.819	.02399	.06899	9.429	136.680	24
14.828	15.159	.02244	.06744	9.756	144.665	25
15.147	15.485	.02102	.06602	10.077	152.625	26
15.451	15.796	.01972	.06472	10.391	160.547	27
15.743	16.094	.01852	.06352	10.698	168.420	28
16.022	16.380	.01741	.06241	10.999	176.232	29
16.289	16.653	.01639	.06139	11.295	183.975	30
16.544	16.914	.01544	.06044	11.583	191.640	31
16.789	17.164	.01456	.05956	11.866	199.220	32
17.023	17.403	.01374	.05874	12.143	206.707	33
17.247	17.632	.01298	.05798	12.414	214.096	34
17.461	17.851	.01227	.05727	12.679	221.380	35
18.402	18.813	.00934	.05434	13.917	256.099	40
19.156	19.584	.00720	.05220	15.020	287.732	45
19.762	20.203	.00560	.05060	15.998	316.145	50
20.248	20.700	.00439	.04939	16.860	341.375	55
20.638	21.099	.00345	.04845	17.617	363.571	60
20.951	21.419	.00273	.04773	18.278	382.947	65
21.202	21.676	.00217	.04717	18.854	399.750	70
21.565	22.047	.00137	.04637	19.785	426.680	80
21.799	22.286	.00087	.04587	20.476	446.359	90
21.950	22.440	.00056	.04556	20.981	460.538	100

N	SINGLE PAYMENT			UNIFORM	
	COMPOUND AMOUNT	PRESENT WORTH		COMPOUND	AMOUNT
	CA	PW	CPW	SCA	CSCA
1	1.050	.9524	.9760	1.000	1.025
2	1.102	.9070	.9295	2.050	2.101
3	1.158	.8638	.8853	3.152	3.231
4	1.216	.8227	.8431	4.310	4.417
5	1.276	.7835	.8030	5.526	5.663
6	1.340	.7462	.7647	6.802	6.971
7	1.407	.7107	.7283	8.142	8.344
8	1.477	.6768	.6936	9.549	9.786
9	1.551	.6446	.6606	11.027	11.300
10	1.629	.6139	.6291	12.578	12.890
11	1.710	.5847	.5992	14.207	14.559
12	1.796	.5568	.5706	15.917	16.312
13	1.886	.5303	.5435	17.713	18.152
14	1.980	.5051	.5176	19.599	20.085
15	2.079	.4810	.4929	21.579	22.114
16	2.183	.4581	.4695	23.657	24.244
17	2.292	.4363	.4471	25.840	26.481
18	2.407	.4155	.4258	28.132	28.830
19	2.527	.3957	.4055	30.539	31.296
20	2.653	.3769	.3862	33.066	33.886
21	2.786	.3589	.3678	35.719	36.605
22	2.925	.3418	.3503	38.505	39.460
23	3.072	.3256	.3336	41.430	42.458
24	3.225	.3101	.3178	44.502	45.606
25	3.386	.2953	.3026	47.727	48.911
26	3.556	.2812	.2882	51.113	52.381
27	3.733	.2678	.2745	54.669	56.025
28	3.920	.2551	.2614	58.403	59.851
29	4.116	.2429	.2490	62.323	63.868
30	4.322	.2314	.2371	66.439	68.086
31	4.538	.2204	.2258	70.761	72.515
32	4.765	.2099	.2151	75.299	77.166
33	5.003	.1999	.2048	80.064	82.049
34	5.253	.1904	.1951	85.067	87.176
35	5.516	.1813	.1858	90.320	92.560
40	7.040	.1420	.1456	120.800	123.795
45	8.985	.1113	.1141	159.700	163.660
50	11.467	.0872	.0894	209.348	214.539
55	14.636	.0683	.0700	272.713	279.475
60	18.679	.0535	.0549	353.584	362.351
65	23.840	.0419	.0430	456.798	468.125
70	30.426	.0329	.0337	588.529	603.122
80	49.561	.0202	.0207	971.229	995.312
90	80.730	.0124	.0127	1594.607	1634.148
100	131.501	.0076	.0078	2610.025	2674.745

I= .05000

ANNUAL SERIES				GRADIENT SERIES		
PRESENT WORTH		SINKING FUND	CAPITAL RECOVERY	UNIFORM SERIES	PRESENT WORTH	N
PW	CSPW	SF	CR	GUS	GPW	
.952	.976	1.00000	1.05000	.000	.000	1
1.859	1.906	.48780	.53780	.488	.907	2
2.723	2.791	.31721	.36721	.967	2.635	3
3.546	3.634	.23201	.28201	1.439	5.103	4
4.329	4.437	.18097	.23097	1.903	8.237	5
5.076	5.202	.14702	.19702	2.358	11.968	6
5.786	5.930	.12282	.17282	2.805	16.232	7
6.463	6.623	.10472	.15472	3.245	20.970	8
7.108	7.284	.09069	.14069	3.676	26.127	9
7.722	7.913	.07950	.12950	4.099	31.652	10
8.306	8.512	.07039	.12039	4.514	37.499	11
8.863	9.083	.06283	.11283	4.922	43.624	12
9.394	9.627	.05646	.10646	5.322	49.988	13
9.899	10.144	.05102	.10102	5.713	56.554	14
10.380	10.637	.04634	.09634	6.097	63.288	15
10.838	11.107	.04227	.09227	6.474	70.160	16
11.274	11.554	.03870	.08870	6.842	77.140	17
11.690	11.979	.03555	.08555	7.203	84.204	18
12.085	12.385	.03275	.08275	7.557	91.328	19
12.462	12.771	.03024	.08024	7.903	98.488	20
12.821	13.139	.02800	.07800	8.242	105.667	21
13.163	13.489	.02597	.07597	8.573	112.846	22
13.489	13.823	.02414	.07414	8.897	120.009	23
13.799	14.141	.02247	.07247	9.214	127.140	24
14.094	14.443	.02095	.07095	9.524	134.228	25
14.375	14.732	.01956	.06956	9.827	141.259	26
14.643	15.006	.01829	.06829	10.122	148.223	27
14.898	15.268	.01712	.06712	10.411	155.110	28
15.141	15.517	.01605	.06605	10.694	161.913	29
15.372	15.754	.01505	.06505	10.969	168.623	30
15.593	15.979	.01413	.06413	11.238	175.233	31
15.803	16.195	.01328	.06328	11.501	181.739	32
16.003	16.399	.01249	.06249	11.757	188.135	33
16.193	16.594	.01176	.06176	12.006	194.417	34
16.374	16.780	.01107	.06107	12.250	200.581	35
17.159	17.585	.00828	.05828	13.377	229.545	40
17.774	18.215	.00626	.05626	14.364	255.315	45
18.256	18.709	.00478	.05478	15.223	277.915	50
18.633	19.096	.00367	.05367	15.966	297.510	55
18.929	19.399	.00283	.05283	16.606	314.343	60
19.161	19.636	.00219	.05219	17.154	328.691	65
19.343	19.822	.00170	.05170	17.621	340.841	70
19.596	20.082	.00103	.05103	18.353	359.646	80
19.752	20.242	.00063	.05063	18.871	372.749	90
19.848	20.340	.00038	.05038	19.234	381.749	100

N	SINGLE PAYMENT			UNIFORM	
	COMPOUND AMOUNT	PRESENT WORTH		COMPOUND	AMOUNT
	CA	PW	CPW	SCA	CSCA
1	1.055	.9479	.9737	1.000	1.027
2	1.113	.8985	.9229	2.055	2.111
3	1.174	.8516	.8748	3.168	3.254
4	1.239	.8072	.8292	4.342	4.461
5	1.307	.7651	.7860	5.581	5.733
6	1.379	.7252	.7450	6.888	7.076
7	1.455	.6874	.7062	8.267	8.492
8	1.535	.6516	.6694	9.722	9.987
9	1.619	.6176	.6345	11.256	11.563
10	1.708	.5854	.6014	12.875	13.226
11	1.802	.5549	.5700	14.583	14.981
12	1.901	.5260	.5403	16.386	16.832
13	2.006	.4986	.5121	18.287	18.785
14	2.116	.4726	.4854	20.293	20.846
15	2.232	.4479	.4601	22.409	23.019
16	2.355	.4246	.4362	24.641	25.313
17	2.485	.4024	.4134	26.996	27.732
18	2.621	.3815	.3919	29.481	30.285
19	2.766	.3616	.3714	32.103	32.978
20	2.918	.3427	.3521	34.868	35.819
21	3.078	.3249	.3337	37.786	38.816
22	3.248	.3079	.3163	40.864	41.978
23	3.426	.2919	.2998	44.112	45.314
24	3.615	.2767	.2842	47.538	48.834
25	3.813	.2622	.2694	51.153	52.547
26	4.023	.2486	.2553	54.966	56.464
27	4.244	.2356	.2420	58.989	60.597
28	4.478	.2233	.2294	63.234	64.957
29	4.724	.2117	.2174	67.711	69.557
30	4.984	.2006	.2061	72.435	74.410
31	5.258	.1902	.1954	77.419	79.529
32	5.547	.1803	.1852	82.677	84.931
33	5.852	.1709	.1755	88.225	90.629
34	6.174	.1620	.1664	94.077	96.641
35	6.514	.1535	.1577	100.251	102.984
40	8.513	.1175	.1207	136.606	140.329
45	11.127	.0899	.0923	184.119	189.137
50	14.542	.0688	.0706	246.217	252.928
55	19.006	.0526	.0540	327.377	336.300
60	24.840	.0403	.0414	433.450	445.264
65	32.465	.0308	.0316	572.083	587.675
70	42.430	.0236	.0242	753.271	773.801
80	72.476	.0138	.0142	1299.571	1334.991
90	123.800	.0081	.0083	2232.731	2293.583
100	211.469	.0047	.0049	3826.702	3930.998

I= .05500

ANNUAL SERIES				GRADIENT SERIES		
PRESENT WORTH		SINKING FUND	CAPITAL RECOVERY	UNIFORM SERIES	PRESENT WORTH	N
PW	CSPW	SF	CR	GUS	GPW	
.948	.974	1.00000	1.05500	.000	.000	1
1.846	1.897	.48662	.54162	.487	.898	2
2.698	2.771	.31565	.37065	.964	2.602	3
3.505	3.601	.23029	.28529	1.433	5.023	4
4.270	4.387	.17918	.23418	1.893	8.084	5
4.996	5.132	.14518	.20018	2.344	11.710	6
5.683	5.838	.12096	.17596	2.786	15.835	7
6.335	6.507	.10286	.15786	3.220	20.396	8
6.952	7.142	.08884	.14384	3.644	25.337	9
7.538	7.743	.07767	.13267	4.060	30.606	10
8.093	8.313	.06857	.12357	4.468	36.155	11
8.619	8.853	.06103	.11603	4.866	41.941	12
9.117	9.366	.05468	.10968	5.256	47.923	13
9.590	9.851	.04928	.10428	5.638	54.067	14
10.038	10.311	.04463	.09963	6.011	60.338	15
10.462	10.747	.04058	.09558	6.376	66.707	16
10.865	11.161	.03704	.09204	6.732	73.146	17
11.246	11.553	.03392	.08892	7.081	79.631	18
11.608	11.924	.03115	.08615	7.421	86.139	19
11.950	12.276	.02868	.08368	7.753	92.651	20
12.275	12.610	.02646	.08146	8.077	99.148	21
12.583	12.926	.02447	.07947	8.393	105.615	22
12.875	13.226	.02267	.07767	8.702	112.036	23
13.152	13.510	.02104	.07604	9.003	118.399	24
13.414	13.780	.01955	.07455	9.296	124.693	25
13.662	14.035	.01819	.07319	9.581	130.907	26
13.898	14.277	.01695	.07195	9.860	137.032	27
14.121	14.506	.01581	.07081	10.131	143.062	28
14.333	14.724	.01477	.06977	10.395	148.989	29
14.534	14.930	.01381	.06881	10.652	154.808	30
14.724	15.125	.01292	.06792	10.902	160.513	31
14.904	15.310	.01210	.06710	11.145	166.102	32
15.075	15.486	.01133	.06633	11.381	171.569	33
15.237	15.652	.01063	.06563	11.611	176.914	34
15.391	15.810	.00997	.06497	11.834	182.134	35
16.046	16.483	.00732	.06232	12.858	206.320	40
16.548	16.999	.00543	.06043	13.738	227.334	45
16.932	17.393	.00406	.05906	14.490	245.331	50
17.225	17.695	.00305	.05805	15.127	260.569	55
17.450	17.925	.00231	.05731	15.665	273.352	60
17.622	18.102	.00175	.05675	16.116	283.992	65
17.753	18.237	.00133	.05633	16.492	292.791	70
17.931	18.420	.00077	.05577	17.063	305.948	80
18.035	18.526	.00045	.05545	17.449	314.690	90
18.096	18.589	.00026	.05526	17.707	320.417	100

N	SINGLE PAYMENT			UNIFORM	
	COMPOUND AMOUNT	PRESENT WORTH		COMPOUND	AMOUNT
	CA	PW	CPW	SCA	CSCA
1	1.060	.9434	.9714	1.000	1.030
2	1.124	.8900	.9164	2.060	2.121
3	1.191	.8396	.8646	3.184	3.278
4	1.262	.7921	.8156	4.375	4.505
5	1.338	.7473	.7695	5.637	5.805
6	1.419	.7050	.7259	6.975	7.183
7	1.504	.6651	.6848	8.394	8.643
8	1.594	.6274	.6461	9.897	10.192
9	1.689	.5919	.6095	11.491	11.833
10	1.791	.5584	.5750	13.181	13.572
11	1.898	.5268	.5424	14.972	15.416
12	2.012	.4970	.5117	16.870	17.371
13	2.133	.4688	.4828	18.882	19.443
14	2.261	.4423	.4554	21.015	21.639
15	2.397	.4173	.4297	23.276	23.967
16	2.540	.3936	.4053	25.673	26.435
17	2.693	.3714	.3824	28.213	29.051
18	2.854	.3503	.3608	30.906	31.824
19	3.026	.3305	.3403	33.760	34.763
20	3.207	.3118	.3211	36.786	37.878
21	3.400	.2942	.3029	39.993	41.181
22	3.604	.2775	.2857	43.392	44.681
23	3.820	.2618	.2696	46.996	48.392
24	4.049	.2470	.2543	50.816	52.325
25	4.292	.2330	.2399	54.865	56.494
26	4.549	.2198	.2263	59.156	60.914
27	4.822	.2074	.2135	63.706	65.598
28	5.112	.1956	.2014	68.528	70.564
29	5.418	.1846	.1900	73.640	75.828
30	5.743	.1741	.1793	79.058	81.407
31	6.088	.1643	.1691	84.802	87.321
32	6.453	.1550	.1596	90.890	93.590
33	6.841	.1462	.1505	97.343	100.235
34	7.251	.1379	.1420	104.184	107.279
35	7.686	.1301	.1340	111.435	114.745
40	10.286	.0972	.1001	154.762	159.360
45	13.765	.0727	.0748	212.744	219.064
50	18.420	.0543	.0559	290.336	298.961
55	24.650	.0406	.0418	394.172	405.882
60	32.988	.0303	.0312	533.128	548.967
65	44.145	.0227	.0233	719.083	740.446
70	59.076	.0169	.0174	967.932	996.688
80	105.796	.0095	.0097	1746.600	1798.489
90	189.465	.0053	.0054	3141.075	3234.392
100	339.302	.0029	.0030	5638.368	5805.876

I= .06000

ANNUAL SERIES				GRADIENT SERIES		
PRESENT WORTH		SINKING FUND	CAPITAL RECOVERY	UNIFORM SERIES	PRESENT WORTH	N
PW	CSPW	SF	CR	GUS	GPW	
.943	.971	1.00000	1.06000	.000	.000	1
1.833	1.688	.48544	.54544	.485	.890	2
2.673	2.752	.31411	.37411	.961	2.569	3
3.465	3.568	.22859	.28859	1.427	4.946	4
4.212	4.338	.17740	.23740	1.884	7.935	5
4.917	5.063	.14336	.20336	2.330	11.459	6
5.582	5.748	.11914	.17914	2.768	15.450	7
6.210	6.394	.10104	.16104	3.195	19.842	8
6.802	7.004	.08702	.14702	3.613	24.577	9
7.360	7.579	.07587	.13587	4.022	29.602	10
7.887	8.121	.06679	.12679	4.421	34.870	11
8.384	8.633	.05928	.11928	4.811	40.337	12
8.853	9.116	.05296	.11296	5.192	45.963	13
9.295	9.571	.04758	.10758	5.564	51.713	14
9.712	10.001	.04296	.10296	5.926	57.555	15
10.106	10.406	.03895	.09895	6.279	63.459	16
10.477	10.789	.03544	.09544	6.624	69.401	17
10.828	11.149	.03236	.09236	6.960	75.357	18
11.158	11.490	.02962	.08962	7.287	81.306	19
11.470	11.811	.02718	.08718	7.605	87.230	20
11.764	12.114	.02500	.08500	7.915	93.114	21
12.042	12.399	.02305	.08305	8.217	98.941	22
12.303	12.669	.02128	.08128	8.510	104.701	23
12.550	12.923	.01968	.07968	8.795	110.381	24
12.783	13.163	.01823	.07823	9.072	115.973	25
13.003	13.389	.01690	.07690	9.341	121.468	26
13.211	13.603	.01570	.07570	9.603	126.860	27
13.406	13.804	.01459	.07459	9.857	132.142	28
13.591	13.994	.01358	.07358	10.103	137.310	29
13.765	14.174	.01265	.07265	10.342	142.359	30
13.929	14.343	.01179	.07179	10.574	147.286	31
14.084	14.502	.01100	.07100	10.799	152.090	32
14.230	14.653	.01027	.07027	11.017	156.768	33
14.368	14.795	.00960	.06960	11.228	161.319	34
14.498	14.929	.00897	.06897	11.432	165.743	35
15.046	15.493	.00646	.06646	12.359	185.957	40
15.456	15.915	.00470	.06470	13.141	203.110	45
15.762	16.230	.00344	.06344	13.796	217.457	50
15.991	16.466	.00254	.06254	14.341	229.322	55
16.161	16.642	.00188	.06188	14.791	239.043	60
16.289	16.773	.00139	.06139	15.160	246.945	65
16.385	16.871	.00103	.06103	15.461	253.327	70
16.509	17.000	.00057	.06057	15.903	262.549	80
16.579	17.071	.00032	.06032	16.189	268.395	90
16.618	17.111	.00018	.06018	16.371	272.047	100

N	SINGLE PAYMENT			UNIFORM	
	COMPOUND AMOUNT	PRESENT WORTH		COMPOUND	AMOUNT
	CA	PW	CPW	SCA	CSCA
1	1.065	.9390	.9692	1.000	1.032
2	1.134	.8817	.9100	2.065	2.131
3	1.208	.8278	.8545	3.199	3.302
4	1.286	.7773	.8023	4.407	4.549
5	1.370	.7299	.7534	5.694	5.877
6	1.459	.6853	.7074	7.064	7.291
7	1.554	.6435	.6642	8.523	8.797
8	1.655	.6042	.6237	10.077	10.401
9	1.763	.5674	.5856	11.732	12.109
10	1.877	.5327	.5499	13.494	13.928
11	1.999	.5002	.5163	15.372	15.866
12	2.129	.4697	.4848	17.371	17.929
13	2.267	.4410	.4552	19.508	20.127
14	2.415	.4141	.4274	21.767	22.467
15	2.572	.3888	.4013	24.182	24.960
16	2.739	.3651	.3768	26.754	27.614
17	2.917	.3428	.3538	29.493	30.441
18	3.107	.3219	.3322	32.410	33.452
19	3.309	.3022	.3120	35.517	36.659
20	3.524	.2838	.2929	38.825	40.074
21	3.753	.2665	.2750	42.349	43.711
22	3.997	.2502	.2583	46.102	47.584
23	4.256	.2349	.2425	50.098	51.709
24	4.533	.2206	.2277	54.355	56.103
25	4.828	.2071	.2138	58.888	60.781
26	5.141	.1945	.2008	63.715	65.764
27	5.476	.1826	.1885	68.857	71.071
28	5.832	.1715	.1770	74.333	76.723
29	6.211	.1610	.1662	80.164	82.742
30	6.614	.1512	.1560	86.375	89.153
31	7.044	.1420	.1465	92.989	95.980
32	7.502	.1333	.1376	100.034	103.250
33	7.990	.1252	.1292	107.536	110.994
34	8.509	.1175	.1213	115.526	119.241
35	9.062	.1103	.1139	124.035	128.024
40	12.416	.0805	.0831	175.632	181.280
45	17.011	.0588	.0607	246.325	254.246
50	23.307	.0429	.0443	343.180	354.216
55	31.932	.0313	.0323	475.880	491.183
60	43.750	.0229	.0236	657.690	678.840
65	59.941	.0167	.0172	906.786	935.947
70	82.124	.0122	.0126	1248.069	1288.205
80	154.159	.0065	.0067	2356.291	2432.067
90	289.377	.0035	.0036	4436.576	4579.252
100	543.201	.0018	.0019	8341.558	8609.813

I= .06500

ANNUAL SERIES				GRADIENT SERIES		
PRESENT WORTH		SINKING FUND	CAPITAL RECOVERY	UNIFORM SERIES	PRESENT WORTH	N
PW	CSPW	SF	CR	GUS	GPW	
.939	.969	1.00000	1.06500	.000	.000	1
1.821	1.879	.48426	.54926	.484	.882	2
2.648	2.734	.31258	.37758	.958	2.537	3
3.426	3.536	.22690	.29190	1.421	4.869	4
4.156	4.289	.17563	.24063	1.874	7.789	5
4.841	4.997	.14157	.20657	2.317	11.216	6
5.485	5.661	.11733	.18233	2.749	15.077	7
6.089	6.285	.09924	.16424	3.171	19.306	8
6.656	6.870	.08524	.15024	3.582	23.845	9
7.189	7.420	.07410	.13910	3.984	28.640	10
7.689	7.936	.06506	.13006	4.375	33.642	11
8.159	8.421	.05757	.12257	4.757	38.808	12
8.600	8.876	.05128	.11628	5.128	44.100	13
9.014	9.304	.04594	.11094	5.490	49.484	14
9.403	9.705	.04135	.10635	5.842	54.927	15
9.768	10.082	.03738	.10238	6.184	60.404	16
10.111	10.436	.03391	.09891	6.517	65.889	17
10.432	10.768	.03085	.09585	6.840	71.361	18
10.735	11.080	.02816	.09316	7.154	76.801	19
11.019	11.373	.02576	.09076	7.460	82.193	20
11.285	11.648	.02361	.08861	7.756	87.523	21
11.535	11.906	.02169	.08669	8.043	92.777	22
11.770	12.149	.01996	.08496	8.322	97.946	23
11.991	12.376	.01840	.08340	8.592	103.020	24
12.198	12.590	.01698	.08198	8.853	107.991	25
12.392	12.791	.01569	.08069	9.107	112.854	26
12.575	12.979	.01452	.07952	9.352	117.602	27
12.746	13.156	.01345	.07845	9.589	122.232	28
12.907	13.323	.01247	.07747	9.819	126.740	29
13.059	13.479	.01158	.07658	10.041	131.125	30
13.201	13.625	.01075	.07575	10.256	135.383	31
13.334	13.763	.01000	.07500	10.463	139.515	32
13.459	13.892	.00930	.07430	10.663	143.521	33
13.577	14.013	.00866	.07366	10.857	147.399	34
13.687	14.127	.00806	.07306	11.043	151.151	35
14.146	14.600	.00569	.07069	11.881	168.060	40
14.480	14.946	.00406	.06906	12.574	182.075	45
14.725	15.198	.00291	.06791	13.143	193.526	50
14.903	15.382	.00210	.06710	13.607	202.776	55
15.033	15.516	.00152	.06652	13.981	210.177	60
15.128	15.614	.00110	.06610	14.282	216.055	65
15.197	15.686	.00080	.06580	14.522	220.691	70
15.285	15.776	.00042	.06542	14.862	227.167	80
15.331	15.824	.00023	.06523	15.073	231.084	90
15.356	15.850	.00012	.06512	15.200	233.418	100

N	SINGLE PAYMENT			UNIFORM	
	COMPOUND AMOUNT	PRESENT WORTH		COMPOUND AMOUNT	
	CA	PW	CPW	SCA	CSCA
1	1.070	.9346	.9669	1.000	1.035
2	1.145	.8734	.9037	2.070	2.142
3	1.225	.8163	.8445	3.215	3.326
4	1.311	.7629	.7893	4.440	4.594
5	1.403	.7130	.7377	5.751	5.950
6	1.501	.6663	.6894	7.153	7.401
7	1.606	.6227	.6443	8.654	8.953
8	1.718	.5820	.6021	10.260	10.615
9	1.838	.5439	.5628	11.978	12.392
10	1.967	.5083	.5259	13.816	14.295
11	2.105	.4751	.4915	15.784	16.330
12	2.252	.4440	.4594	17.888	18.507
13	2.410	.4150	.4293	20.141	20.838
14	2.579	.3878	.4012	22.550	23.331
15	2.759	.3624	.3750	25.129	25.999
16	2.952	.3387	.3505	27.888	28.853
17	3.159	.3166	.3275	30.840	31.907
18	3.380	.2959	.3061	33.999	35.176
19	3.617	.2765	.2861	37.379	38.672
20	3.670	.2584	.2674	40.995	42.414
21	4.141	.2415	.2499	44.865	46.418
22	4.430	.2257	.2335	49.006	50.702
23	4.741	.2109	.2182	53.436	55.285
24	5.072	.1971	.2040	58.177	60.190
25	5.427	.1842	.1906	63.249	65.438
26	5.607	.1722	.1782	68.676	71.053
27	6.214	.1609	.1665	74.484	77.061
28	6.649	.1504	.1556	80.698	83.490
29	7.114	.1406	.1454	87.347	90.369
30	7.612	.1314	.1359	94.461	97.730
31	8.145	.1228	.1270	102.073	105.605
32	8.715	.1147	.1187	110.218	114.032
33	9.325	.1072	.1109	118.933	123.049
34	9.978	.1002	.1037	128.259	132.697
35	10.677	.0937	.0969	138.237	143.021
40	14.974	.0668	.0691	199.635	206.544
45	21.002	.0476	.0493	285.749	295.638
50	29.457	.0339	.0351	406.529	420.597
55	41.315	.0242	.0250	575.929	595.859
60	57.946	.0173	.0179	813.520	841.673
65	81.273	.0123	.0127	1146.755	1186.439
70	113.989	.0088	.0091	1614.134	1669.992
80	224.234	.0045	.0046	3189.063	3299.421
90	441.103	.0023	.0023	6287.185	6504.756
100	867.716	.0012	.0012	12381.662	12810.134

I= .07000

ANNUAL SERIES				GRADIENT SERIES		
PRESENT WORTH		SINKING FUND	CAPITAL RECOVERY	UNIFORM SERIES	PRESENT WORTH	N
PW	CSPW	SF	CR	GUS	GPW	
.935	.967	1.00000	1.07000	.000	.000	1
1.808	1.871	.48309	.55309	.483	.873	2
2.624	2.715	.31105	.38105	.955	2.506	3
3.387	3.504	.22523	.29523	1.416	4.795	4
4.100	4.242	.17389	.24389	1.865	7.647	5
4.767	4.931	.13980	.20980	2.303	10.978	6
5.389	5.576	.11555	.18555	2.730	14.715	7
5.971	6.178	.09747	.16747	3.147	18.789	8
6.515	6.741	.08349	.15349	3.552	23.140	9
7.024	7.267	.07238	.14238	3.946	27.716	10
7.499	7.758	.06336	.13336	4.330	32.466	11
7.943	8.218	.05590	.12590	4.703	37.351	12
8.358	8.647	.04965	.11965	5.065	42.330	13
8.745	9.048	.04434	.11434	5.417	47.372	14
9.108	9.423	.03979	.10979	5.758	52.446	15
9.447	9.774	.03586	.10586	6.090	57.527	16
9.763	10.101	.03243	.10243	6.411	62.592	17
10.059	10.407	.02941	.09941	6.722	67.622	18
10.336	10.693	.02675	.09675	7.024	72.599	19
10.594	10.961	.02439	.09439	7.316	77.509	20
10.836	11.210	.02229	.09229	7.599	82.339	21
11.061	11.444	.02041	.09041	7.872	87.079	22
11.272	11.662	.01871	.08871	8.137	91.720	23
11.469	11.866	.01719	.08719	8.392	96.255	24
11.654	12.057	.01581	.08581	8.639	100.676	25
11.826	12.235	.01456	.08456	8.877	104.981	26
11.987	12.402	.01343	.08343	9.107	109.166	27
12.137	12.557	.01239	.08239	9.329	113.226	28
12.278	12.703	.01145	.08145	9.543	117.162	29
12.409	12.838	.01059	.08059	9.749	120.972	30
12.532	12.965	.00980	.07980	9.947	124.655	31
12.647	13.084	.00907	.07907	10.138	128.212	32
12.754	13.195	.00841	.07841	10.322	131.643	33
12.854	13.299	.00780	.07780	10.499	134.951	34
12.948	13.396	.00723	.07723	10.669	138.135	35
13.332	13.793	.00501	.07501	11.423	152.293	40
13.606	14.076	.00350	.07350	12.036	163.756	45
13.801	14.278	.00246	.07246	12.529	172.905	50
13.940	14.422	.00174	.07174	12.921	180.124	55
14.039	14.525	.00123	.07123	13.232	185.768	60
14.110	14.598	.00087	.07087	13.476	190.145	65
14.160	14.650	.00062	.07062	13.666	193.519	70
14.222	14.714	.00031	.07031	13.927	198.075	80
14.253	14.747	.00016	.07016	14.081	200.704	90
14.269	14.763	.00008	.07008	14.170	202.200	100

N	SINGLE PAYMENT			UNIFORM	
	COMPOUND AMOUNT	PRESENT WORTH		COMPOUND AMOUNT	
	CA	PW	CPW	SCA	CSCA
1	1.075	.9302	.9647	1.000	1.037
2	1.156	.8653	.8974	2.075	2.152
3	1.242	.8050	.8348	3.231	3.350
4	1.335	.7488	.7765	4.473	4.639
5	1.436	.6966	.7224	5.808	6.024
6	1.543	.6480	.6720	7.244	7.512
7	1.659	.6028	.6251	8.787	9.113
8	1.783	.5607	.5815	10.446	10.833
9	1.917	.5216	.5409	12.230	12.683
10	2.061	.4852	.5032	14.147	14.671
11	2.216	.4513	.4681	16.208	16.809
12	2.382	.4199	.4354	18.424	19.106
13	2.560	.3906	.4050	20.806	21.576
14	2.752	.3633	.3768	23.366	24.232
15	2.959	.3380	.3505	26.118	27.086
16	3.181	.3144	.3260	29.077	30.154
17	3.419	.2925	.3033	32.255	33.453
18	3.676	.2720	.2821	35.677	36.999
19	3.951	.2531	.2624	39.353	40.811
20	4.248	.2354	.2441	43.305	44.909
21	4.566	.2190	.2271	47.553	49.314
22	4.909	.2037	.2113	52.119	54.050
23	5.277	.1895	.1965	57.028	59.141
24	5.673	.1763	.1828	62.305	64.613
25	6.098	.1640	.1701	67.978	70.496
26	6.556	.1525	.1582	74.076	76.821
27	7.047	.1419	.1472	80.632	83.619
28	7.576	.1320	.1369	87.679	90.928
29	8.144	.1228	.1273	95.255	98.784
30	8.755	.1142	.1185	103.399	107.230
31	9.412	.1063	.1102	112.154	116.309
32	10.117	.0988	.1025	121.566	126.070
33	10.876	.0919	.0953	131.683	136.562
34	11.692	.0855	.0887	142.560	147.841
35	12.569	.0796	.0825	154.252	159.966
40	18.044	.0554	.0575	227.257	235.676
45	25.905	.0386	.0400	332.065	344.367
50	37.190	.0269	.0279	482.530	500.407
55	53.391	.0187	.0194	698.543	724.422
60	76.649	.0130	.0135	1008.657	1046.025
65	110.040	.0091	.0094	1453.865	1507.728
70	157.977	.0063	.0066	2093.020	2170.562
80	325.595	.0031	.0032	4327.927	4488.269
90	671.061	.0015	.0015	8934.142	9265.135
100	1383.077	.0007	.0007	18427.696	19110.406

I = .07500

ANNUAL SERIES				GRADIENT SERIES		
PRESENT WORTH		SINKING FUND	CAPITAL RECOVERY	UNIFORM SERIES	PRESENT WORTH	N
PW	CSPW	SF	CR	GUS	GPW	
.930	.965	1.00000	1.07500	.000	.000	1
1.796	1.862	.48193	.55693	.482	.865	2
2.601	2.697	.30954	.38454	.952	2.475	3
3.349	3.473	.22357	.29857	1.410	4.722	4
4.046	4.196	.17216	.24716	1.856	7.508	5
4.694	4.868	.13804	.21304	2.290	10.748	6
5.297	5.493	.11380	.18880	2.712	14.364	7
5.857	6.074	.09573	.17073	3.122	18.289	8
6.379	6.615	.08177	.15677	3.521	22.462	9
6.864	7.118	.07069	.14569	3.909	26.829	10
7.315	7.586	.06170	.13670	4.284	31.342	11
7.735	8.022	.05428	.12928	4.649	35.960	12
8.126	8.427	.04806	.12306	5.002	40.647	13
8.489	8.804	.04280	.11780	5.344	45.370	14
8.827	9.154	.03829	.11329	5.676	50.102	15
9.142	9.480	.03439	.10939	5.997	54.818	16
9.434	9.783	.03100	.10600	6.307	59.497	17
9.706	10.066	.02803	.10303	6.606	64.122	18
9.959	10.328	.02541	.10041	6.896	68.677	19
10.194	10.572	.02309	.09809	7.175	73.150	20
10.413	10.799	.02103	.09603	7.445	77.529	21
10.617	11.011	.01919	.09419	7.705	81.807	22
10.807	11.207	.01754	.09254	7.956	85.976	23
10.983	11.390	.01605	.09105	8.197	90.031	24
11.147	11.560	.01471	.08971	8.430	93.966	25
11.299	11.718	.01350	.08850	8.653	97.780	26
11.441	11.865	.01240	.08740	8.869	101.469	27
11.573	12.002	.01141	.08641	9.075	105.033	28
11.696	12.129	.01050	.08550	9.274	108.471	29
11.810	12.248	.00967	.08467	9.465	111.783	30
11.917	12.358	.00892	.08392	9.648	114.971	31
12.015	12.461	.00823	.08323	9.824	118.035	32
12.107	12.556	.00759	.08259	9.992	120.977	33
12.193	12.645	.00701	.08201	10.153	123.800	34
12.273	12.727	.00648	.08148	10.308	126.505	35
12.594	13.061	.00440	.07940	10.986	138.368	40
12.819	13.294	.00301	.07801	11.526	147.753	45
12.975	13.456	.00207	.07707	11.952	155.071	50
13.084	13.568	.00143	.07643	12.284	160.713	55
13.159	13.647	.00099	.07599	12.540	165.021	60
13.212	13.702	.00069	.07569	12.737	168.286	65
13.249	13.740	.00048	.07548	12.887	170.744	70
13.292	13.785	.00023	.07523	13.087	173.956	80
13.313	13.807	.00011	.07511	13.199	175.725	90
13.324	13.817	.00005	.07505	13.261	176.685	100

N	SINGLE PAYMENT			UNIFORM	
	COMPOUND AMOUNT	PRESENT WORTH		COMPOUND	AMOUNT
	CA	PW	CPW	SCA	CSCA
1	1.080	.9259	.9625	1.000	1.039
2	1.166	.8573	.8912	2.080	2.162
3	1.260	.7938	.8252	3.246	3.375
4	1.360	.7350	.7641	4.506	4.684
5	1.469	.6806	.7075	5.867	6.098
6	1.587	.6302	.6551	7.336	7.626
7	1.714	.5835	.6065	8.923	9.275
8	1.851	.5403	.5616	10.637	11.057
9	1.999	.5002	.5200	12.488	12.981
10	2.159	.4632	.4815	14.487	15.059
11	2.332	.4289	.4458	16.645	17.303
12	2.518	.3971	.4128	18.977	19.726
13	2.720	.3677	.3822	21.495	22.344
14	2.937	.3405	.3539	24.215	25.171
15	3.172	.3152	.3277	27.152	28.224
16	3.426	.2919	.3034	30.324	31.522
17	3.700	.2703	.2809	33.750	35.083
18	3.996	.2502	.2601	37.450	38.929
19	4.316	.2317	.2409	41.446	43.083
20	4.661	.2145	.2230	45.762	47.569
21	5.034	.1987	.2065	50.423	52.414
22	5.437	.1839	.1912	55.457	57.647
23	5.871	.1703	.1770	60.893	63.298
24	6.341	.1577	.1639	66.765	69.401
25	6.848	.1460	.1518	73.106	75.993
26	7.396	.1352	.1405	79.954	83.112
27	7.988	.1252	.1301	87.351	90.800
28	8.627	.1159	.1205	95.339	99.103
29	9.317	.1073	.1116	103.966	108.071
30	10.063	.0994	.1033	113.283	117.756
31	10.868	.0920	.0956	123.346	128.216
32	11.737	.0852	.0886	134.214	139.513
33	12.676	.0789	.0820	145.951	151.714
34	13.690	.0730	.0759	158.627	164.890
35	14.785	.0676	.0703	172.317	179.121
40	21.725	.0460	.0478	259.057	269.286
45	31.920	.0313	.0326	386.506	401.768
50	46.902	.0213	.0222	573.770	596.427
55	68.914	.0145	.0151	848.923	882.445
60	101.257	.0099	.0103	1253.213	1302.699
65	148.780	.0067	.0070	1847.248	1920.190
70	218.606	.0046	.0048	2720.080	2827.488
80	471.955	.0021	.0022	5886.935	6119.393
90	1018.915	.0010	.0010	12723.939	13226.368
100	2199.761	.0005	.0005	27484.516	28569.796

I= .08000

ANNUAL SERIES				GRADIENT SERIES		
PRESENT WORTH		SINKING FUND	CAPITAL RECOVERY	UNIFORM SERIES	PRESENT WORTH	N
PW	CSPW	SF	CR	GUS	GPW	
.926	.962	1.00000	1.08000	.000	.000	1
1.783	1.854	.48077	.56077	.481	.857	2
2.577	2.679	.30803	.38803	.949	2.445	3
3.312	3.443	.22192	.30192	1.404	4.650	4
3.993	4.150	.17046	.25046	1.846	7.372	5
4.623	4.805	.13632	.21632	2.276	10.523	6
5.206	5.412	.11207	.19207	2.694	14.024	7
5.747	5.974	.09401	.17401	3.099	17.806	8
6.247	6.494	.08008	.16008	3.491	21.808	9
6.710	6.975	.06903	.14903	3.871	25.977	10
7.139	7.421	.06008	.14008	4.240	30.266	11
7.536	7.834	.05270	.13270	4.596	34.634	12
7.904	8.216	.04652	.12652	4.940	39.046	13
8.244	8.570	.04130	.12130	5.273	43.472	14
8.559	8.897	.03683	.11683	5.594	47.886	15
8.851	9.201	.03298	.11298	5.905	52.264	16
9.122	9.482	.02963	.10963	6.204	56.588	17
9.372	9.742	.02670	.10670	6.492	60.843	18
9.604	9.983	.02413	.10413	6.770	65.013	19
9.818	10.206	.02185	.10185	7.037	69.090	20
10.017	10.412	.01983	.09983	7.294	73.063	21
10.201	10.604	.01803	.09803	7.541	76.926	22
10.371	10.781	.01642	.09642	7.779	80.673	23
10.529	10.945	.01498	.09498	8.007	84.300	24
10.675	11.096	.01368	.09368	8.225	87.804	25
10.810	11.237	.01251	.09251	8.435	91.184	26
10.935	11.367	.01145	.09145	8.636	94.439	27
11.051	11.487	.01049	.09049	8.829	97.569	28
11.158	11.599	.00962	.08962	9.013	100.574	29
11.258	11.702	.00883	.08883	9.190	103.456	30
11.350	11.798	.00811	.08811	9.358	106.216	31
11.435	11.687	.00745	.08745	9.520	108.857	32
11.514	11.969	.00685	.08685	9.674	111.382	33
11.587	12.044	.00630	.08630	9.821	113.792	34
11.655	12.115	.00580	.08580	9.961	116.092	35
11.925	12.395	.00386	.08386	10.570	126.042	40
12.108	12.587	.00259	.08259	11.045	133.733	45
12.233	12.717	.00174	.08174	11.411	139.593	50
12.319	12.805	.00118	.08118	11.690	144.006	55
12.377	12.865	.00080	.08080	11.902	147.300	60
12.416	12.906	.00054	.08054	12.060	149.739	65
12.443	12.934	.00037	.08037	12.178	151.533	70
12.474	12.966	.00017	.08017	12.330	153.800	80
12.488	12.981	.00008	.08008	12.412	154.993	90
12.494	12.988	.00004	.08004	12.455	155.611	100

N	SINGLE PAYMENT			UNIFORM	
	COMPOUND AMOUNT	PRESENT WORTH		COMPOUND	AMOUNT
	CA	PW	CPW	SCA	CSCA
1	1.085	.9217	.9603	1.000	1.042
2	1.177	.8495	.8851	2.085	2.172
3	1.277	.7829	.8157	3.262	3.399
4	1.386	.7216	.7518	4.540	4.730
5	1.504	.6650	.6929	5.925	6.174
6	1.631	.6129	.6386	7.429	7.740
7	1.770	.5649	.5886	9.060	9.440
8	1.921	.5207	.5425	10.831	11.285
9	2.084	.4799	.5000	12.751	13.286
10	2.261	.4423	.4608	14.835	15.457
11	2.453	.4076	.4247	17.096	17.813
12	2.662	.3757	.3915	19.549	20.369
13	2.888	.3463	.3608	22.211	23.142
14	3.133	.3191	.3325	25.099	26.151
15	3.400	.2941	.3065	28.232	29.416
16	3.689	.2711	.2825	31.632	32.958
17	4.002	.2499	.2603	35.321	36.801
18	4.342	.2303	.2399	39.323	40.972
19	4.712	.2122	.2211	43.665	45.496
20	5.112	.1956	.2038	48.377	50.405
21	5.547	.1803	.1878	53.489	55.731
22	6.018	.1662	.1731	59.036	61.511
23	6.530	.1531	.1596	65.054	67.781
24	7.085	.1412	.1471	71.533	74.584
25	7.687	.1301	.1355	78.668	81.966
26	8.340	.1199	.1249	86.355	89.975
27	9.049	.1105	.1151	94.695	98.665
28	9.818	.1019	.1061	103.744	108.093
29	10.653	.0939	.0978	113.562	118.323
30	11.558	.0865	.0901	124.215	129.422
31	12.541	.0797	.0831	135.773	141.465
32	13.607	.0735	.0766	148.314	154.531
33	14.763	.0677	.0706	161.920	168.708
34	16.018	.0624	.0650	176.684	184.091
35	17.380	.0575	.0600	192.702	200.780
40	26.133	.0383	.0399	295.683	308.078
45	39.295	.0254	.0265	450.530	469.418
50	59.086	.0169	.0176	683.368	712.017
55	88.846	.0113	.0117	1033.477	1076.802
60	133.593	.0075	.0078	1559.920	1625.315
65	200.878	.0050	.0052	2351.509	2450.090
70	302.052	.0033	.0034	3541.788	3690.267
80	682.935	.0015	.0015	8022.759	8359.091
90	1544.104	.0006	.0007	18154.160	18915.222
100	3491.193	.0003	.0003	41061.090	42782.462

I= .08500

ANNUAL SERIES				GRADIENT SERIES		
PRESENT WORTH		SINKING FUND	CAPITAL RECOVERY	UNIFORM SERIES	PRESENT WORTH	N
PW	CSPW	SF	CR	GUS	GPW	
.922	.960	1.00000	1.08500	.000	.000	1
1.771	1.845	.47962	.56462	.480	.849	2
2.554	2.661	.30654	.39154	.946	2.415	3
3.276	3.413	.22029	.30529	1.398	4.580	4
3.941	4.106	.16877	.25377	1.837	7.240	5
4.554	4.744	.13461	.21961	2.263	10.305	6
5.119	5.333	.11037	.19537	2.675	13.694	7
5.639	5.876	.09233	.17733	3.075	17.339	8
6.119	6.376	.07842	.16342	3.461	21.178	9
6.561	6.836	.06741	.15241	3.834	25.159	10
6.969	7.261	.05849	.14349	4.195	29.235	11
7.345	7.653	.05115	.13615	4.543	33.368	12
7.691	8.013	.04502	.13002	4.879	37.523	13
8.010	8.346	.03984	.12484	5.202	41.672	14
8.304	8.652	.03542	.12042	5.514	45.790	15
8.575	8.935	.03161	.11661	5.814	49.856	16
8.825	9.195	.02831	.11331	6.102	53.854	17
9.055	9.435	.02543	.11043	6.379	57.769	18
9.268	9.656	.02290	.10790	6.646	61.589	19
9.463	9.860	.02067	.10567	6.901	65.306	20
9.644	10.048	.01870	.10370	7.146	68.912	21
9.810	10.221	.01694	.10194	7.381	72.401	22
9.963	10.381	.01537	.10037	7.605	75.771	23
10.104	10.528	.01397	.09897	7.820	79.017	24
10.234	10.663	.01271	.09771	8.026	82.139	25
10.354	10.788	.01158	.09658	8.223	85.137	26
10.465	10.903	.01056	.09556	8.410	88.010	27
10.566	11.009	.00964	.09464	8.589	90.760	28
10.660	11.107	.00881	.09381	8.760	93.389	29
10.747	11.197	.00805	.09305	8.923	95.898	30
10.827	11.280	.00737	.09237	9.079	98.290	31
10.900	11.357	.00674	.09174	9.226	100.568	32
10.968	11.428	.00618	.09118	9.367	102.736	33
11.030	11.493	.00566	.09066	9.501	104.796	34
11.088	11.553	.00519	.09019	9.628	106.752	35
11.315	11.789	.00338	.08838	10.173	115.105	40
11.465	11.946	.00222	.08722	10.590	121.413	45
11.566	12.050	.00146	.08646	10.904	126.110	50
11.632	12.120	.00097	.08597	11.139	129.567	55
11.677	12.166	.00064	.08564	11.312	132.088	60
11.706	12.197	.00043	.08543	11.440	133.912	65
11.726	12.217	.00028	.08528	11.532	135.224	70
11.747	12.240	.00012	.08512	11.647	136.828	80
11.757	12.250	.00006	.08506	11.706	137.633	90
11.761	12.254	.00002	.08502	11.736	138.032	100

N	SINGLE PAYMENT			UNIFORM	
	COMPOUND AMOUNT	PRESENT WORTH		COMPOUND AMOUNT	
	CA	PW	CPW	SCA	CSCA
1	1.090	.9174	.9581	1.000	1.044
2	1.188	.8417	.8790	2.090	2.183
3	1.295	.7722	.8064	3.278	3.423
4	1.412	.7084	.7398	4.573	4.776
5	1.539	.6499	.6788	5.985	6.250
6	1.677	.5963	.6227	7.523	7.857
7	1.828	.5470	.5713	9.200	9.609
8	1.993	.5019	.5241	11.028	11.518
9	2.172	.4604	.4808	13.021	13.599
10	2.367	.4224	.4411	15.193	15.867
11	2.580	.3875	.4047	17.560	18.339
12	2.813	.3555	.3713	20.141	21.034
13	3.066	.3262	.3406	22.953	23.971
14	3.342	.2992	.3125	26.019	27.173
15	3.642	.2745	.2867	29.361	30.663
16	3.970	.2519	.2630	33.003	34.467
17	4.328	.2311	.2413	36.974	38.614
18	4.717	.2120	.2214	41.301	43.133
19	5.142	.1945	.2031	46.018	48.060
20	5.604	.1784	.1863	51.160	53.429
21	6.109	.1637	.1710	56.765	59.282
22	6.659	.1502	.1568	62.873	65.662
23	7.258	.1378	.1439	69.532	72.616
24	7.911	.1264	.1320	76.790	80.196
25	8.623	.1160	.1211	84.701	88.458
26	9.399	.1064	.1111	93.324	97.463
27	10.245	.0976	.1019	102.723	107.279
28	11.167	.0895	.0935	112.968	117.979
29	12.172	.0822	.0858	124.135	129.641
30	13.268	.0754	.0787	136.308	142.353
31	14.462	.0691	.0722	149.575	156.209
32	15.763	.0634	.0663	164.037	171.313
33	17.182	.0582	.0608	179.800	187.775
34	18.728	.0534	.0558	196.982	205.719
35	20.414	.0490	.0512	215.711	225.278
40	31.409	.0318	.0332	337.882	352.869
45	48.327	.0207	.0216	525.859	549.183
50	74.358	.0134	.0140	815.084	851.236
55	114.408	.0087	.0091	1260.092	1315.982
60	176.031	.0057	.0059	1944.792	2031.051
65	270.846	.0037	.0039	2998.288	3131.274
70	416.730	.0024	.0025	4619.223	4824.103
80	986.552	.0010	.0011	10950.574	11436.273
90	2335.527	.0004	.0004	25939.184	27089.684
100	5529.041	.0002	.0002	61422.675	64147.001

I= .09000

ANNUAL SERIES				GRADIENT SERIES		
PRESENT WORTH		SINKING FUND	CAPITAL RECOVERY	UNIFORM SERIES	PRESENT WORTH	N
PW	CSPW	SF	CR	GUS	GPW	
.917	.958	1.00000	1.09000	.000	.000	1
1.759	1.837	.47847	.56847	.478	.842	2
2.531	2.644	.30505	.39505	.943	2.386	3
3.240	3.383	.21867	.30867	1.393	4.511	4
3.890	4.062	.16709	.25709	1.828	7.111	5
4.486	4.685	.13292	.22292	2.250	10.092	6
5.033	5.256	.10869	.19869	2.657	13.375	7
5.535	5.780	.09067	.18067	3.051	16.888	8
5.995	6.261	.07680	.16680	3.431	20.571	9
6.418	6.702	.06582	.15582	3.798	24.373	10
6.805	7.107	.05695	.14695	4.151	28.248	11
7.161	7.478	.04965	.13965	4.491	32.159	12
7.487	7.819	.04357	.13357	4.818	36.073	13
7.786	8.131	.03843	.12843	5.133	39.963	14
8.061	8.418	.03406	.12406	5.435	43.807	15
8.313	8.681	.03030	.12030	5.724	47.585	16
8.544	8.923	.02705	.11705	6.002	51.282	17
8.756	9.144	.02421	.11421	6.269	54.886	18
8.950	9.347	.02173	.11173	6.524	58.387	19
9.129	9.533	.01955	.10955	6.767	61.777	20
9.292	9.704	.01762	.10762	7.001	65.051	21
9.442	9.861	.01590	.10590	7.223	68.205	22
9.580	10.005	.01438	.10438	7.436	71.236	23
9.707	10.137	.01302	.10302	7.638	74.143	24
9.823	10.258	.01181	.10181	7.832	76.926	25
9.929	10.369	.01072	.10072	8.016	79.586	26
10.027	10.471	.00973	.09973	8.191	82.124	27
10.116	10.565	.00885	.09885	8.357	84.542	28
10.198	10.651	.00806	.09806	8.515	86.842	29
10.274	10.729	.00734	.09734	8.666	89.028	30
10.343	10.802	.00669	.09669	8.808	91.102	31
10.406	10.868	.00610	.09610	8.944	93.069	32
10.464	10.929	.00556	.09556	9.072	94.931	33
10.518	10.984	.00508	.09508	9.193	96.693	34
10.567	11.035	.00464	.09464	9.308	98.359	35
10.757	11.234	.00296	.09296	9.796	105.376	40
10.881	11.364	.00190	.09190	10.160	110.556	45
10.962	11.448	.00123	.09123	10.430	114.325	50
11.014	11.503	.00079	.09079	10.626	117.036	55
11.048	11.538	.00051	.09051	10.768	118.968	60
11.070	11.561	.00033	.09033	10.870	120.334	65
11.084	11.576	.00022	.09022	10.943	121.294	70
11.100	11.592	.00009	.09009	11.030	122.431	80
11.106	11.599	.00004	.09004	11.073	122.976	90
11.109	11.602	.00002	.09002	11.093	123.234	100

N	SINGLE PAYMENT			UNIFORM	
	COMPOUND AMOUNT	PRESENT WORTH		COMPOUND	AMOUNT
	CA	PW	CPW	SCA	CSCA
1	1.095	.9132	.9560	1.000	1.047
2	1.199	.8340	.8730	2.095	2.193
3	1.313	.7617	.7973	3.294	3.448
4	1.438	.6956	.7281	4.607	4.822
5	1.574	.6352	.6649	6.045	6.327
6	1.724	.5801	.6073	7.619	7.975
7	1.888	.5298	.5546	9.343	9.780
8	2.067	.4838	.5065	11.230	11.756
9	2.263	.4418	.4625	13.297	13.919
10	2.478	.4035	.4224	15.560	16.288
11	2.714	.3685	.3857	18.039	18.882
12	2.971	.3365	.3523	20.752	21.723
13	3.254	.3073	.3217	23.724	24.833
14	3.563	.2807	.2938	26.977	28.239
15	3.901	.2563	.2683	30.540	31.969
16	4.272	.2341	.2450	34.442	36.053
17	4.678	.2138	.2238	38.714	40.525
18	5.122	.1952	.2044	43.391	45.421
19	5.609	.1783	.1866	48.513	50.783
20	6.142	.1628	.1704	54.122	56.654
21	6.725	.1487	.1557	60.264	63.083
22	7.364	.1358	.1421	66.989	70.123
23	8.064	.1240	.1298	74.353	77.831
24	8.830	.1133	.1186	82.416	86.272
25	9.668	.1034	.1083	91.246	95.515
26	10.587	.0945	.0989	100.914	105.635
27	11.593	.0863	.0903	111.501	116.717
28	12.694	.0788	.0825	123.094	128.852
29	13.900	.0719	.0753	135.788	142.140
30	15.220	.0657	.0688	149.688	156.690
31	16.666	.0600	.0628	164.908	172.622
32	18.250	.0548	.0574	181.574	190.068
33	19.983	.0500	.0524	199.824	209.172
34	21.882	.0457	.0478	219.807	230.090
35	23.960	.0417	.0437	241.688	252.995
40	37.719	.0265	.0278	386.520	404.602
45	59.379	.0168	.0176	614.519	643.268
50	93.477	.0107	.0112	973.445	1018.984
55	147.156	.0068	.0071	1538.479	1610.452
60	231.658	.0043	.0045	2427.978	2541.563
65	364.685	.0027	.0029	3828.262	4007.354
70	574.101	.0017	.0018	6032.643	6314.859
80	1422.753	.0007	.0007	14965.822	15665.947
90	3525.906	.0003	.0003	37104.273	38840.072
100	8737.998	.0001	.0001	91968.395	96270.826

I= .09500

ANNUAL SERIES				GRADIENT SERIES		
PRESENT WORTH		SINKING FUND	CAPITAL RECOVERY	UNIFORM SERIES	PRESENT WORTH	N
PW	CSPW	SF	CR	GUS	GPW	
.913	.956	1.00000	1.09500	.000	.000	1
1.747	1.829	.47733	.57233	.477	.834	2
2.509	2.626	.30358	.39858	.940	2.357	3
3.204	3.354	.21706	.31206	1.387	4.444	4
3.840	4.019	.16544	.26044	1.819	6.985	5
4.420	4.627	.13125	.22625	2.237	9.886	6
4.950	5.181	.10704	.20204	2.639	13.064	7
5.433	5.688	.08905	.18405	3.028	16.451	8
5.875	6.150	.07520	.17020	3.402	19.986	9
6.279	6.573	.06427	.15927	3.761	23.617	10
6.647	6.958	.05544	.15044	4.107	27.302	11
6.984	7.311	.04819	.14319	4.439	31.004	12
7.291	7.632	.04215	.13715	4.758	34.692	13
7.572	7.926	.03707	.13207	5.064	38.341	14
7.828	8.194	.03274	.12774	5.356	41.930	15
8.062	8.439	.02903	.12403	5.636	45.441	16
8.276	8.663	.02583	.12083	5.904	48.861	17
8.471	8.868	.02305	.11805	6.160	52.180	18
8.650	9.054	.02061	.11561	6.404	55.390	19
8.812	9.225	.01848	.11348	6.636	58.483	20
8.961	9.380	.01659	.11159	6.858	61.457	21
9.097	9.522	.01493	.10993	7.069	64.309	22
9.221	9.652	.01345	.10845	7.270	67.037	23
9.334	9.771	.01213	.10713	7.461	69.642	24
9.438	9.879	.01096	.10596	7.642	72.124	25
9.532	9.978	.00991	.10491	7.814	74.486	26
9.618	10.068	.00897	.10397	7.977	76.729	27
9.697	10.151	.00812	.10312	8.132	78.856	28
9.769	10.226	.00736	.10236	8.278	80.870	29
9.835	10.295	.00668	.10168	8.417	82.775	30
9.895	10.358	.00606	.10106	8.548	84.576	31
9.950	10.415	.00551	.10051	8.671	86.274	32
10.000	10.467	.00500	.10000	8.788	87.876	33
10.045	10.515	.00455	.09955	8.898	89.384	34
10.087	10.559	.00414	.09914	9.002	90.803	35
10.247	10.727	.00259	.09759	9.437	96.703	40
10.349	10.833	.00163	.09663	9.755	100.960	45
10.414	10.901	.00103	.09603	9.986	103.988	50
10.455	10.944	.00065	.09565	10.150	106.116	55
10.481	10.971	.00041	.09541	10.266	107.599	60
10.497	10.989	.00026	.09526	10.348	108.623	65
10.508	11.000	.00017	.09517	10.404	109.327	70
10.519	11.011	.00007	.09507	10.470	110.134	80
10.523	11.016	.00003	.09503	10.501	110.503	90
10.525	11.017	.00001	.09501	10.515	110.670	100

N	SINGLE PAYMENT			UNIFORM	
	COMPOUND AMOUNT	PRESENT WORTH		COMPOUND AMOUNT	
	CA	PW	CPW	SCA	CSCA
1	1.100	.9091	.9538	1.000	1.049
2	1.210	.8264	.8671	2.100	2.203
3	1.331	.7513	.7883	3.310	3.473
4	1.464	.6830	.7166	4.641	4.869
5	1.611	.6209	.6515	6.105	6.406
6	1.772	.5645	.5922	7.716	8.095
7	1.949	.5132	.5384	9.487	9.954
8	2.144	.4665	.4895	11.436	11.999
9	2.358	.4241	.4450	13.579	14.248
10	2.594	.3855	.4045	15.937	16.722
11	2.853	.3505	.3677	18.531	19.443
12	3.138	.3186	.3343	21.384	22.437
13	3.452	.2897	.3039	24.523	25.729
14	3.797	.2633	.2763	27.975	29.352
15	4.177	.2394	.2512	31.772	33.336
16	4.595	.2176	.2283	35.950	37.719
17	5.054	.1978	.2076	40.545	42.540
18	5.560	.1799	.1887	45.599	47.843
19	6.116	.1635	.1716	51.159	53.676
20	6.727	.1486	.1560	57.275	60.093
21	7.400	.1351	.1418	64.002	67.152
22	8.140	.1228	.1289	71.403	74.916
23	8.954	.1117	.1172	79.543	83.457
24	9.850	.1015	.1065	88.497	92.852
25	10.835	.0923	.0968	98.347	103.186
26	11.918	.0839	.0880	109.182	114.554
27	13.110	.0763	.0800	121.100	127.059
28	14.421	.0693	.0728	134.210	140.814
29	15.863	.0630	.0661	148.631	155.944
30	17.449	.0573	.0601	164.494	172.588
31	19.194	.0521	.0547	181.943	190.896
32	21.114	.0474	.0497	201.138	211.035
33	23.225	.0431	.0452	222.252	233.188
34	25.548	.0391	.0411	245.477	257.556
35	28.102	.0356	.0373	271.024	284.360
40	45.259	.0221	.0232	442.593	464.371
45	72.890	.0137	.0144	718.905	754.279
50	117.391	.0085	.0089	1163.909	1221.180
55	189.059	.0053	.0055	1880.591	1973.128
60	304.482	.0033	.0034	3034.816	3184.147
65	490.371	.0020	.0021	4893.707	5134.506
70	789.747	.0013	.0013	7887.470	8275.579
80	2048.400	.0005	.0005	20474.002	21481.443
90	5313.023	.0002	.0002	53120.226	55734.053

I= .10000

ANNUAL SERIES				GRADIENT SERIES		
PRESENT	WORTH	SINKING FUND	CAPITAL RECOVERY	UNIFORM SERIES	PRESENT WORTH	N
PW	CSPW	SF	CR	GUS	GPW	
.909	.954	1.00000	1.10000	.000	.000	1
1.736	1.821	.47619	.57619	.476	.826	2
2.487	2.609	.30211	.40211	.937	2.329	3
3.170	3.326	.21547	.31547	1.381	4.378	4
3.791	3.977	.16380	.26380	1.810	6.862	5
4.355	4.570	.12961	.22961	2.224	9.684	6
4.868	5.108	.10541	.20541	2.622	12.763	7
5.335	5.597	.08744	.18744	3.004	16.029	8
5.759	6.042	.07364	.17364	3.372	19.421	9
6.145	6.447	.06275	.16275	3.725	22.891	10
6.495	6.815	.05396	.15396	4.064	26.396	11
6.814	7.149	.04676	.14676	4.388	29.901	12
7.103	7.453	.04078	.14078	4.699	33.377	13
7.367	7.729	.03575	.13575	4.996	36.800	14
7.606	7.980	.03147	.13147	5.279	40.152	15
7.824	8.209	.02782	.12782	5.549	43.416	16
8.022	8.416	.02466	.12466	5.807	46.582	17
8.201	8.605	.02193	.12193	6.053	49.640	18
8.365	8.777	.01955	.11955	6.286	52.583	19
8.514	8.932	.01746	.11746	6.508	55.407	20
8.649	9.074	.01562	.11562	6.719	58.110	21
8.772	9.203	.01401	.11401	6.919	60.689	22
8.883	9.320	.01257	.11257	7.108	63.146	23
8.985	9.427	.01130	.11130	7.288	65.481	24
9.077	9.524	.01017	.11017	7.458	67.696	25
9.161	9.612	.00916	.10916	7.619	69.794	26
9.237	9.692	.00826	.10826	7.770	71.777	27
9.307	9.765	.00745	.10745	7.914	73.650	28
9.370	9.831	.00673	.10673	8.049	75.415	29
9.427	9.891	.00608	.10608	8.176	77.077	30
9.479	9.945	.00550	.10550	8.296	78.640	31
9.526	9.995	.00497	.10497	8.409	80.108	32
9.569	10.040	.00450	.10450	8.515	81.486	33
9.609	10.081	.00407	.10407	8.615	82.777	34
9.644	10.119	.00369	.10369	8.709	83.987	35
9.779	10.260	.00226	.10226	9.096	88.953	40
9.863	10.348	.00139	.10139	9.374	92.454	45
9.915	10.403	.00086	.10086	9.570	94.889	50
9.947	10.437	.00053	.10053	9.708	96.562	55
9.967	10.458	.00033	.10033	9.802	97.701	60
9.980	10.471	.00020	.10020	9.867	98.471	65
9.987	10.479	.00013	.10013	9.911	98.987	70
9.995	10.487	.00005	.10005	9.961	99.561	80
9.998	10.490	.00002	.10002	9.983	99.812	90

N	SINGLE PAYMENT			UNIFORM	
	COMPOUND AMOUNT	PRESENT WORTH		COMPOUND	AMOUNT
	CA	PW	CPW	SCA	CSCA
1	1.110	.9009	.9496	1.000	1.054
2	1.232	.8116	.8555	2.110	2.224
3	1.368	.7312	.7707	3.342	3.523
4	1.518	.6587	.6943	4.710	4.964
5	1.685	.5935	.6255	6.228	6.564
6	1.870	.5346	.5635	7.913	8.340
7	2.076	.4817	.5077	9.783	10.312
8	2.305	.4339	.4574	11.859	12.500
9	2.558	.3909	.4121	14.164	14.929
10	2.839	.3522	.3712	16.722	17.626
11	3.152	.3173	.3344	19.561	20.619
12	3.498	.2858	.3013	22.713	23.941
13	3.883	.2575	.2714	26.212	27.628
14	4.310	.2320	.2445	30.095	31.721
15	4.785	.2090	.2203	34.405	36.265
16	5.311	.1883	.1985	39.190	41.308
17	5.895	.1696	.1788	44.501	46.906
18	6.544	.1528	.1611	50.396	53.120
19	7.263	.1377	.1451	56.939	60.017
20	8.062	.1240	.1307	64.203	67.673
21	8.949	.1117	.1178	72.265	76.171
22	9.934	.1007	.1061	81.214	85.603
23	11.026	.0907	.0956	91.148	96.074
24	12.239	.0817	.0861	102.174	107.696
25	13.585	.0736	.0776	114.413	120.597
26	15.080	.0663	.0699	127.999	134.916
27	16.739	.0597	.0630	143.079	150.811
28	18.580	.0538	.0567	159.817	168.454
29	20.624	.0485	.0511	178.397	188.038
30	22.892	.0437	.0460	199.021	209.777
31	25.410	.0394	.0415	221.913	233.906
32	28.206	.0355	.0374	247.324	260.690
33	31.308	.0319	.0337	275.529	290.420
34	34.752	.0288	.0303	306.837	323.420
35	38.575	.0259	.0273	341.590	360.050
40	65.001	.0154	.0162	581.826	613.270
45	109.530	.0091	.0096	986.639	1039.960
50	184.565	.0054	.0057	1668.771	1758.957
55	311.002	.0032	.0034	2818.204	2970.510
60	524.057	.0019	.0020	4755.066	5012.046
65	883.067	.0011	.0012	8018.790	8452.154
70	1488.019	.0007	.0007	13518.356	14248.936
80	4225.113	.0002	.0002	38401.025	40476.352

I= .11000

ANNUAL SERIES				GRADIENT SERIES		
PRESENT WORTH		SINKING FUND	CAPITAL RECOVERY	UNIFORM SERIES	PRESENT WORTH	N
PW	CSPW	SF	CR	GUS	GPW	
.901	.950	1.00000	1.11000	.000	.000	1
1.713	1.805	.47393	.58393	.474	.812	2
2.444	2.576	.29921	.40921	.931	2.274	3
3.102	3.270	.21233	.32233	1.370	4.250	4
3.696	3.896	.16057	.27057	1.792	6.624	5
4.231	4.459	.12638	.23638	2.198	9.297	6
4.712	4.967	.10222	.21222	2.586	12.187	7
5.146	5.424	.08432	.19432	2.958	15.225	8
5.537	5.836	.07060	.18060	3.314	18.352	9
5.889	6.208	.05980	.16980	3.654	21.522	10
6.207	6.542	.05112	.16112	3.979	24.695	11
6.492	6.843	.04403	.15403	4.288	27.839	12
6.750	7.115	.03815	.14815	4.582	30.929	13
6.982	7.359	.03323	.14323	4.862	33.945	14
7.191	7.579	.02907	.13907	5.127	36.871	15
7.379	7.778	.02552	.13552	5.379	39.695	16
7.549	7.957	.02247	.13247	5.618	42.409	17
7.702	8.118	.01984	.12984	5.844	45.007	18
7.839	8.263	.01756	.12756	6.057	47.486	19
7.963	8.394	.01558	.12558	6.259	49.842	20
8.075	8.511	.01384	.12384	6.449	52.077	21
8.176	8.618	.01231	.12231	6.628	54.191	22
8.266	8.713	.01097	.12097	6.797	56.186	23
8.348	8.799	.00979	.11979	6.956	58.066	24
8.422	8.877	.00874	.11874	7.104	59.832	25
8.488	8.947	.00781	.11781	7.244	61.490	26
8.548	9.810	.00699	.11699	7.375	63.043	27
8.602	9.066	.00626	.11626	7.498	64.497	28
8.650	9.118	.00561	.11561	7.613	65.854	29
8.894	9.164	.00502	.11502	7.721	67.121	30
8.733	9.205	.00451	.11451	7.821	68.302	31
8.769	9.242	.00404	.11404	7.915	69.401	32
8.801	9.276	.00363	.11363	8.002	70.423	33
8.829	9.306	.00326	.11326	8.084	71.372	34
8.855	9.334	.00293	.11293	8.159	72.254	35
8.951	9.435	.00172	.11172	8.466	75.779	40
9.008	9.495	.00101	.11101	8.676	78.155	45
9.042	9.530	.00060	.11060	8.819	79.734	50
9.062	9.551	.00035	.11035	8.913	80.771	55
9.074	9.564	.00021	.11021	8.976	81.446	60
9.081	9.571	.00012	.11012	9.017	81.882	65
9.085	9.576	.00007	.11007	9.044	82.161	70
9.089	9.580	.00003	.11003	9.072	82.453	80

N	SINGLE PAYMENT			UNIFORM	
	COMPOUND AMOUNT	PRESENT WORTH		COMPOUND	AMOUNT
	CA	PW	CPW	SCA	CSCA
1	1.120	.8929	.9454	1.000	1.059
2	1.254	.7972	.8441	2.120	2.245
3	1.405	.7118	.7537	3.374	3.573
4	1.574	.6355	.6729	4.779	5.061
5	1.762	.5674	.6008	6.353	6.727
6	1.974	.5066	.5365	8.115	8.593
7	2.211	.4523	.4790	10.089	10.683
8	2.476	.4039	.4277	12.300	13.024
9	2.773	.3606	.3818	14.776	15.645
10	3.106	.3220	.3409	17.549	18.582
11	3.479	.2875	.3044	20.655	21.870
12	3.896	.2567	.2718	24.133	25.554
13	4.363	.2292	.2427	28.029	29.679
14	4.887	.2046	.2167	32.393	34.299
15	5.474	.1827	.1935	37.280	39.474
16	6.130	.1631	.1727	42.753	45.270
17	6.866	.1456	.1542	48.884	51.761
18	7.690	.1300	.1377	55.750	59.032
19	8.613	.1161	.1229	63.440	67.174
20	9.646	.1037	.1098	72.052	76.294
21	10.804	.0926	.0980	81.699	86.508
22	12.100	.0826	.0875	92.503	97.948
23	13.552	.0738	.0781	104.603	110.761
24	15.179	.0659	.0698	118.155	125.111
25	17.000	.0588	.0623	133.334	141.183
26	19.040	.0525	.0556	150.334	159.184
27	21.325	.0469	.0497	169.374	179.345
28	23.884	.0419	.0443	190.699	201.925
29	26.750	.0374	.0396	214.583	227.215
30	29.960	.0334	.0353	241.333	255.539
31	33.555	.0298	.0316	271.293	287.263
32	37.582	.0266	.0282	304.848	322.793
33	42.092	.0238	.0252	342.429	362.587
34	47.143	.0212	.0225	384.521	407.157
35	52.800	.0189	.0201	431.663	457.074
40	93.051	.0107	.0114	767.091	812.248
45	163.988	.0061	.0065	1358.230	1438.185
50	289.002	.0035	.0037	2400.018	2541.300
55	509.321	.0020	.0021	4236.005	4485.366
60	897.597	.0011	.0012	7471.641	7911.474
65	1581.872	.0006	.0007	13173.937	13949.447
70	2787.800	.0004	.0004	23223.332	24590.419
80	8658.483	.0001	.0001	72145.692	76392.690

I= .12000

ANNUAL SERIES				GRADIENT SERIES		
PRESENT WORTH		SINKING FUND	CAPITAL RECOVERY	UNIFORM SERIES	PRESENT WORTH	N
PW	CSPW	SF	CR	GUS	GPW	
.893	.945	1.00000	1.12000	.000	.000	1
1.690	1.790	.47170	.59170	.472	.797	2
2.402	2.543	.29635	.41635	.925	2.221	3
3.037	3.216	.20923	.32923	1.359	4.127	4
3.605	3.817	.15741	.27741	1.775	6.397	5
4.111	4.353	.12323	.24323	2.172	8.930	6
4.564	4.832	.09912	.21912	2.551	11.644	7
4.968	5.260	.08130	.20130	2.913	14.471	8
5.328	5.642	.06768	.18768	3.257	17.356	9
5.650	5.983	.05698	.17698	3.585	20.254	10
5.938	6.287	.04842	.16842	3.895	23.129	11
6.194	6.559	.04144	.16144	4.190	25.952	12
6.424	6.802	.03568	.15568	4.468	28.702	13
6.628	7.018	.03087	.15087	4.732	31.362	14
6.811	7.212	.02682	.14682	4.980	33.920	15
6.974	7.385	.02339	.14339	5.215	36.367	16
7.120	7.539	.02046	.14046	5.435	38.697	17
7.250	7.676	.01794	.13794	5.643	40.908	18
7.366	7.799	.01576	.13576	5.838	42.998	19
7.469	7.909	.01388	.13388	6.020	44.968	20
7.562	8.007	.01224	.13224	6.191	46.819	21
7.645	8.095	.01081	.13081	6.351	48.554	22
7.718	8.173	.00956	.12956	6.501	50.178	23
7.784	8.243	.00846	.12846	6.641	51.693	24
7.843	8.305	.00750	.12750	6.771	53.105	25
7.896	8.360	.00665	.12665	6.892	54.418	26
7.943	8.410	.00590	.12590	7.005	55.637	27
7.984	8.454	.00524	.12524	7.110	56.767	28
8.022	8.494	.00466	.12466	7.207	57.814	29
8.055	8.529	.00414	.12414	7.297	58.782	30
8.085	8.561	.00369	.12369	7.381	59.676	31
8.112	8.589	.00328	.12328	7.459	60.501	32
8.135	8.614	.00292	.12292	7.530	61.261	33
8.157	8.637	.00260	.12260	7.596	61.961	34
8.176	8.657	.00232	.12232	7.658	62.605	35
8.244	8.729	.00130	.12130	7.899	65.116	40
8.283	8.770	.00074	.12074	8.057	66.734	45
8.304	8.793	.00042	.12042	8.160	67.762	50
8.317	8.807	.00024	.12024	8.225	68.408	55
8.324	8.814	.00013	.12013	8.266	68.810	60
8.328	8.818	.00008	.12008	8.292	69.058	65
8.330	8.821	.00004	.12004	8.308	69.210	70
8.332	8.823	.00001	.12001	8.324	69.359	80

N	SINGLE PAYMENT			UNIFORM	
	COMPOUND AMOUNT	PRESENT WORTH		COMPOUND AMOUNT	
	CA	PW	CPW	SCA	CSCA
1	1.130	.8850	.9413	1.000	1.064
2	1.277	.7831	.8330	2.130	2.266
3	1.443	.6931	.7372	3.407	3.624
4	1.630	.6133	.6524	4.850	5.159
5	1.842	.5428	.5773	6.480	6.893
6	2.082	.4803	.5109	8.323	8.853
7	2.353	.4251	.4521	10.405	11.067
8	2.658	.3762	.4001	12.757	13.570
9	3.004	.3329	.3541	15.416	16.397
10	3.395	.2946	.3133	18.420	19.593
11	3.836	.2607	.2773	21.814	23.203
12	4.335	.2307	.2454	25.650	27.283
13	4.898	.2042	.2172	29.985	31.894
14	5.535	.1807	.1922	34.883	37.104
15	6.254	.1599	.1701	40.417	42.991
16	7.067	.1415	.1505	46.672	49.644
17	7.986	.1252	.1332	53.739	57.161
18	9.024	.1108	.1179	61.725	65.656
19	10.197	.0981	.1043	70.749	75.254
20	11.523	.0868	.0923	80.947	86.101
21	13.021	.0768	.0817	92.470	98.358
22	14.714	.0680	.0723	105.491	112.208
23	16.627	.0601	.0640	120.205	127.859
24	18.788	.0532	.0566	136.831	145.544
25	21.231	.0471	.0501	155.620	165.529
26	23.991	.0417	.0443	176.850	188.111
27	27.109	.0369	.0392	200.841	213.629
28	30.633	.0326	.0347	227.950	242.465
29	34.616	.0289	.0307	258.583	275.049
30	39.116	.0256	.0272	293.199	311.869
31	44.201	.0226	.0241	332.315	353.476
32	49.947	.0200	.0213	376.516	400.491
33	56.440	.0177	.0188	426.463	453.619
34	63.777	.0157	.0167	482.903	513.653
35	72.069	.0139	.0148	546.681	581.491
40	132.782	.0075	.0080	1013.704	1078.253
45	244.641	.0041	.0043	1874.165	1993.505
50	450.736	.0022	.0024	3459.507	3679.796
55	830.452	.0012	.0013	6380.398	6786.678
60	1530.053	.0007	.0007	11761.950	12510.907
65	2819.024	.0004	.0004	21677.110	23057.429
70	5193.870	.0002	.0002	39945.151	42488.711

I= .13000

ANNUAL SERIES				GRADIENT SERIES		
PRESENT WORTH		SINKING FUND	CAPITAL RECOVERY	UNIFORM SERIES	PRESENT WORTH	N
PW	CSPW	SF	CR	GUS	GPW	
.885	.941	1.00000	1.13000	.000	.000	1
1.668	1.774	.46948	.59948	.469	.783	2
2.361	2.512	.29352	.42352	.919	2.169	3
2.974	3.164	.20619	.33619	1.348	4.009	4
3.517	3.741	.15431	.28431	1.757	6.180	5
3.998	4.252	.12015	.25015	2.147	8.582	6
4.423	4.704	.09611	.22611	2.517	11.132	7
4.799	5.104	.07839	.20839	2.869	13.765	8
5.132	5.458	.06487	.19487	3.201	16.428	9
5.426	5.772	.05429	.18429	3.516	19.080	10
5.687	6.049	.04584	.17584	3.813	21.687	11
5.918	6.294	.03899	.16899	4.094	24.224	12
6.122	6.512	.03335	.16335	4.357	26.674	13
6.302	6.704	.02867	.15867	4.605	29.023	14
6.462	6.874	.02474	.15474	4.837	31.262	15
6.604	7.024	.02143	.15143	5.055	33.384	16
6.729	7.158	.01861	.14861	5.259	35.388	17
6.840	7.275	.01620	.14620	5.449	37.271	18
6.938	7.380	.01413	.14413	5.627	39.037	19
7.025	7.472	.01235	.14235	5.792	40.685	20
7.102	7.554	.01081	.14081	5.945	42.221	21
7.170	7.626	.00948	.13948	6.088	43.649	22
7.230	7.690	.00832	.13832	6.220	44.972	23
7.283	7.747	.00731	.13731	6.343	46.196	24
7.330	7.797	.00643	.13643	6.457	47.326	25
7.372	7.841	.00565	.13565	6.561	48.369	26
7.409	7.880	.00498	.13498	6.658	49.328	27
7.441	7.915	.00439	.13439	6.747	50.209	28
7.470	7.946	.00387	.13387	6.830	51.018	29
7.496	7.973	.00341	.13341	6.905	51.759	30
7.518	7.997	.00301	.13301	6.975	52.438	31
7.538	8.018	.00266	.13266	7.039	53.059	32
7.556	8.037	.00234	.13234	7.097	53.626	33
7.572	8.054	.00207	.13207	7.151	54.143	34
7.586	8.069	.00183	.13183	7.200	54.615	35
7.634	8.121	.00099	.13099	7.389	56.409	40
7.661	8.149	.00053	.13053	7.508	57.515	45
7.675	8.164	.00029	.13029	7.581	58.187	50
7.683	8.172	.00016	.13016	7.626	58.591	55
7.687	8.177	.00009	.13009	7.653	58.831	60
7.690	8.179	.00005	.13005	7.669	58.973	65
7.691	8.181	.00003	.13003	7.679	59.057	70

N	SINGLE PAYMENT			UNIFORM	
	COMPOUND AMOUNT	PRESENT WORTH		COMPOUND	AMOUNT
	CA	PW	CPW	SCA	CSCA
1	1.140	.8772	.9373	1.000	1.068
2	1.300	.7695	.8222	2.140	2.287
3	1.482	.6750	.7212	3.440	3.675
4	1.689	.5921	.6326	4.921	5.258
5	1.925	.5194	.5549	6.610	7.063
6	2.195	.4556	.4868	8.536	9.120
7	2.502	.3996	.4270	10.730	11.465
8	2.853	.3506	.3746	13.233	14.139
9	3.252	.3075	.3286	16.085	17.187
10	3.707	.2697	.2882	19.337	20.661
11	4.226	.2366	.2528	23.045	24.622
12	4.818	.2076	.2218	27.271	29.138
13	5.492	.1821	.1945	32.089	34.286
14	6.261	.1597	.1706	37.581	40.154
15	7.138	.1401	.1497	43.842	46.844
16	8.137	.1229	.1313	50.980	54.471
17	9.276	.1078	.1152	59.118	63.165
18	10.575	.0946	.1010	68.394	73.077
19	12.056	.0829	.0886	78.969	84.376
20	13.743	.0728	.0777	91.025	97.258
21	15.668	.0638	.0682	104.768	111.942
22	17.861	.0560	.0598	120.436	128.682
23	20.362	.0491	.0525	138.297	147.766
24	23.212	.0431	.0460	158.659	169.522
25	26.462	.0378	.0404	181.871	194.324
26	30.167	.0331	.0354	208.333	222.598
27	34.390	.0291	.0311	238.499	254.830
28	39.204	.0255	.0273	272.889	291.574
29	44.693	.0224	.0239	312.094	333.463
30	50.950	.0196	.0210	356.787	381.217
31	58.083	.0172	.0184	407.737	435.655
32	66.215	.0151	.0161	465.820	497.716
33	75.485	.0132	.0142	532.035	568.464
34	86.053	.0116	.0124	607.520	649.118
35	98.100	.0102	.0109	693.573	741.063
40	188.884	.0053	.0057	1342.025	1433.916
45	363.679	.0027	.0029	2590.565	2767.945
50	700.233	.0014	.0015	4994.521	5336.505
55	1348.239	.0007	.0008	9623.134	10282.047
60	2595.919	.0004	.0004	18535.133	19804.267
65	4998.220	.0002	.0002	35694.426	38138.487
70	9623.645	.0001	.0001	68733.178	73439.461

I= .14000

ANNUAL SERIES				GRADIENT SERIES		
PRESENT WORTH		SINKING FUND	CAPITAL RECOVERY	UNIFORM SERIES	PRESENT WORTH	N
PW	CSPW	SF	CR	GUS	GPW	
.877	.937	1.00000	1.14000	.000	.000	1
1.647	1.759	.46729	.60729	.467	.769	2
2.322	2.481	.29073	.43073	.913	2.119	3
2.914	3.113	.20320	.34320	1.337	3.896	4
3.433	3.668	.15128	.29128	1.740	5.973	5
3.889	4.155	.11716	.25716	2.122	8.251	6
4.288	4.582	.09319	.23319	2.483	10.649	7
4.639	4.956	.07557	.21557	2.825	13.103	8
4.946	5.285	.06217	.20217	3.146	15.563	9
5.216	5.573	.05171	.19171	3.449	17.991	10
5.453	5.826	.04339	.18339	3.733	20.357	11
5.660	6.048	.03667	.17667	4.000	22.640	12
5.842	6.242	.03116	.17116	4.249	24.825	13
6.002	6.413	.02661	.16661	4.482	26.901	14
6.142	6.563	.02281	.16281	4.699	28.862	15
6.265	6.694	.01962	.15962	4.901	30.706	16
6.373	6.809	.01692	.15692	5.089	32.430	17
6.467	6.910	.01462	.15462	5.263	34.038	18
6.550	6.999	.01266	.15266	5.424	35.531	19
6.623	7.077	.01099	.15099	5.573	36.914	20
6.687	7.145	.00954	.14954	5.711	38.190	21
6.743	7.205	.00830	.14830	5.838	39.366	22
6.792	7.257	.00723	.14723	5.955	40.446	23
6.835	7.303	.00630	.14630	6.062	41.437	24
6.873	7.344	.00550	.14550	6.161	42.344	25
6.906	7.379	.00480	.14480	6.251	43.173	26
6.935	7.410	.00419	.14419	6.334	43.929	27
6.961	7.437	.00366	.14366	6.410	44.618	28
6.983	7.461	.00320	.14320	6.479	45.244	29
7.003	7.482	.00280	.14280	6.542	45.813	30
7.020	7.501	.00245	.14245	6.600	46.330	31
7.035	7.517	.00215	.14215	6.652	46.798	32
7.048	7.531	.00188	.14188	6.700	47.222	33
7.060	7.543	.00165	.14165	6.743	47.605	34
7.070	7.554	.00144	.14144	6.782	47.952	35
7.105	7.592	.00075	.14075	6.930	49.238	40
7.123	7.611	.00039	.14039	7.019	49.996	45
7.133	7.621	.00020	.14020	7.071	50.438	50
7.138	7.626	.00010	.14010	7.102	50.691	55
7.140	7.629	.00005	.14005	7.120	50.836	60
7.141	7.630	.00003	.14003	7.130	50.917	65
7.142	7.631	.00001	.14001	7.136	50.963	70

N	SINGLE PAYMENT			UNIFORM	
	COMPOUND AMOUNT	PRESENT WORTH		COMPOUND AMOUNT	
	CA	PW	CPW	SCA	CSCA
1	1.150	.8696	.9333	1.000	1.073
2	1.322	.7561	.8115	2.150	2.307
3	1.521	.6575	.7057	3.472	3.727
4	1.749	.5718	.6136	4.993	5.359
5	2.011	.4972	.5336	6.742	7.236
6	2.313	.4323	.4640	8.754	9.395
7	2.660	.3759	.4035	11.067	11.877
8	3.059	.3269	.3508	13.727	14.732
9	3.518	.2843	.3051	16.786	18.015
10	4.046	.2472	.2653	20.304	21.791
11	4.652	.2149	.2307	24.349	26.133
12	5.350	.1869	.2006	29.002	31.126
13	6.153	.1625	.1744	34.352	36.868
14	7.076	.1413	.1517	40.505	43.472
15	8.137	.1229	.1319	47.580	51.066
16	9.358	.1069	.1147	55.717	59.799
17	10.761	.0929	.0997	65.075	69.842
18	12.375	.0808	.0867	75.836	81.392
19	14.232	.0703	.0754	88.212	94.674
20	16.367	.0611	.0656	102.444	109.948
21	18.822	.0531	.0570	118.810	127.513
22	21.645	.0462	.0496	137.632	147.714
23	24.891	.0402	.0431	159.276	170.944
24	28.625	.0349	.0375	184.168	197.659
25	32.919	.0304	.0326	212.793	228.381
26	37.857	.0264	.0284	245.712	263.711
27	43.535	.0230	.0247	283.569	304.341
28	50.066	.0200	.0214	327.104	351.066
29	57.575	.0174	.0186	377.170	404.799
30	66.212	.0151	.0162	434.745	466.592
31	76.144	.0131	.0141	500.957	537.654
32	87.565	.0114	.0123	577.100	619.375
33	100.700	.0099	.0107	664.666	713.355
34	115.805	.0086	.0093	765.365	821.431
35	133.176	.0075	.0081	881.170	945.719
40	267.864	.0037	.0040	1779.090	1909.415
45	538.769	.0019	.0020	3585.128	3847.752
50	1083.657	.0009	.0010	7217.716	7746.440
55	2179.622	.0005	.0005	14524.148	15588.093
60	4383.999	.0002	.0002	29219.992	31360.460
65	8817.787	.0001	.0001	58778.583	63084.322

I= .15000

ANNUAL SERIES				GRADIENT SERIES		
PRESENT WORTH		SINKING FUND	CAPITAL RECOVERY	UNIFORM SERIES	PRESENT WORTH	N
PW	CSPW	SF	CR	GUS	GPW	
.870	.933	1.00000	1.15000	.000	.000	1
1.626	1.745	.46512	.61512	.465	.756	2
2.283	2.450	.28798	.43798	.907	2.071	3
2.855	3.064	.20027	.35027	1.326	3.786	4
3.352	3.598	.14832	.29832	1.723	5.775	5
3.784	4.062	.11424	.26424	2.097	7.937	6
4.160	4.465	.09036	.24036	2.450	10.192	7
4.487	4.816	.07285	.22285	2.781	12.481	8
4.772	5.121	.05957	.20957	3.092	14.755	9
5.019	5.386	.04925	.19925	3.383	16.979	10
5.234	5.617	.04107	.19107	3.655	19.129	11
5.421	5.818	.03448	.18448	3.908	21.185	12
5.583	5.992	.02911	.17911	4.144	23.135	13
5.724	6.144	.02469	.17469	4.362	24.972	14
5.847	6.276	.02102	.17102	4.565	26.693	15
5.954	6.390	.01795	.16795	4.752	28.296	16
6.047	6.490	.01537	.16537	4.925	29.783	17
6.128	6.577	.01319	.16319	5.084	31.156	18
6.198	6.652	.01134	.16134	5.231	32.421	19
6.259	6.718	.00976	.15976	5.365	33.582	20
6.312	6.775	.00842	.15842	5.488	34.645	21
6.359	6.824	.00727	.15727	5.601	35.615	22
6.399	6.868	.00628	.15628	5.704	36.499	23
6.434	6.905	.00543	.15543	5.798	37.302	24
6.464	6.938	.00470	.15470	5.883	38.031	25
6.491	6.966	.00407	.15407	5.961	38.692	26
6.514	6.991	.00353	.15353	6.032	39.289	27
6.534	7.012	.00306	.15306	6.096	39.828	28
6.551	7.031	.00265	.15265	6.154	40.315	29
6.566	7.047	.00230	.15230	6.207	40.753	30
6.579	7.061	.00200	.15200	6.254	41.147	31
6.591	7.073	.00173	.15173	6.297	41.501	32
6.600	7.084	.00150	.15150	6.336	41.818	33
6.609	7.093	.00131	.15131	6.371	42.103	34
6.617	7.101	.00113	.15113	6.402	42.359	35
6.642	7.128	.00056	.15056	6.517	43.283	40
6.654	7.142	.00028	.15028	6.583	43.805	45
6.661	7.148	.00014	.15014	6.620	44.096	50
6.664	7.152	.00007	.15007	6.641	44.256	55
6.665	7.153	.00003	.15003	6.653	44.343	60
6.666	7.154	.00002	.15002	6.659	44.390	65

N	SINGLE PAYMENT			UNIFORM	
	COMPOUND AMOUNT	PRESENT WORTH		COMPOUND	AMOUNT
	CA	PW	CPW	SCA	CSCA
1	1.160	.8621	.9293	1.000	1.078
2	1.346	.7432	.8011	2.160	2.329
3	1.561	.6407	.6906	3.506	3.779
4	1.811	.5523	.5954	5.066	5.462
5	2.100	.4761	.5133	6.877	7.414
6	2.436	.4104	.4425	8.977	9.678
7	2.826	.3538	.3814	11.414	12.304
8	3.278	.3050	.3288	14.240	15.351
9	3.803	.2630	.2835	17.519	18.885
10	4.411	.2267	.2444	21.321	22.985
11	5.117	.1954	.2107	25.733	27.741
12	5.936	.1685	.1816	30.850	33.257
13	6.886	.1452	.1566	36.786	39.656
14	7.988	.1252	.1350	43.672	47.079
15	9.266	.1079	.1163	51.660	55.690
16	10.748	.0930	.1003	60.925	65.679
17	12.468	.0802	.0865	71.673	77.265
18	14.463	.0691	.0745	84.141	90.706
19	16.777	.0596	.0643	98.603	106.296
20	19.461	.0514	.0554	115.380	124.382
21	22.574	.0443	.0478	134.841	145.361
22	26.186	.0382	.0412	157.415	169.697
23	30.376	.0329	.0355	183.601	197.926
24	35.236	.0284	.0306	213.978	230.673
25	40.874	.0245	.0264	249.214	268.658
26	47.414	.0211	.0227	290.088	312.721
27	55.000	.0182	.0196	337.502	363.835
28	63.800	.0157	.0169	392.503	423.127
29	74.009	.0135	.0146	456.303	491.905
30	85.850	.0116	.0126	530.312	571.688
31	99.586	.0100	.0108	616.162	664.236
32	115.520	.0087	.0093	715.747	771.591
33	134.003	.0075	.0080	831.267	896.124
34	155.443	.0064	.0069	965.270	1040.582
35	180.314	.0055	.0060	1120.713	1208.153
40	378.721	.0026	.0028	2360.757	2544.948
45	795.444	.0013	.0014	4965.274	5352.673
50	1670.704	.0006	.0006	10435.649	11249.857
55	3509.049	.0003	.0003	21925.305	23635.957
60	7370.201	.0001	.0001	46057.509	49650.998

I= .16000

ANNUAL SERIES				GRADIENT SERIES		
PRESENT WORTH		SINKING FUND	CAPITAL RECOVERY	UNIFORM SERIES	PRESENT WORTH	N
PW	CSPW	SF	CR	GUS	GPW	
.862	.929	1.00000	1.16000	.000	.000	1
1.605	1.730	.46296	.62296	.463	.743	2
2.246	2.421	.28526	.44526	.901	2.024	3
2.798	3.016	.19738	.35738	1.316	3.681	4
3.274	3.530	.14541	.30541	1.706	5.586	5
3.685	3.972	.11139	.27139	2.073	7.638	6
4.039	4.354	.08761	.24761	2.417	9.761	7
4.344	4.682	.07022	.23022	2.739	11.896	8
4.607	4.966	.05708	.21708	3.039	14.000	9
4.833	5.210	.04690	.20690	3.319	16.040	10
5.029	5.421	.03886	.19886	3.578	17.994	11
5.197	5.603	.03241	.19241	3.819	19.847	12
5.342	5.759	.02718	.18718	4.041	21.590	13
5.468	5.894	.02290	.18290	4.246	23.217	14
5.575	6.010	.01936	.17936	4.435	24.728	15
5.668	6.111	.01641	.17641	4.609	26.124	16
5.749	6.197	.01395	.17395	4.768	27.407	17
5.818	6.272	.01188	.17188	4.913	28.583	18
5.877	6.336	.01014	.17014	5.046	29.656	19
5.929	6.391	.00867	.16867	5.167	30.632	20
5.973	6.439	.00742	.16742	5.277	31.518	21
6.011	6.480	.00635	.16635	5.377	32.320	22
6.044	6.516	.00545	.16545	5.467	33.044	23
6.073	6.546	.00467	.16467	5.549	33.697	24
6.097	6.573	.00401	.16401	5.623	34.284	25
6.118	6.596	.00345	.16345	5.690	34.811	26
6.136	6.615	.00296	.16296	5.750	35.284	27
6.152	6.632	.00255	.16255	5.804	35.707	28
6.166	6.647	.00219	.16219	5.853	36.086	29
6.177	6.659	.00189	.16189	5.896	36.423	30
6.187	6.670	.00162	.16162	5.936	36.725	31
6.196	6.679	.00140	.16140	5.971	36.993	32
6.203	6.687	.00120	.16120	6.002	37.232	33
6.210	6.694	.00104	.16104	6.030	37.444	34
6.215	6.700	.00089	.16089	6.055	37.633	35
6.233	6.720	.00042	.16042	6.144	38.299	40
6.242	6.729	.00020	.16020	6.193	38.660	45
6.246	6.734	.00010	.16010	6.220	38.852	50
6.248	6.736	.00005	.16005	6.234	38.953	55
6.249	6.737	.00002	.16002	6.242	39.006	60

N	SINGLE PAYMENT			UNIFORM	
	COMPOUND AMOUNT	PRESENT WORTH		COMPOUND AMOUNT	
	CA	PW	CPW	SCA	CSCA
1	1.170	.8547	.9255	1.000	1.083
2	1.369	.7305	.7910	2.170	2.350
3	1.602	.6244	.6761	3.539	3.832
4	1.874	.5337	.5778	5.141	5.566
5	2.192	.4561	.4939	7.014	7.595
6	2.565	.3898	.4221	9.207	9.969
7	3.001	.3332	.3608	11.772	12.746
8	3.511	.2848	.3084	14.773	15.996
9	4.108	.2434	.2636	18.285	19.798
10	4.807	.2080	.2253	22.393	24.247
11	5.624	.1778	.1925	27.200	29.451
12	6.580	.1520	.1646	32.824	35.541
13	7.699	.1299	.1406	39.404	42.666
14	9.007	.1110	.1202	47.103	51.002
15	10.539	.0949	.1027	56.110	60.755
16	12.330	.0811	.0878	66.649	72.166
17	14.426	.0693	.0751	78.979	85.517
18	16.879	.0592	.0641	93.406	101.137
19	19.748	.0506	.0548	110.285	119.414
20	23.106	.0433	.0469	130.033	140.797
21	27.034	.0370	.0401	153.139	165.815
22	31.629	.0316	.0342	180.172	195.086
23	37.006	.0270	.0293	211.801	229.334
24	43.297	.0231	.0250	248.808	269.403
25	50.658	.0197	.0214	292.105	316.284
26	59.270	.0169	.0183	342.763	371.135
27	69.345	.0144	.0156	402.032	435.311
28	81.134	.0123	.0133	471.378	510.397
29	94.927	.0105	.0114	552.512	598.247
30	111.065	.0090	.0097	647.439	701.032
31	129.946	.0077	.0083	758.504	821.290
32	152.036	.0066	.0071	888.449	961.992
33	177.883	.0056	.0061	1040.486	1126.614
34	208.123	.0048	.0052	1218.368	1319.221
35	243.503	.0041	.0044	1426.491	1544.571
40	533.869	.0019	.0020	3134.522	3393.987
45	1170.479	.0009	.0009	6879.291	7448.736
50	2566.215	.0004	.0004	15089.502	16338.561
55	5626.294	.0002	.0002	33089.963	35829.040

I= .17000

ANNUAL SERIES				GRADIENT SERIES		
PRESENT WORTH		SINKING FUND	CAPITAL RECOVERY	UNIFORM SERIES	PRESENT WORTH	N
PW	CSPW	SF	CR	GUS	GPW	
.855	.925	1.00000	1.17000	.000	.000	1
1.585	1.716	.46083	.63083	.461	.731	2
2.210	2.392	.28257	.45257	.896	1.979	3
2.743	2.970	.19453	.36453	1.305	3.580	4
3.199	3.464	.14256	.31256	1.689	5.405	5
3.589	3.886	.10861	.27861	2.049	7.354	6
3.922	4.247	.08495	.25495	2.385	9.353	7
4.207	4.555	.06769	.23769	2.697	11.346	8
4.451	4.819	.05469	.22469	2.987	13.294	9
4.659	5.044	.04466	.21466	3.255	15.166	10
4.836	5.237	.03676	.20676	3.503	16.944	11
4.988	5.401	.03047	.20047	3.732	18.616	12
5.118	5.542	.02538	.19538	3.942	20.175	13
5.229	5.662	.02123	.19123	4.134	21.618	14
5.324	5.765	.01782	.18782	4.310	22.946	15
5.405	5.853	.01500	.18500	4.470	24.163	16
5.475	5.928	.01266	.18266	4.616	25.272	17
5.534	5.992	.01071	.18071	4.749	26.279	18
5.584	6.047	.00907	.17907	4.869	27.190	19
5.628	6.094	.00769	.17769	4.978	28.013	20
5.665	6.134	.00653	.17653	5.076	28.753	21
5.696	6.168	.00555	.17555	5.164	29.417	22
5.723	6.197	.00472	.17472	5.244	30.011	23
5.746	6.222	.00402	.17402	5.315	30.542	24
5.766	6.244	.00342	.17342	5.379	31.016	25
5.783	6.262	.00292	.17292	5.436	31.438	26
5.798	6.277	.00249	.17249	5.487	31.813	27
5.810	6.291	.00212	.17212	5.533	32.146	28
5.820	6.302	.00181	.17181	5.574	32.441	29
5.829	6.312	.00154	.17154	5.610	32.702	30
5.837	6.320	.00132	.17132	5.642	32.932	31
5.844	6.327	.00113	.17113	5.670	33.136	32
5.849	6.333	.00096	.17096	5.696	33.316	33
5.854	6.339	.00082	.17082	5.718	33.475	34
5.858	6.343	.00070	.17070	5.738	33.614	35
5.871	6.357	.00032	.17032	5.807	34.097	40
5.877	6.364	.00015	.17015	5.844	34.346	45
5.880	6.367	.00007	.17007	5.863	34.474	50
5.881	6.368	.00003	.17003	5.873	34.538	55

N	SINGLE PAYMENT			UNIFORM	
	COMPOUND AMOUNT	PRESENT WORTH		COMPOUND	AMOUNT
	CA	PW	CPW	SCA	CSCA
1	1.180	.8475	.9216	1.000	1.088
2	1.392	.7182	.7810	2.180	2.371
3	1.643	.6086	.6619	3.572	3.885
4	1.939	.5158	.5609	5.215	5.672
5	2.288	.4371	.4754	7.154	7.780
6	2.700	.3704	.4029	9.442	10.268
7	3.185	.3139	.3414	12.142	13.204
8	3.759	.2660	.2893	15.327	16.668
9	4.435	.2255	.2452	19.086	20.756
10	5.234	.1911	.2078	23.521	25.580
11	6.176	.1619	.1761	28.755	31.272
12	7.288	.1372	.1492	34.931	37.988
13	8.599	.1163	.1265	42.219	45.914
14	10.147	.0985	.1072	50.818	55.266
15	11.974	.0835	.0908	60.965	66.301
16	14.129	.0708	.0770	72.939	79.323
17	16.672	.0600	.0652	87.068	94.688
18	19.673	.0508	.0553	103.740	112.819
19	23.214	.0431	.0468	123.414	134.214
20	27.393	.0365	.0397	146.628	159.461
21	32.324	.0309	.0336	174.021	189.251
22	38.142	.0262	.0285	206.345	224.404
23	45.008	.0222	.0242	244.487	265.884
24	53.109	.0188	.0205	289.494	314.831
25	62.669	.0160	.0174	342.603	372.588
26	73.949	.0135	.0147	405.272	440.741
27	87.260	.0115	.0125	479.221	521.162
28	102.967	.0097	.0106	566.481	616.058
29	121.501	.0082	.0090	669.447	728.036
30	143.371	.0070	.0076	790.948	860.171
31	169.177	.0059	.0064	934.319	1016.089
32	199.629	.0050	.0054	1103.496	1200.072
33	235.563	.0042	.0046	1303.125	1417.173
34	277.964	.0036	.0039	1538.688	1673.351
35	327.997	.0030	.0033	1816.652	1975.642
40	750.378	.0013	.0014	4163.213	4527.571
45	1716.684	.0006	.0006	9531.577	10365.766
50	3927.357	.0003	.0003	21813.094	23722.141
55	8984.841	.0001	.0001	49910.228	54278.293

I = .18000

ANNUAL SERIES				GRADIENT SERIES		
PRESENT WORTH		SINKING FUND	CAPITAL RECOVERY	UNIFORM SERIES	PRESENT WORTH	N
PW	CSPW	SF	CR	GUS	GPW	
.847	.922	1.00000	1.18000	.000	.000	1
1.566	1.703	.45872	.63872	.459	.718	2
2.174	2.365	.27992	.45992	.890	1.935	3
2.690	2.925	.19174	.37174	1.295	3.483	4
3.127	3.401	.13978	.31978	1.673	5.231	5
3.498	3.804	.10591	.28591	2.025	7.083	6
3.812	4.145	.08236	.26236	2.353	8.967	7
4.078	4.434	.06524	.24524	2.656	10.829	8
4.303	4.680	.05239	.23239	2.936	12.633	9
4.494	4.887	.04251	.22251	3.194	14.352	10
4.656	5.063	.03478	.21478	3.430	15.972	11
4.793	5.213	.02863	.20863	3.647	17.481	12
4.910	5.339	.02369	.20369	3.845	18.877	13
5.008	5.446	.01968	.19968	4.025	20.158	14
5.092	5.537	.01640	.19640	4.189	21.327	15
5.162	5.614	.01371	.19371	4.337	22.389	16
5.222	5.679	.01149	.19149	4.471	23.348	17
5.273	5.735	.00964	.18964	4.592	24.212	18
5.316	5.782	.00810	.18810	4.700	24.988	19
5.353	5.821	.00682	.18682	4.798	25.681	20
5.384	5.855	.00575	.18575	4.885	26.300	21
5.410	5.883	.00485	.18485	4.963	26.851	22
5.432	5.908	.00409	.18409	5.033	27.339	23
5.451	5.928	.00345	.18345	5.095	27.772	24
5.467	5.945	.00292	.18292	5.150	28.155	25
5.480	5.960	.00247	.18247	5.199	28.494	26
5.492	5.973	.00209	.18209	5.243	28.791	27
5.502	5.983	.00177	.18177	5.281	29.054	28
5.510	5.992	.00149	.18149	5.315	29.284	29
5.517	6.000	.00126	.18126	5.345	29.486	30
5.523	6.006	.00107	.18107	5.371	29.664	31
5.528	6.012	.00091	.18091	5.394	29.819	32
5.532	6.016	.00077	.18077	5.415	29.955	33
5.536	6.020	.00065	.18065	5.433	30.074	34
5.539	6.023	.00055	.18055	5.449	30.177	35
5.548	6.034	.00024	.18024	5.502	30.527	40
5.552	6.038	.00010	.18010	5.529	30.701	45
5.554	6.040	.00005	.18005	5.543	30.786	50
5.555	6.041	.00002	.18002	5.549	30.827	55

N	SINGLE PAYMENT			UNIFORM	
	COMPOUND AMOUNT	PRESENT WORTH		COMPOUND	AMOUNT
	CA	PW	CPW	SCA	CSCA
1	1.190	.8403	.9179	1.000	1.092
2	1.416	.7062	.7713	2.190	2.392
3	1.685	.5934	.6482	3.606	3.939
4	2.005	.4987	.5447	5.291	5.779
5	2.386	.4190	.4577	7.297	7.970
6	2.840	.3521	.3846	9.683	10.576
7	3.379	.2959	.3232	12.523	13.678
8	4.021	.2487	.2716	15.902	17.369
9	4.785	.2090	.2282	19.923	21.761
10	5.695	.1756	.1918	24.709	26.988
11	6.777	.1476	.1612	30.404	33.208
12	8.064	.1240	.1354	37.180	40.610
13	9.596	.1042	.1138	45.244	49.418
14	11.420	.0876	.0956	54.841	59.900
15	13.590	.0736	.0804	66.261	72.373
16	16.172	.0618	.0675	79.850	87.216
17	19.244	.0520	.0568	96.022	104.879
18	22.901	.0437	.0477	115.266	125.899
19	27.252	.0367	.0401	138.166	150.912
20	32.429	.0308	.0337	165.418	180.677
21	38.591	.0259	.0283	197.847	216.098
22	45.923	.0218	.0238	236.438	258.249
23	54.649	.0183	.0200	282.362	308.409
24	65.032	.0154	.0168	337.010	368.099
25	77.388	.0129	.0141	402.042	439.130
26	92.092	.0109	.0119	479.431	523.657
27	109.589	.0091	.0100	571.522	624.244
28	130.411	.0077	.0084	681.112	743.942
29	155.189	.0064	.0070	811.523	886.383
30	184.675	.0054	.0059	966.712	1055.889
31	219.764	.0046	.0050	1151.387	1257.600
32	261.519	.0038	.0042	1371.151	1497.636
33	311.207	.0032	.0035	1632.670	1783.279
34	370.337	.0027	.0029	1943.877	2123.194
35	440.701	.0023	.0025	2314.214	2527.693
40	1051.668	.0010	.0010	5529.829	6039.940
45	2509.651	.0004	.0004	13203.424	14421.402
50	5988.914	.0002	.0002	31515.336	34422.536

I= .19000

ANNUAL SERIES				GRADIENT SERIES		
PRESENT WORTH		SINKING FUND	CAPITAL RECOVERY	UNIFORM SERIES	PRESENT WORTH	N
PW	CSPW	SF	CR	GUS	GPW	
.840	.918	1.00000	1.19000	.000	.000	1
1.547	1.689	.45662	.64662	.457	.706	2
2.140	2.337	.27731	.46731	.885	1.893	3
2.639	2.882	.18899	.37899	1.284	3.389	4
3.058	3.340	.13705	.32705	1.657	5.065	5
3.410	3.724	.10327	.29327	2.002	6.826	6
3.706	4.048	.07985	.26985	2.321	8.601	7
3.954	4.319	.06289	.25289	2.615	10.342	8
4.163	4.547	.05019	.24019	2.886	12.014	9
4.339	4.739	.04047	.23047	3.133	13.594	10
4.486	4.900	.03289	.22289	3.359	15.070	11
4.611	5.036	.02690	.21690	3.564	16.434	12
4.715	5.150	.02210	.21210	3.751	17.684	13
4.802	5.245	.01823	.20823	3.920	18.823	14
4.876	5.326	.01509	.20509	4.072	19.853	15
4.938	5.393	.01252	.20252	4.209	20.781	16
4.990	5.450	.01041	.20041	4.331	21.612	17
5.033	5.498	.00868	.19868	4.441	22.354	18
5.070	5.538	.00724	.19724	4.539	23.015	19
5.101	5.571	.00605	.19605	4.627	23.601	20
5.127	5.600	.00505	.19505	4.705	24.119	21
5.149	5.623	.00423	.19423	4.773	24.576	22
5.167	5.643	.00354	.19354	4.834	24.979	23
5.182	5.660	.00297	.19297	4.888	25.333	24
5.195	5.674	.00249	.19249	4.936	25.643	25
5.206	5.686	.00209	.19209	4.978	25.914	26
5.215	5.696	.00175	.19175	5.015	26.151	27
5.223	5.705	.00147	.19147	5.047	26.358	28
5.229	5.712	.00123	.19123	5.075	26.539	29
5.235	5.718	.00103	.19103	5.100	26.696	30
5.239	5.723	.00087	.19087	5.121	26.832	31
5.243	5.727	.00073	.19073	5.140	26.951	32
5.246	5.730	.00061	.19061	5.157	27.054	33
5.249	5.733	.00051	.19051	5.171	27.143	34
5.251	5.736	.00043	.19043	5.184	27.220	35
5.258	5.743	.00018	.19018	5.225	27.474	40
5.261	5.746	.00008	.19008	5.245	27.595	45
5.262	5.748	.00003	.19003	5.255	27.652	50

N	S I N G L E P A Y M E N T			U N I F O R M	
	COMPOUND AMOUNT	PRESENT WORTH		COMPOUND	AMOUNT
	CA	PW	CPW	SCA	CSCA
1	1.200	.8333	.9141	1.000	1.097
2	1.440	.6944	.7618	2.200	2.413
3	1.728	.5787	.6348	3.640	3.993
4	2.074	.4823	.5290	5.368	5.888
5	2.488	.4019	.4408	7.442	8.163
6	2.986	.3349	.3674	9.930	10.893
7	3.583	.2791	.3061	12.916	14.168
8	4.300	.2326	.2551	16.499	18.099
9	5.160	.1938	.2126	20.799	22.816
10	6.192	.1615	.1772	25.959	28.476
11	7.430	.1346	.1476	32.150	35.268
12	8.916	.1122	.1230	39.581	43.418
13	10.699	.0935	.1025	48.497	53.199
14	12.839	.0779	.0854	59.196	64.936
15	15.407	.0649	.0712	72.035	79.020
16	18.488	.0541	.0593	87.442	95.921
17	22.186	.0451	.0494	105.931	116.202
18	26.623	.0376	.0412	128.117	140.539
19	31.948	.0313	.0343	154.740	169.744
20	38.338	.0261	.0286	186.688	204.790
21	46.005	.0217	.0238	225.026	246.845
22	55.206	.0181	.0199	271.031	297.311
23	66.247	.0151	.0166	326.237	357.870
24	79.497	.0126	.0138	392.484	430.541
25	95.396	.0105	.0115	471.981	517.746
26	114.475	.0087	.0096	567.377	622.392
27	137.371	.0073	.0080	681.853	747.967
28	164.845	.0061	.0067	819.223	898.658
29	197.814	.0051	.0055	984.068	1079.486
30	237.376	.0042	.0046	1181.882	1296.480
31	284.852	.0035	.0039	1419.258	1556.873
32	341.822	.0029	.0032	1704.109	1869.345
33	410.186	.0024	.0027	2045.931	2244.311
34	492.224	.0020	.0022	2456.118	2694.270
35	590.668	.0017	.0019	2948.341	3234.221
40	1469.772	.0007	.0007	7343.858	8055.940
45	3657.262	.0003	.0003	18281.310	20053.920
50	9100.438	.0001	.0001	45497.191	49908.734

I= .20000

ANNUAL SERIES				GRADIENT SERIES		
PRESENT WORTH		SINKING FUND	CAPITAL RECOVERY	UNIFORM SERIES	PRESENT WORTH	N
PW	CSPW	SF	CR	GUS	GPW	
.833	.914	1.00000	1.20000	.000	.000	1
1.528	1.676	.45455	.65455	.455	.694	2
2.106	2.311	.27473	.47473	.879	1.852	3
2.589	2.840	.18629	.38629	1.274	3.299	4
2.991	3.281	.13438	.33438	1.641	4.906	5
3.326	3.648	.10071	.30071	1.979	6.581	6
3.605	3.954	.07742	.27742	2.290	8.255	7
3.837	4.209	.06061	.26061	2.576	9.883	8
4.031	4.427	.04808	.24808	2.836	11.434	9
4.192	4.599	.03852	.23852	3.074	12.887	10
4.327	4.747	.03110	.23110	3.289	14.233	11
4.439	4.870	.02526	.22526	3.484	15.467	12
4.533	4.972	.02062	.22062	3.660	16.588	13
4.611	5.058	.01689	.21689	3.817	17.601	14
4.675	5.129	.01388	.21388	3.959	18.509	15
4.730	5.188	.01144	.21144	4.085	19.321	16
4.775	5.238	.00944	.20944	4.198	20.042	17
4.812	5.279	.00781	.20781	4.298	20.680	18
4.843	5.313	.00646	.20646	4.386	21.244	19
4.870	5.342	.00536	.20536	4.464	21.739	20
4.891	5.366	.00444	.20444	4.533	22.174	21
4.909	5.385	.00369	.20369	4.594	22.555	22
4.925	5.402	.00307	.20307	4.647	22.887	23
4.937	5.416	.00255	.20255	4.694	23.176	24
4.948	5.427	.00212	.20212	4.735	23.428	25
4.956	5.437	.00176	.20176	4.771	23.646	26
4.964	5.445	.00147	.20147	4.802	23.835	27
4.970	5.452	.00122	.20122	4.829	23.999	28
4.975	5.457	.00102	.20102	4.853	24.141	29
4.979	5.462	.00085	.20085	4.873	24.263	30
4.982	5.466	.00070	.20070	4.891	24.368	31
4.985	5.469	.00059	.20059	4.906	24.459	32
4.988	5.471	.00049	.20049	4.919	24.537	33
4.990	5.474	.00041	.20041	4.931	24.604	34
4.992	5.476	.00034	.20034	4.941	24.661	35
4.997	5.481	.00014	.20014	4.973	24.847	40
4.999	5.483	.00005	.20005	4.988	24.932	45
4.999	5.484	.00002	.20002	4.995	24.970	50

N	SINGLE PAYMENT			UNIFORM	
	COMPOUND AMOUNT	PRESENT WORTH		COMPOUND	AMOUNT
	CA	PW	CPW	SCA	CSCA
1	1.250	.8000	.8963	1.000	1.120
2	1.563	.6400	.7170	2.250	2.521
3	1.953	.5120	.5736	3.812	4.271
4	2.441	.4096	.4589	5.766	6.460
5	3.052	.3277	.3671	8.207	9.195
6	3.815	.2621	.2937	11.259	12.614
7	4.768	.2097	.2350	15.073	16.888
8	5.960	.1678	.1880	19.842	22.230
9	7.451	.1342	.1504	25.802	28.908
10	9.313	.1074	.1203	33.253	37.255
11	11.642	.0859	.0962	42.566	47.689
12	14.552	.0687	.0770	54.208	60.732
13	18.190	.0550	.0616	68.760	77.035
14	22.737	.0440	.0493	86.949	97.414
15	28.422	.0352	.0394	109.687	122.888
16	35.527	.0281	.0315	138.109	154.731
17	44.409	.0225	.0252	173.636	194.534
18	55.511	.0180	.0202	218.045	244.287
19	69.389	.0144	.0161	273.556	306.480
20	86.736	.0115	.0129	342.945	384.220
21	108.420	.0092	.0103	429.681	481.395
22	135.525	.0074	.0083	538.101	602.864
23	169.407	.0059	.0066	673.626	754.701
24	211.758	.0047	.0053	843.033	944.49
25	264.698	.0038	.0042	1054.791	1181.741
26	330.872	.0030	.0034	1319.489	1478.29
27	413.590	.0024	.0027	1650.361	1848.99
28	516.988	.0019	.0022	2063.952	2312.35
29	646.235	.0015	.0017	2580.939	2891.56
30	807.794	.0012	.0014	3227.174	3615.581
31	1009.742	.0010	.0011	4034.968	4520.59
32	1262.177	.0008	.0009	5044.710	5651.86
33	1577.722	.0006	.0007	6306.887	7065.95
34	1972.152	.0005	.0006	7884.609	8833.56
35	2465.190	.0004	.0005	9856.761	11043.07
40	7523.164	.0001	.0001	30088.655	33709.97

I= .25000

ANNUAL SERIES				GRADIENT SERIES		
PRESENT WORTH		SINKING FUND	CAPITAL RECOVERY	UNIFORM SERIES	PRESENT WORTH	N
PW	CSPW	SF	CR	GUS	GPW	
.800	.896	1.00000	1.25000	.000	.000	1
1.440	1.613	.44444	.69444	.444	.640	2
1.952	2.187	.26230	.51230	.852	1.664	3
2.362	2.646	.17344	.42344	1.225	2.893	4
2.689	3.013	.12185	.37185	1.563	4.204	5
2.951	3.307	.08882	.33882	1.868	5.514	6
3.161	3.542	.06634	.31634	2.142	6.773	7
3.329	3.730	.05040	.30040	2.387	7.947	8
3.463	3.880	.03876	.28876	2.605	9.021	9
3.571	4.000	.03007	.28007	2.797	9.987	10
3.656	4.096	.02349	.27349	2.966	10.846	11
3.725	4.173	.01845	.26845	3.115	11.602	12
3.780	4.235	.01454	.26454	3.244	12.262	13
3.824	4.284	.01150	.26150	3.356	12.833	14
3.859	4.324	.00912	.25912	3.453	13.326	15
3.887	4.355	.00724	.25724	3.537	13.748	16
3.910	4.381	.00576	.25576	3.608	14.108	17
3.928	4.401	.00459	.25459	3.670	14.415	18
3.942	4.417	.00366	.25366	3.722	14.674	19
3.954	4.430	.00292	.25292	3.767	14.893	20
3.963	4.440	.00233	.25233	3.805	15.078	21
3.970	4.448	.00186	.25186	3.836	15.233	22
3.976	4.455	.00148	.25148	3.863	15.362	23
3.981	4.460	.00119	.25119	3.886	15.471	24
3.985	4.464	.00095	.25095	3.905	15.562	25
3.988	4.468	.00076	.25076	3.921	15.637	26
3.990	4.471	.00061	.25061	3.935	15.700	27
3.992	4.473	.00048	.25048	3.946	15.752	28
3.994	4.474	.00039	.25039	3.955	15.796	29
3.995	4.476	.00031	.25031	3.963	15.832	30
3.996	4.477	.00025	.25025	3.969	15.861	31
3.997	4.478	.00020	.25020	3.975	15.886	32
3.997	4.479	.00016	.25016	3.979	15.906	33
3.998	4.479	.00013	.25013	3.983	15.923	34
3.998	4.480	.00010	.25010	3.986	15.937	35
3.999	4.481	.00003	.25003	3.995	15.977	40

N	SINGLE PAYMENT			UNIFORM	
	COMPOUND AMOUNT	PRESENT WORTH		COMPOUND	AMOUNT
	CA	PW	CPW	SCA	CSCA
1	1.300	.7692	.8796	1.000	1.143
2	1.690	.5917	.6766	2.300	2.630
3	2.197	.4552	.5205	3.990	4.562
4	2.856	.3501	.4004	6.187	7.075
5	3.713	.2693	.3080	9.043	10.340
6	4.827	.2072	.2369	12.756	14.586
7	6.275	.1594	.1822	17.583	20.105
8	8.157	.1226	.1402	23.858	27.280
9	10.604	.0943	.1078	32.015	36.607
10	13.786	.0725	.0829	42.619	48.733
11	17.922	.0558	.0638	56.405	64.497
12	23.298	.0429	.0491	74.327	84.989
13	30.288	.0330	.0378	97.625	111.629
14	39.374	.0254	.0290	127.913	146.261
15	51.186	.0195	.0223	167.286	191.283
16	66.542	.0150	.0172	218.472	249.812
17	86.504	.0116	.0132	285.014	325.899
18	112.455	.0089	.0102	371.518	424.812
19	146.192	.0068	.0078	483.973	553.399
20	190.050	.0053	.0060	630.165	720.562
21	247.065	.0040	.0046	820.215	937.874
22	321.184	.0031	.0036	1067.280	1220.379
23	417.539	.0024	.0027	1388.464	1587.636
24	542.801	.0018	.0021	1806.003	2065.071
25	705.641	.0014	.0016	2348.803	2685.735
26	917.333	.0011	.0012	3054.444	3492.600
27	1192.533	.0008	.0010	3971.778	4541.523
28	1550.293	.0006	.0007	5164.311	5905.123
29	2015.381	.0005	.0006	6714.604	7677.803
30	2619.996	.0004	.0004	8729.985	9982.288
31	3405.994	.0003	.0003	11349.981	12978.118
32	4427.793	.0002	.0003	14755.975	16872.697
33	5756.130	.0002	.0002	19183.768	21935.649
34	7482.970	.0001	.0002	24939.899	28517.487
35	9727.860	.0001	.0001	32422.868	37073.877

I= .30000

ANNUAL SERIES				GRADIENT SERIES		
PRESENT WORTH		SINKING FUND	CAPITAL RECOVERY	UNIFORM SERIES	PRESENT WORTH	N
PW	CSPW	SF	CR	GUS	GPW	
.769	.880	1.00000	1.30000	.000	.000	1
1.361	1.556	.43478	.73478	.435	.592	2
1.816	2.077	.25063	.55063	.827	1.502	3
2.166	2.477	.16163	.46163	1.178	2.552	4
2.436	2.785	.11058	.41058	1.490	3.630	5
2.643	3.022	.07839	.37839	1.765	4.666	6
2.802	3.204	.05687	.35687	2.006	5.622	7
2.925	3.344	.04192	.34192	2.216	6.480	8
3.019	3.452	.03124	.33124	2.396	7.234	9
3.092	3.535	.02346	.32346	2.551	7.887	10
3.147	3.599	.01773	.31773	2.683	8.445	11
3.190	3.648	.01345	.31345	2.795	8.917	12
3.223	3.686	.01024	.31024	2.889	9.314	13
3.249	3.715	.00782	.30782	2.969	9.644	14
3.268	3.737	.00598	.30598	3.034	9.917	15
3.283	3.754	.00458	.30458	3.089	10.143	16
3.295	3.767	.00351	.30351	3.135	10.328	17
3.304	3.778	.00269	.30269	3.172	10.479	18
3.311	3.785	.00207	.30207	3.202	10.602	19
3.316	3.791	.00159	.30159	3.228	10.702	20
3.320	3.796	.00122	.30122	3.248	10.783	21
3.323	3.800	.00094	.30094	3.265	10.848	22
3.325	3.802	.00072	.30072	3.278	10.901	23
3.327	3.804	.00055	.30055	3.289	10.943	24
3.329	3.806	.00043	.30043	3.298	10.977	25
3.330	3.807	.00033	.30033	3.305	11.005	26
3.331	3.808	.00025	.30025	3.311	11.026	27
3.331	3.809	.00019	.30019	3.315	11.044	28
3.332	3.810	.00015	.30015	3.319	11.058	29
3.332	3.810	.00011	.30011	3.322	11.069	30
3.332	3.810	.00009	.30009	3.324	11.078	31
3.333	3.811	.00007	.30007	3.326	11.085	32
3.333	3.811	.00005	.30005	3.328	11.090	33
3.333	3.811	.00004	.30004	3.329	11.094	34
3.333	3.811	.00003	.30003	3.330	11.098	35

N	SINGLE PAYMENT			UNIFORM	
	COMPOUND AMOUNT	PRESENT WORTH		COMPOUND	AMOUNT
	CA	PW	CPW	SCA	CSCA
1	1.350	.7407	.8639	1.000	1.166
2	1.822	.5487	.6399	2.350	2.741
3	2.460	.4064	.4740	4.172	4.866
4	3.322	.3011	.3511	6.633	7.736
5	4.484	.2230	.2601	9.954	11.609
6	6.053	.1652	.1927	14.438	16.839
7	8.172	.1224	.1427	20.492	23.899
8	11.032	.0906	.1057	28.664	33.430
9	14.894	.0671	.0783	39.696	46.296
10	20.107	.0497	.0580	54.590	63.666
11	27.144	.0368	.0430	74.697	87.116
12	36.644	.0273	.0318	101.841	118.773
13	49.470	.0202	.0236	138.485	161.509
14	66.784	.0150	.0175	187.954	219.204
15	90.158	.0111	.0129	254.736	297.091
16	121.714	.0082	.0096	344.897	402.240
17	164.314	.0061	.0071	466.611	544.190
18	221.824	.0045	.0053	630.925	735.822
19	299.462	.0033	.0039	852.748	994.526
20	404.274	.0025	.0029	1152.210	1343.777
21	545.769	.0018	.0021	1556.484	1815.265
22	736.789	.0014	.0016	2102.253	2451.774
23	994.665	.0010	.0012	2839.042	3311.061
24	1342.797	.0007	.0009	3833.706	4471.099
25	1812.776	.0006	.0006	5176.504	6037.149
26	2447.248	.0004	.0005	6989.280	8151.318
27	3303.785	.0003	.0004	9436.528	11005.446
28	4460.109	.0002	.0003	12740.313	14858.518
29	6021.148	.0002	.0002	17200.422	20060.165
30	8128.549	.0001	.0001	23221.570	27082.390

I= .35000

ANNUAL SERIES				GRADIENT SERIES		
PRESENT WORTH		SINKING FUND	CAPITAL RECOVERY	UNIFORM SERIES	PRESENT WORTH	N
PW	CSPW	SF	CR	GUS	GPW	
.741	.864	1.00000	1.35000	.000	.000	1
1.289	1.504	.42553	.77553	.426	.549	2
1.696	1.978	.23966	.58966	.803	1.362	3
1.997	2.329	.15076	.50076	1.134	2.265	4
2.220	2.589	.10046	.45046	1.422	3.157	5
2.385	2.782	.06926	.41926	1.670	3.983	6
2.508	2.924	.04880	.39880	1.881	4.717	7
2.598	3.030	.03489	.38489	2.060	5.352	8
2.665	3.108	.02519	.37519	2.209	5.889	9
2.715	3.166	.01832	.36832	2.334	6.336	10
2.752	3.209	.01339	.36339	2.436	6.705	11
2.779	3.241	.00982	.35982	2.520	7.005	12
2.799	3.265	.00722	.35722	2.589	7.247	13
2.814	3.282	.00532	.35532	2.644	7.442	14
2.825	3.295	.00393	.35393	2.689	7.597	15
2.834	3.305	.00290	.35290	2.725	7.721	16
2.840	3.312	.00214	.35214	2.753	7.818	17
2.844	3.317	.00158	.35158	2.776	7.895	18
2.848	3.321	.00117	.35117	2.793	7.955	19
2.850	3.324	.00087	.35087	2.808	8.002	20
2.852	3.326	.00064	.35064	2.819	8.038	21
2.853	3.328	.00048	.35048	2.827	8.067	22
2.854	3.329	.00035	.35035	2.834	8.089	23
2.855	3.330	.00026	.35026	2.839	8.106	24
2.856	3.330	.00019	.35019	2.843	8.119	25
2.856	3.331	.00014	.35014	2.847	8.130	26
2.856	3.331	.00011	.35011	2.849	8.137	27
2.857	3.331	.00008	.35008	2.851	8.143	28
2.857	3.332	.00006	.35006	2.852	8.148	29
2.857	3.332	.00004	.35004	2.853	8.152	30

N	SINGLE PAYMENT			UNIFORM	
	COMPOUND AMOUNT	PRESENT WORTH		COMPOUND AMOUNT	
	CA	PW	CPW	SCA	CSCA
1	1.400	.7143	.8491	1.000	1.189
2	1.960	.5102	.6065	2.400	2.853
3	2.744	.3644	.4332	4.360	5.183
4	3.842	.2603	.3095	7.104	8.445
5	5.378	.1859	.2210	10.946	13.012
6	7.530	.1328	.1579	16.324	19.406
7	10.541	.0949	.1128	23.853	28.357
8	14.758	.0678	.0806	34.395	40.889
9	20.661	.0484	.0575	49.153	58.433
10	28.925	.0346	.0411	69.814	82.995
11	40.496	.0247	.0294	98.739	117.382
12	56.694	.0176	.0210	139.235	165.523
13	79.371	.0126	.0150	195.929	232.921
14	111.120	.0090	.0107	275.300	327.278
15	155.568	.0064	.0076	386.420	459.378
16	217.795	.0046	.0055	541.988	644.319
17	304.913	.0033	.0039	759.784	903.235
18	426.879	.0023	.0028	1064.697	1265.718
19	597.630	.0017	.0020	1491.576	1773.194
20	836.683	.0012	.0014	2089.206	2483.660
21	1171.356	.0009	.0010	2925.889	3478.312
22	1639.898	.0006	.0007	4097.245	4870.826
23	2295.857	.0004	.0005	5737.142	6820.346
24	3214.200	.0003	.0004	8032.999	9549.673
25	4499.880	.0002	.0003	11247.199	13370.730
26	6299.831	.0002	.0002	15747.079	18720.211
27	8819.764	.0001	.0001	22046.910	26209.485

I= .40000

ANNUAL SERIES				GRADIENT SERIES		
PRESENT WORTH		SINKING FUND	CAPITAL RECOVERY	UNIFORM SERIES	PRESENT WORTH	N
PW	CSPW	SF	CR	GUS	GPW	
.714	.849	1.00000	1.40000	.000	.000	1
1.224	1.456	.41667	.81667	.417	.510	2
1.589	1.889	.22936	.62936	.780	1.239	3
1.849	2.198	.14077	.54077	1.092	2.020	4
2.035	2.419	.09136	.49136	1.358	2.764	5
2.168	2.577	.06126	.46126	1.581	3.428	6
2.263	2.690	.04192	.44192	1.766	3.997	7
2.331	2.771	.02907	.42907	1.919	4.471	8
2.379	2.828	.02034	.42034	2.042	4.858	9
2.414	2.869	.01432	.41432	2.142	5.170	10
2.438	2.899	.01013	.41013	2.221	5.417	11
2.456	2.920	.00718	.40718	2.285	5.611	12
2.469	2.935	.00510	.40510	2.334	5.762	13
2.478	2.945	.00363	.40363	2.373	5.879	14
2.484	2.953	.00259	.40259	2.403	5.969	15
2.489	2.958	.00185	.40185	2.426	6.038	16
2.492	2.962	.00132	.40132	2.444	6.090	17
2.494	2.965	.00094	.40094	2.458	6.130	18
2.496	2.967	.00067	.40067	2.468	6.160	19
2.497	2.968	.00048	.40048	2.476	6.183	20
2.498	2.969	.00034	.40034	2.482	6.200	21
2.498	2.970	.00024	.40024	2.487	6.213	22
2.499	2.971	.00017	.40017	2.490	6.222	23
2.499	2.971	.00012	.40012	2.493	6.229	24
2.499	2.971	.00009	.40009	2.494	6.235	25
2.500	2.972	.00006	.40006	2.496	6.239	26
2.500	2.972	.00005	.40005	2.497	6.242	27

N	SINGLE PAYMENT			UNIFORM	
	COMPOUND AMOUNT	PRESENT WORTH		COMPOUND	AMOUNT
	CA	PW	CPW	SCA	CSCA
1	1.450	.6897	.8352	1.000	1.211
2	2.102	.4756	.5760	2.450	2.967
3	3.049	.3280	.3973	4.552	5.514
4	4.421	.2262	.2740	7.601	9.206
5	6.410	.1560	.1889	12.022	14.559
6	9.294	.1076	.1303	18.431	22.322
7	13.476	.0742	.0899	27.725	33.578
8	19.541	.0512	.0620	41.202	49.900
9	28.334	.0353	.0427	60.743	73.566
10	41.085	.0243	.0295	89.077	107.881
11	59.573	.0168	.0203	130.162	157.639
12	86.381	.0116	.0140	189.735	229.787
13	125.252	.0080	.0097	276.115	334.403
14	181.615	.0055	.0067	401.367	486.095
15	263.342	.0038	.0046	582.982	706.049
16	381.846	.0026	.0032	846.324	1024.982
17	553.676	.0018	.0022	1228.170	1487.434
18	802.831	.0012	.0015	1781.846	2157.991
19	1164.105	.0009	.0010	2584.677	3130.298
20	1687.952	.0006	.0007	3748.782	4540.143
21	2447.530	.0004	.0005	5436.734	6584.419
22	3548.919	.0003	.0003	7884.264	9548.619
23	5145.932	.0002	.0002	11433.182	13846.708
24	7461.602	.0001	.0002	16579.115	20078.938

I= .45000

ANNUAL SERIES				GRADIENT SERIES		
PRESENT WORTH		SINKING FUND	CAPITAL RECOVERY	UNIFORM SERIES	PRESENT WORTH	N
PW	CSPW	SF	CR	GUS	GPW	
.690	.835	1.00000	1.45000	.000	.000	1
1.165	1.411	.40816	.85816	.408	.476	2
1.493	1.809	.21966	.66966	.758	1.132	3
1.720	2.083	.13156	.58156	1.053	1.810	4
1.876	2.271	.08318	.53318	1.298	2.434	5
1.983	2.402	.05426	.50426	1.499	2.972	6
2.057	2.492	.03607	.48607	1.661	3.418	7
2.109	2.554	.02427	.47427	1.791	3.776	8
2.144	2.596	.01646	.46646	1.893	4.058	9
2.168	2.626	.01123	.46123	1.973	4.277	10
2.185	2.646	.00768	.45768	2.034	4.445	11
2.196	2.660	.00527	.45527	2.082	4.572	12
2.204	2.670	.00362	.45362	2.118	4.668	13
2.210	2.677	.00249	.45249	2.145	4.740	14
2.214	2.681	.00172	.45172	2.165	4.793	15
2.216	2.684	.00118	.45118	2.180	4.832	16
2.218	2.686	.00081	.45081	2.191	4.861	17
2.219	2.688	.00056	.45056	2.200	4.882	18
2.220	2.689	.00039	.45039	2.206	4.898	19
2.221	2.690	.00027	.45027	2.210	4.909	20
2.221	2.690	.00018	.45018	2.214	4.917	21
2.222	2.691	.00013	.45013	2.216	4.923	22
2.222	2.691	.00009	.45009	2.218	4.927	23
2.222	2.691	.00006	.45006	2.219	4.930	24

N	SINGLE PAYMENT			UNIFORM	
	COMPOUND AMOUNT	PRESENT WORTH		COMPOUND	AMOUNT
	CA	PW	CPW	SCA	CSCA
1	1.500	.6667	.8221	1.000	1.233
2	2.250	.4444	.5481	2.500	3.083
3	3.375	.2963	.3654	4.750	5.857
4	5.062	.1975	.2436	8.125	10.019
5	7.594	.1317	.1624	13.187	16.262
6	11.391	.0878	.1083	20.781	25.626
7	17.086	.0585	.0722	32.172	39.673
8	25.629	.0390	.0481	49.258	60.742
9	38.443	.0260	.0321	74.887	92.347
10	57.665	.0173	.0214	113.330	139.753
11	86.498	.0116	.0143	170.995	210.863
12	129.746	.0077	.0095	257.493	317.528
13	194.620	.0051	.0063	387.239	477.524
14	291.929	.0034	.0042	581.859	717.520
15	437.894	.0023	.0028	873.788	1077.513
16	656.841	.0015	.0019	1311.682	1617.503
17	985.261	.0010	.0013	1968.523	2427.487
18	1477.892	.0007	.0008	2953.784	3642.464
19	2216.838	.0005	.0006	4431.676	5464.928
20	3325.257	.0003	.0004	6648.513	8198.626
21	4987.885	.0002	.0002	9973.770	12299.172
22	7481.828	.0001	.0002	14961.655	18449.991

I= .50000

ANNUAL SERIES				GRADIENT SERIES		
PRESENT WORTH		SINKING FUND	CAPITAL RECOVERY	UNIFORM SERIES	PRESENT WORTH	N
PW	CSPW	SF	CR	GUS	GPW	
.667	.822	1.00000	1.50000	.000	.000	1
1.111	1.370	.40000	.90000	.400	.444	2
1.407	1.736	.21053	.71053	.737	1.037	3
1.605	1.979	.12308	.62308	1.015	1.630	4
1.737	2.142	.07583	.57583	1.242	2.156	5
1.824	2.250	.04812	.54812	1.423	2.595	6
1.883	2.322	.03108	.53108	1.565	2.947	7
1.922	2.370	.02030	.52030	1.675	3.220	8
1.948	2.402	.01335	.51335	1.760	3.428	9
1.965	2.424	.00882	.50882	1.824	3.584	10
1.977	2.438	.00585	.50585	1.871	3.699	11
1.985	2.447	.00388	.50388	1.907	3.784	12
1.990	2.454	.00258	.50258	1.933	3.846	13
1.993	2.458	.00172	.50172	1.952	3.890	14
1.995	2.461	.00114	.50114	1.966	3.922	15
1.997	2.463	.00076	.50076	1.976	3.945	16
1.998	2.464	.00051	.50051	1.983	3.961	17
1.999	2.465	.00034	.50034	1.988	3.973	18
1.999	2.465	.00023	.50023	1.991	3.981	19
1.999	2.466	.00015	.50015	1.994	3.987	20
2.000	2.466	.00010	.50010	1.996	3.991	21
2.000	2.466	.00007	.50007	1.997	3.994	22

SELECTED BIBLIOGRAPHY

GENERAL REFERENCES

Barish, Norman N., *Economic Analysis for Engineering and Managerial Decision Making*. New York: McGraw-Hill Book Company, Inc. 1962.

Beranek, William, *Analysis for Financial Decisions*. Homewood, Illinois: Richard D. Irwin, Inc., 1963.

Bierman, H. J., and S. Smidt, *The Capital Budgeting Decision*. New York: The Macmillan Company, 1960. 2nd Edition (1966).

Bierman, H. J., *et al.*, *Quantitative Analysis for Business Decisions*. Homewood, Illinois: Richard D. Irwin, Inc., 1965.

Bullinger, C. E., *Engineering Economy*. New York: McGraw-Hill Book Company, Inc., 1958.

Carr, Charles R. and Charles W. Howe, *Quantitative Decision Procedures in Management and Economics*. New York: McGraw-Hill Book Company, Inc., 1964.

Cohen, Jerome B. and Edward D. Zinbarg, *Investment Analysis and Portfolio Management*. Homewood, Illinois: Richard D. Irwin, Inc., 1967.

"The Capital Expenditure Control Program, A Summary of Practice," Accounting Practice Report No. 7, N.A.A. Bulletin, Vol. 40, March 1959, Section 3.

Dean, Joel, *Capital Budgeting*. New York: Columbia University Press, 1951.

———, *Managerial Economics*. Englewood Cliffs, New Jersey: Prentice-Hall, Inc., 1951.

DeGarmo, E. P., *Engineering Economy*, 4th Edition. New York: The Macmillan Company, 1967.

Eisner, R., *Determinants of Capital Expenditures*, University of Illinois Bulletin. Urbana, Illinois: University of Illinois Press, 1956.

Fleischer, Gerald A., "Two Major Issues Associated with the Rate of Return Method for Capital Allocation: The 'Ranking Error' and 'Preliminary Selection,'" *The Journal of Industrial Engineering*, Vol. 17, No. 4, April 1966, pp. 202–08.

Gordon, Myron and Eli Shapiro, "Capital Equipment Analysis and the Required Rate of Profit," *Management Science*, Vol. 3, No. 1, 1956, pp. 102–10.

Grant, E. L., Lawrence F. Bell, and W. G. Ireson, *Principles of Engineering Economy*, 4th Edition (Rev.). New York: The Ronald Press Company, 1964.

Hackney, John W., *Control and Management of Capital Projects*. New York: John Wiley and Sons, Inc., 1965.

Hanssman, F., *Operations Research Techniques for Capital Investment*. New York: John Wiley & Sons, Inc., 1968.

Harlan, N. E., C. J. Christenson, and R. F. Vancil, *Managerial Economics*. Homewood, Illinois: Richard D. Irwin, Inc., 1962.

Hertz, David B., "Risk Analysis in Capital Expenditure Decisions," *Harvard Business Review*, Vol. 42, No. 1, January–February 1964, pp. 89–106.

Hirschleifer, J., "On the Theory of Optimal Investment," *Journal of Political Economy*, Vol. 66, No. 4, August 1958, pp. 329–52.

Hunt, P., C. M. Williams, and G. Donaldson, *Basic Business Finance*. Homewood, Illinois: Richard D. Irwin, Inc., 1961.

Istvan, Donald F., *Capital-Expenditure Decisions: How They are Made in Large Corporations*, Indiana Business Report No. 33. Indiana: Indiana University, 1961.

Kempster, John H., *Financial Analysis to Guide Capital Expenditures*. New York: National Association of Accountants, 1967.

Lesourne, Jacques, *Economic Analysis and Industrial Management*, 2nd ed. Englewood Cliffs, New Jersey: Prentice-Hall, Inc., 1963.

Lorie, J. H., and L. J. Savage, "Three Problems in Rationing Capital," *Journal of Business*, Vol. 28, No. 4, October 1955, pp. 229–39.

Lutz, F. and V. Lutz, *The Theory of Investment of the Firm*. Princeton: Princeton University Press, 1951.

Manne, Alan S., *Economic Analysis for Business Decisions*. New York: McGraw-Hill Book Company, Inc., 1961.

Massé, Pierre, *Optimal Investment Decisions: Rules for Action and Criteria for Choice*. Englewood Cliffs, New Jersey: Prentice-Hall, Inc., 1962.

Meyer, J. R., and E. Kuh, *The Investment Decision: An Empirical Study*. Massachusetts: Harvard University Press, 1957.

Mock, Edward J., *Financial Decision-Making*. Pennsylvania: International Textbook Company, 1967.

Morris, William T., *The Analysis of Management Decisions*. Homewood, Illinois: Richard D. Irwin, Inc., 1964.

Quirin, G. David, *The Capital Expenditure Decision.* Homewood, Illinois: Richard D. Irwin, Inc., 1967.

Rakowski, M., *Efficiency of Investment in a Socialist Economy.* New York: Pergamon Press, 1966.

Robichek, Alexander A. and Stewart C. Meyers, *Optimal Financing Decisions.* Englewood Cliffs, New Jersey: Prentice-Hall, Inc., 1965.

Rosenthal, Stanley, *Engineering Economics and Practice.* New York: The Macmillan Company, 1964.

Roscoe, E. S., *Project Economy.* Homewood, Illinois: Richard D. Irwin, Inc., 1961.

Schweyer, Herbert E., *Analytical Models for Managerial and Engineering Economics.* New York: Reinhold Publishing Corporation, 1964.

Smith, Gerald W., "A Brief History of Interest Calculations," *The Journal of Industrial Engineering*, Vol. 18, No. 10, October 1967, pp. 569–574.

Taylor, George A., *Managerial and Engineering Economy: Economic Decision-Making.* Princeton, New Jersey: D. van Nostrand Company, Inc., 1964.

Terborgh, George, *Business Investment Management.* Machinery and Allied Products Institute, Washington, D.C., 1967.

Thuesen, H. G. and W. J. Fabrycky, *Engineering Economy.* Englewood Cliffs, New Jersey: Prentice-Hall, Inc., 1964.

U.S. Agency for International Development, *Feasibility Studies: Economic and Technical Soundness Analysis: Capital Projects.* Washington, D.C., 1962.

Van Horne, James C., *Financial Management and Policy.* New Jersey: Prentice-Hall, Inc., 1968.

Vandell, R. F. and R. F. Vancil, *Cases in Capital Budgeting.* Homewood, Illinois; Richard D. Irwin, Inc., 1962.

Weston, J. Fred, *Managerial Finance.* New York: Holt, Rinehart, and Winston, Inc., 1962.

COST OF CAPITAL AND CAPITAL STRUCTURE[1]

Barges, Alexander, *The Effect of Capital Structure on the Cost of Capital.* Englewood Cliffs, New Jersey: Prentice-Hall, Inc., 1963.

Fisher, Lawrence and James H. Lorie, "Rates of Return on Investments in Common Stock, the Year by Year Record 1926-65," *Journal of Business*, Vol. 41, No. 3, July 1968, pp. 291–316.

Guthmann, Harry G. and Herbert E. Dougall, *Corporate Financial Policy.* Englewood Cliffs, New Jersey: Prentice-Hall, Inc., 1962.

[1] The topics which follow are also discussed in many of the citations listed under "General References." In any event, the bibliography is by no means complete. It is simply intended to serve as a starting point for students interested in additional study in these areas.

Hunt, P., C. M. Williams, and G. Donaldson, *Basic Business Finance*. Homewood, Illinois: Irwin, 1966.

Lintner, J., "The Cost of Capital and Optimal Financing of Corporate Growth," *Journal of Finance*, Vol. 18, No. 2, May 1963, pp. 292–310.

Miller, M. H. and F. Modigliani, "Dividend Policy, Growth and the Valuation of Shares," *Journal of Business*, Vol. 34, No. 4, Oct. 1961, pp. 411–433.

———, "The Cost of Capital, Corporation Finance and the Theory of Investment," *American Economic Review*, Vol. 48, No. 3, June 1958, pp. 261–97.

Porterfield, James T., *Investment Decisions and Capital Costs*. Englewood Cliffs, New Jersey: Prentice-Hall, Inc., 1965.

Solomon, Ezra, *The Management of Corporate Capital*. Glencoe, Illinois: The Free Press, 1959.

———, *The Theory of Financial Management*. New York: Columbia University Press, 1963.

MATHEMATICAL PROGRAMMING – SELECTION PROCEDURES

Charnes, A., W. W. Cooper and M. H. Miller, "Application of Linear Programming to Financial Budgeting and the Costing of Funds," *Journal of Business*, Vol. 32, No. 1, Jan. 1959, pp. 20–46.

Cord, Joel, "A Method for Allocating Funds to Investment Projects when Returns are Subject to Uncertainty," *Management Science*, Vol. 10, No. 2, January 1964, pp. 335–41.

Everett, Hugh, "Generalized LaGrange Multiplier Method for Solving Problems of Optimum Allocation," *Journal of the Operations Research Society of America*, Vol. 11, No. 3, May 1963, pp. 399–417.

Markowitz, H., *Portfolio Selection: Efficient Diversification of Investments*. New York: John Wiley and Sons, Inc., 1959.

Sharpe, W., "A Simplified Model for Portfolio Analysis," *Management Science*, Vol. 9, No. 2, Jan. 1963, pp. 277–93.

Weingartner, H. Martin, *Mathematical Programming and the Analysis of Capital Budgeting Problems*. Illinois: Markham Publishing Co., 1967.

RETIREMENT AND REPLACEMENT

Alchian, A. A., *Economic Replacement Policy*. Santa Monica, California: RAND Corporation, RM-2153, 1958.

Dean, Burton V., "Replacement Theory," *Progress in Operations Research*, Vol. I, ORSA Publication No. 5, (edited by R. L. Ackoff), 1963, Chapter 9.

Derman, C., "On Optimal Replacement Rules when Changes of State are Markovian," *Mathematical Optimization Techniques*, (edited by R. Bellman, Berkeley, U. of Calif. Press), 1963, pp. 201–10.

Dreyfus, Stuart E., "A Generalized Equipment Replacement Study," *Journal of the Society for Industrial and Applied Mathematics*, Vol. 8, No. 3, Sept. 1960, pp. 425–35.

Naik, M. D. and K. P. Nair, "Multistage Replacement Strategies," *Journal of the Operations Research Society of America*, Vol. 13, No. 2, March–April 1965, pp. 279–290.

Reisman, A. and E. S. Buffa, "A General Model for Investment Policy," *Management Science*, Vol. 8, No. 3, April 1962, pp. 304–10.

Terborgh, George, *Business Investment Policy*. Washington, D.C.: Machinery and Allied Products Institute, 1958.

———, *Dynamic Equipment Policy*. New York: McGraw-Hill Book Company, Inc., 1949.

RISK AND UNCERTAINTY

Bennion, Edward G., "Capital Budgeting and Game Theory," *Harvard Business Review*, Vol. 34, No. 6, November–December 1956, pp. 115–23.

Egerton, R. A. D., *Investment Decisions under Uncertainty*. Liverpool, England: Liverpool Univ. Press, 1960.

Farrar, Donald, *The Investment Decision under Uncertainty*. Englewood Cliffs, New Jersey: Prentice-Hall, Inc., 1962.

Ferguson, Earl J. and James E. Shamblin, "Break-Even Analysis," *The Journal of Industrial Engineering*, Vol. 18, No. 8, August 1967, pp. xvii-xx.

Fishburn, Peter C., *Decision and Value Theory*. New York: John Wiley and Sons, 1964.

Grayson, Jr., C. Jackson, *Decisions under Uncertainty*. Boston: Harvard Business School Press, 1960.

Hertz, David B., "Risk Analysis in Capital Expenditure Decisions," *Harvard Business Review*, Vol. 42, No. 1, January–February 1964, pp. 89–106.

Hespos, R. F. and P. A. Strassmann, "Stochastic Decision Trees for the Analysis of Investment Decisions," *Management Science*, Vol. 11, No. 10, August 1965, pp. 244–59.

Hester, Donald D. and James Tobin, *Risk Aversion and Portfolio Choice; Cowles Monograph 19*. New York: John Wiley and Sons, 1967.

Hillier, F. S., "The Derivation of Probabilistic Information for Evaluation of Risky Investments," *Management Science*, Vol. 9, No. 3, April 1963, pp. 443–57.

Lintner, J., "The Valuation of Risk Assets and the Selection of Risky Investments in Stock Portfolios and Capital Budgets," *Review of Economies and Statistics*, Vol. 47, No. 1, Feb. 1965, pp. 13–37.

Luce, R. Duncan and Howard Raiffa, *Games and Decisions: Introduction and Critical Survey*. New York, John Wiley & Sons, Inc., 1957.

Markowitz, Harry M., *Portfolio Selection: Efficient Diversification of Investments*, Cowles Commission Monograph 16. New York: John Wiley & Sons, Inc., 1959.

Schlaifer, Robert, *Analysis of Decisions under Uncertainty, Vol. I.* New York: McGraw-Hill Book Co., 1967.

Teichroew, Robichek, and Montalbano, "Mathematical Analysis of Rates of Return under Uncertainty," *Management Science*, Vol. 11, No. 3, Jan. 1965, pp. 395–404.

Terry, Herbert, "Comparative Evaluation of Performance Using Multiple Criteria," *Management Science*, Vol. 9, No. 3, 1963.

Thrall, R. M., C. H. Coombs, and R. L. Davis, *Decision Processes*. New York: John Wiley & Sons, 1954.

Van Horne, J., "Capital Budgeting Decisions Involving Combinations of Risky Investments," *Management Science*, Vol. 13, No. 10, Oct. 1966, pp. 84–92.

von Neumann, J. and O. Morgenstern, *Theory of Games and Economic Behavior*. Princeton, New Jersey: Princeton University Press, 1947.

TAXES AND DEPRECIATION

Caplin, Mortimer M. and Robert A. Klayman, "Depreciation — 1965 Model," *The Journal of Accountancy*, Vol. 119, No. 4, April 1965, pp. 34–42.

Davidson, Sidney, and David F. Drake, "The 'Best' Tax Depreciation Method — 1964," *Journal of Business*, Vol. 37, No. 3, July 1964, pp. 258–260.

"Depreciation: A Special Report," *Journal of Taxation*, Vol. 18, No. 5, May 1963, pp. 258–281.

Grant, E. L. and Paul T. Norton, *Depreciation*. Revised Printing, New York: The Ronald Press Company, 1955.

Lasser, J. K., *Your Income Tax*. New York: Simon and Schuster (see latest edition).

Schoomer, B. Alva, "Optimal Depreciation Strategies for Income Tax Purposes," *Management Science*, Vol. 12, No. 12, August 1966, pp. 552–580.

U.S. Treasury Department, *Your Federal Income Tax: 1967 Edition for Individuals*, IRS Pub. No. 17, (revised annually).

———, *Tax Guide . . . for Small Business* (Individuals, Corporation, Partnerships), IRS Pub. No. 334 (revised annually).

———, *Depreciation, Investment Credit, Amortization, Depletion*, IRS Pub. No. 5050, December 1965.

———, *Depreciation Guidelines and Rules: Revenue Procedure 62–21*, IRS Pub. No. 456 (see latest edition).

———, *Tables for Applying Revenue Procedure 62–21*, IRS Pub. No. 457, August 1962.

———, *Regulations Relating to Depreciation: Treasury Decision No. 6182* (Part 1 of Title 26 [1954], Code of Federal Regulations, IRS Pub. No. 311) (see latest edition).

INDEX

University of Bristol
WITHDRAWN